T0373871

ANDAZA

To Mummy, Daddy and Ayaana

Sumayya Usmani

ANDAZA

A memoir of food, flavour and freedom in the Pakistani kitchen

murdoch books
London | Sydney

Contents

ABOUT ANDAZA

When I imagine my mother, I see her in the kitchen, immersed in the act of preparing a meal, measuring spices with her fingers. My memories of my Nani (maternal grandmother) – Nani Mummy, as I called her – are of her crouched over her white enamel cooker, stirring rice pudding. In my reminiscences of my Dadi (paternal grandmother), she is always in the kitchen, silently commanding my five aunts as they cooked large family meals.

Both of my grandmothers, and my mother, cooked without recipes, recollecting and recreating meals using their senses. I grew up around this way of cooking called *andaza*, which translates as 'estimation', but really encompasses what I like to think of as the art of sensory cooking. Even as a young child I was fascinated by the idea that a recipe could turn out differently when it was cooked by someone else, that we all had a different 'flavour in our hands' that made a dish unique to us – this felt like alchemy to me.

In my family, the processes involved in creating a meal were sometimes laborious and painstaking, beginning with the careful selection of produce at the market each week, but no one questioned them and there were never any complaints. No meal was just a one-dish affair; daily meals involved simple dishes, but there were always many of them to share, each with an abundance of flavour and texture. Mealtimes meant more than just eating together; they were a time to savour the labour and the bounty laid out before us.

I began to appreciate that part of our role as women was to provide nourishment and nurturing. The kitchen was a space exclusive to the women in the family, who would gather there to cook or to keep each other company, to laugh and joke, to share recipes and stories. There was always life in the kitchen – it was almost a sacred space, the female domain, willingly occupied not from a sense of duty but rather a sense of ownership and togetherness. The kitchen was a place of effortlessness, of belonging and of strength, and as a child it was my place of consistency and comfort.

Growing up, I always felt a little displaced. I was born in Karachi and lived there until I was a year old, but then led a wandering life aboard merchant ships as a child, interspersed with spells in Karachi and short bursts in England between voyages, before spending my adolescence and adulthood back in Karachi. I struggled with conformity, convention and what it meant to not have had a 'normal' childhood. My teenage years in Pakistan took place during a turbulent time of martial law and restrictions, followed by political strife. The kitchen was the one place I felt secure, there was something about its dependability in my life that made it feel like home.

There was such familiarity and security in knowing that the same aromas, flavours and textures my mother made on the ships could be recreated in another place, at another time. So whenever I yearned for a sense of belonging, I gravitated towards the kitchen. For me, home was never just a place; it was a sensory experience that began in the kitchen.

This is my coming-of-age story, a story about how cooking offered strength in times of weakness and ease in times of sadness, and about how trusting my senses in the kitchen helped me to trust my intuition and equipped me with the confidence to navigate life's challenges. It's also a book that explores the hidden world of Pakistani women, based on several generations of my family and what the kitchen means to them. Although this is my personal story, I hope it will resonate with other free-spirited cooks and believers in the magic created in the kitchen.

The kitchen was a place of effortlessness, of belonging and of strength, and as a child it was my place of consistency and comfort.

CHAPTER 1

You can't cook with words

Early in my life I learn that recipes don't need to be written. Like storytelling, they guide you through an unfamiliar terrain – and, like all good stories, they evolve with each storyteller's instinct and imagination, and cease to exist if they aren't shared.

Sea of Japan, October 1977

BURNT FUDGE

Furious waves crashed against the hull as the ship rolled and pitched. The wind outside our cabin shook the steel doors and whistled through the crevices of the portholes. A light flickered above Mummy's head.

She was making sticky, impossible fudge, stirring butter, sugar, saffron and condensed milk together while the ship swayed to and fro. Taking a pinch of saffron, she ground it between her fingertips. The crushed flecks looked like stars dancing in a caramel sea. The electric frying pan was on high, and smoke swirled around the low metal ceiling of her makeshift galley. Meanwhile, I was holding on to a mattress, tied to either side of the floor, my pink and white polka-dot nightie soaked with tears.

'Gogi,' I wept. 'Please come back, Gogi.' My howling mingled with the howling of the wind outside.

'It's ok, Somi,' Mummy said, calling me by my family nickname. 'He wanted to swim back to his family. The fudge is nearly done; I promise you'll feel better.'

She lowered the dial on the frying pan. The darkened sugar smelt potent, like freshly ground spice. She scraped the ball of sticky fudge together, trying to save what she could.

I continued to choke on my tears; my four-year-old heart felt broken.

'We will get you Gogi's brother when we reach Singapore,' Mummy said, touching my cheek, as she switched off the frying pan.

Until a few weeks ago, I would run on the decks with Gogi, sharing my hiding places behind foghorns and cuddling up with him in my hammock while I read books. I'd play with him in my sandpit and tell him my secrets, sharing my cakes with him. As the captain's only child, I was allowed to go anywhere, and all the cadets on board humoured me. I was their little touch of reality in an unreal setting.

On the day of Gogi's demise, I had been showing him the wheel on the bridge, pretending to sail the vessel. I walked out onto the portside deck, where Daddy would shoot down the stars every evening with the sextant. On the horizon, the sun was setting, the sea like a floor of glass. I chewed on Gogi's furry rabbit ear and sat down on the deck, beneath an orange and pink sky. One of the senior cadets was on duty on the deck. He had friendly eyes and always talked to me.

'Why do you carry this dirty floppy toy around?' he asked.

'Because he's my only friend,' I replied, looking out to the sunset.

'Why don't you freshen him up with a bath? If you throw him into the sea, he'll swim back to you all clean!' The cadet smirked as he tried to tug Gogi out of my hands. I pulled him back quickly.

'Ok, I'll do it!' I said. I whispered words of comfort in Gogi's damp ear.

The ocean, to me, was what land was to other children. I didn't understand the permanence of loss or the fathomlessness of the ocean. I hesitated for a moment. I looked back at the friendly-eyed cadet who gave me a reassuring pat on the shoulder and nodded his head confidently. Gogi had seen many adventures and survived them.

Then I flung him over the side of the ship. I watched Gogi tumble into the water, his lifeless body slowly sucking up sea water as the ship moved past, and away. I ran to the stern to follow him, watching as he disappeared from view, swallowed by the all-encompassing sea. I waited for his return, wet, cold but clean. It wasn't until later, in bed, that fear shot through my heart. My bunny rabbit wasn't coming back, was he?

Meanwhile, the fudge had stuck to the pan; it was deep caramel and ochre. The saffron had added a depth of colour and flavour to the fudge. Even during a storm, Mummy was committed to making this sweet treat for me. Without saying a word, she pressed a layer of the musky fudge into a stainless-steel baking tin and scored it quickly.

'Don't worry, it's caramelised,' she said, 'not burnt. Eat it and everything will be ok.'

At first bite it was crumbly, but very quickly its warmth melted in my mouth, turning into a spiced, bitter nectar. For a moment, everything seemed suddenly still. The fudge was heady like black cardamom, mysterious like liquorice and my sense of loss receded.

Ever since, Mummy has baked and cooked to console me, if only for a few moments. That fateful evening, I learnt that there was something comforting about this small corner of our living quarters – this cooking space warmed my heart in a way no other place could. There were no sweetie shops, no bakeries and no land for weeks ahead. Mummy's makeshift galley, with her single electric frying pan, was my one refuge, my one place of consolation. Together we made treats to distract me from staring longingly at the sea.

Above her frying pan were shelves bursting with recipes in many forms. Le Cordon Bleu cookery school books, brown-edged copies of *Family Circle* magazine, cuttings

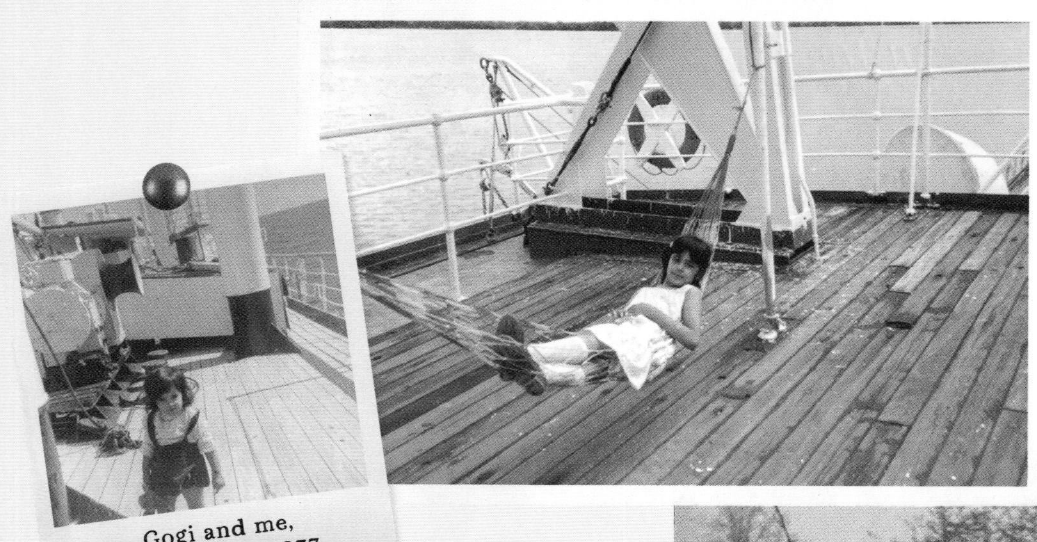

Gogi and me,
on the deck, 1977

I would run on the decks with Gogi, sharing my hiding places behind foghorns ... As the captain's only child, I was allowed to go anywhere.

tucked in a notebook, and an edition of *Betty Crocker's Cookbook* – an anniversary present from Daddy, with an inscription scrawled in his near-indecipherable handwriting, '*To my sweetheart, with all my love, with the hope that she does not fatten me with all these recipes – Shaiq*'.

I always wondered how Mummy could conjure up such decadent meals, merely by flicking through books, glancing at the pictures and lists of ingredients, and ignoring their detailed instructions. She would put the books to one side, head to the galley and create cream-filled meringues and mustard-coloured pullao rice as if by magic. Her way of measuring was her hands.

'Why don't you use any of the books or measure anything, Mummy?' I'd ask.

'You can't cook with words,' she'd say. 'You need to trust your senses – nobody can cook well otherwise. You'll never need to weigh and measure if you let your senses guide you. I just buy books for ideas.'

She'd pour rice in a bowl and hold it in her hands to estimate its weight. Next she'd open her spice box and select a few spices, then sniff them and pop a few different ones in her mouth to test how fresh they were – this would help her to gauge whether they would flavour the rice adequately. Each time she'd cook this rice, she'd select a different proportion of spices and play with the flavours until she was sure the balance was perfect.

Mummy spent her time making up her own recipes – collecting local herbs and spices from every port we went to and experimenting with them. On land she'd seek out cooks in restaurants or ask people at the markets how unusual ingredients were used. Most of the time she concocted spontaneous recipes that she would never be able to replicate. Every meal was different – every story she told in her cooking was different.

Almost everything she cooked had some spice, but merely a hint, to enhance and not overpower. I'd watch as she took spices from a tin and created intoxicating aromas just by adding them to a hot pan. Their roasted scent filled our cabin with the magical perfume of faraway places, and their delicate flavours were etched onto my mind and my palate. Of course I didn't learn to cook with spices until much later, but these flavour memories were locked away, waiting to be called upon when I needed them, saffron, cardamom and cumin being the first flavours I remember.

The night my mother made that fudge is the strongest memory I have of food during all our years of sailing. Mummy wasn't like other captains' wives who loved being free of household chores. She hated the ship's food and disliked staff hovering around her. She missed cooking her own meals in the sovereignty of her own kitchen.

She kept simple cooking utensils in a spare room, so she could cook for us, every day. To avert months of boredom she tackled every recipe in her Cordon Bleu series, every cake in *Betty Crocker* – and she cooked everything from biryani and naan to lemon meringue pie and brioche. Sometimes we would catch flying fish with nets on the lower decks and she would flash-fry them with salt, pepper and chilli powder, or we'd grill corn cobs on our tin-can barbecue.

Exploring new lands was thrilling, but her cooking on the ship meant more to me than any of that: it wasn't just an expression of love but the creation of a home in the most unhomely of places. Mummy taught me that it didn't matter which ingredients were used, or how authentic food was to a particular cuisine, what mattered – and what created a lasting memory – was the act of nurturing another with a meal made by one's own hands. Through her cooking, I learnt that making food was about relationships and people – especially, perhaps, the relationship between mother and daughter.

RECIPES ARE STORIES

On board the ship, the endless weeks of open skies and unchanging horizons seemed interchangeable, indistinguishable from one another. I spent time in my hammock, escaping to Narnia or watching the sea, hoping to catch a glimpse of a dolphin's fin.

Sometimes I'd sneak into Daddy's smoking room, looking for pipe-cleaners. The wooden-panelled room smelt like burnt orange zest and French toast. The side cabinet had an array of briarwood and meerschaum pipes propped against a wooden stand. A box of Montecristos sat on a small table, next to Daddy's black leather tobacco pouch filled with Erinmore tobacco and multi-coloured pipe-cleaners, which I'd steal to make bendy finger puppets and bracelets, or tiny flowers and fruit.

We rose early every morning. Breakfast was at 6 a.m. in the officers' mess, usually parathas and oily spiced omelettes with heavily sweetened cooked chai – Mummy shook her head in disgust at how unhealthy it all was. I would get a bowl of cardboard-flavoured Fauji cornflakes or Quaker porridge oats with long-life milk. We always had so much long-life milk that when cartons neared their expiry date, Mummy and I would take baths in it, imagining we were Cleopatra.

For the crew, food was mere fodder, and every meal in the galley tasted like mutton korma, under different names. We rarely sat with the crew in the mess for lunch or dinner, as the Pakistani food the ship's cook made lacked creativity or any kind of adventurousness. But with limited ingredients, Mummy became a master of creating meals using tinned vegetables and store-cupboard basics – she just let her heart guide her and improvised when she needed to.

'Recipes are stories,' she'd say, 'and ingredients are characters. You can make up your own story as you go along.' Mummy herself was like an oral storyteller, making up tales on the spot for me to devour. We had few other distractions on-board, and I watched with fascination as the stories unfolded, different each time they were told.

This life of sailing wasn't what my mother had signed up for. Daddy was in the Pakistan Navy when they married, as his father had thought it a good career for his eldest son. But having fought in two wars with India and nearly lost his life in one, he and Mummy soon grew wary of the risks of a naval career.

Before he joined the navy, it had been my father's dream to read Law, and so at the end of 1974 he resigned his commission and became a master mariner in the interim. The merchant navy offered a salary that could sustain a family, and an income that would help him take his master's Law degree in the UK.

Mummy probably agreed to this stint on merchant ships as it offered the chance for us to live a life of adventure. I may have grown up lacking friendship, structure and school, but I gained an education like no other, developing a sense of freedom and a penchant for unusual flavours.

Before they embarked on this life of adventure, in the first year of their marriage, my parents lived in a one-bedroom flat in Brackner House, a Victorian building in the Clifton area of Karachi. It was here that Mummy really learnt to cook. She'd make daily phone calls to her mother to ask her for recipes. It would always be 'a handful of this' or 'a pinch of that' – just a rough list of ingredients, methods and timings, guided by smells or moments in the cooking process, such as 'when the ginger and garlic doesn't smell raw', 'when the cinnamon and cumin smell warm and not burnt' and 'when the oil comes to the top of the sauce'.

With this vague guidance, Mummy had begun cooking. She had learnt that the flavours she created were her own, and constantly evolving; it was a lesson I picked up from her very early on.

MY CHICKEN ODESA

I'd never really had a proper birthday party until I turned six. At the time, we were on a voyage to Sri Lanka, on the M.V. *Ohrmazd* – once a passenger liner, now a merchant vessel. This was the largest ship I had ever been on, and I spent a lot of time exploring the areas I was told not to: the derelict guest cabins, and the dining-room bar that was filled with cobwebs and a stale smell of disuse. Outside the bar was an empty, rust-stained open-air pool, with shattered floor lights and mouldy sky-blue tiles. Daddy had the pool cleaned and filled with sea water so that I could float about in it. I didn't know how to swim, so I would jump in wearing a ship's life jacket, accidentally swallowing water. Intensely briny, the water was heavy and dense. Our life on board was engulfed in this brininess. My hair and skin would be sticky from it; even when I opened my mouth to eat, I'd taste the salty air.

I wanted to help Mummy cook on my birthday. I'd decided I wanted to try making a recipe I'd learnt on our previous voyage, when we'd gone to Odesa. My parents went out every night to a local nightclub that had no problem with me tagging along, so I'd sit next to them and quietly observe everyone around me. Mummy would order every Russian dish she had ever heard of – there were stews and breads, but nothing that excited me as I found all the food bland. Every night I noticed the same two ladies sitting near our table. I'd never seen such striking women, with scarlet lips and cascading blonde hair, and I was enchanted by the way they ate without disturbing their lipstick. They sliced pieces of crumbed chicken effortlessly, the crumbs falling off the plate and begging to be gathered up by a licked finger.

One night, one of the ladies caught me staring at them and called me over. For the rest of that evening, they conversed with me in their broken English and shared the recipe for the chicken Odesa they were eating. And when our last night came around, they gave me a large stuffed lion, which I cherished for many years.

So, back on the M.V. *Ohrmazd*, I decided to make the chicken Odesa for my birthday party. I pounded several chicken breasts between plastic bags. In a bowl, I softened some butter, mixing in garlic granules, salt, dried marjoram and parsley. The heat from my fingertips loosened the herbed butter as I smeared it liberally over the chicken pieces and then tumbled them into flour. Next, I dredged the chicken through beaten egg and breadcrumbs. Mummy helped me to fry each piece in her electric frying pan and lay them in large stainless-steel trays, ready for my party. The glistening coating on the chicken filled my heart with pride. I may have chopped onions for a biryani or helped to bake a cake before, but I had never cooked anything from scratch.

At my birthday party, instead of noisy six-year-olds, my guests were groups of uniformed men, smiling politely to hide their disinterest. Crepe paper chains and foil chandeliers hung from the cobwebbed ceiling fan; balloons were dotted around the rosewood-panelled bar. The faint, musty smell of mothballs filled the room, and the sea breeze seeped through the corroded portholes.

Mummy had baked a pink sponge cake in the shape of a cat, with matching pink buttercream, pastel hundreds and thousands, and chocolate finger biscuits for whiskers. Always dressed to perfection, even in a place otherwise untouched by fashion, Mummy wore a navy-blue safari suit she had stitched using a Vogue pattern. Her tiny waist was cinched with a fabric belt, her hair was like a sheet of silk falling across her shoulders. The paper tablecloth was covered with ribbon sandwiches, shami kebabs and my chicken Odesa. The crew stood around awkwardly as I cut the cake, all of them singing happy birthday in reserved voices. No one wanted to be the first to pick up a plate, but Mummy nudged them to start eating. Within minutes, they began piling their plates with chicken and sandwiches.

'Madam, your food makes me miss my mother's cooking,' said one of the cadets as he ate a shami kebab, while reaching for a slice of cake with his other hand.

'Thank you,' said Mummy. 'I'm happy I can feed you something that reminds you of home.'

Mummy beamed. She loved nothing more than being a hostess, hungry for appreciation beyond her family. I sat in the corner with my slice of cake. Though I knew no different, I was aware that this was an odd way to celebrate a birthday. At the same time, I had discovered that using my own hands to create something to eat offered me the freedom to express myself in a way nothing else did.

A SCHOOL OF DESPAIR

Months of cabin fever would be washed away with each sighting of land. As the anchor dropped, we'd climb down the gangway to a speedboat that would take us to new places. We would discover marketplaces in Abidjan, or head to Istanbul to explore the city where East meets West. At restaurants overlooking the Bosporus, we would eat grilled fish and wash it down with *ayran*, a yoghurt drink. After weeks of no fresh fruit, we'd have fresh coconut water and cashews in Kandy, or fresh papaya in Djibouti. As we sailed along the Nile, pedlars came aboard from tiny wooden boats and set up shop on deck, selling Egyptian souvenirs and the sweetest figs I've ever eaten. We visited Iran just before the revolution, exploring the spice markets in Minab and discovering the best saffron.

In Osaka, a ship chandler's wife gave me the most beautiful present I have ever received: a wooden box with a sliding lid, carved with Japanese calligraphy. Inside lay eight sugared-violet jelly sweets, each in its own individual section, on a small square of delicate, translucent rice paper. A tiny two-pronged wooden fork sat alongside. I ate each one slowly, to savour its floral, sweet-pea-like flavour. I refused to share the sweets, keeping them hidden under my pillow for weeks; I couldn't bear to eat the final one, so I gave it to Mummy.

At every port we went to, I saw children in groups, heading off to school in the mornings. I watched girls in school uniform, with pigtails in ribbons, walking down the streets of Colombo. I gazed with envy at Dutch children, laughing and skipping together, matching scarves around their necks. School looked like a place I would love. I longed to be around others my age, to play freely and form friendships instead of merely reading about them. I wanted to be taught by a teacher who would be patient and kind, rather than studying a correspondence course with Daddy, who was sometimes neither, at least as a tutor. I loved seeing schools – though all that changed when we went to North Korea.

At the time, in 1977, Daddy was sailing a government-owned vessel instructed to convey missiles from North Korea to Pakistan. After the 1971 war with India, Zulfikar Ali Bhutto, then the Pakistani prime minister, felt threatened about the prospect of further conflict. Because Bhutto was seen as a socialist, he wasn't popular with America, and as a result US aid had dried up, leaving North Korea as the only nation open to supplying arms and ammunition to Pakistan.

Rust and engine fumes filled my nose as I jumped off the last steps of the wooden ladder onto a boat that would ferry us to the dock, where a car awaited to take us to Nampo. As official state guests, we were being taken on a tour of the city. My father had told our escort that I loved seeing local schools, so our first visit was to a boarding school. It was winter, and as we drove down immaculate roads, the biting wind chilled the car. The branches of the bare trees looked like soldiers standing at attention.

We arrived at a state school, an imposing lodge-style building. The main hall smelt like sour vinegar and the reception area resembled a hospital waiting room. A woman wearing a high-necked tunic met us; she had steely eyes, and dark hair twisted tightly into a bun.

There was chanting in the distance, which grew louder as we walked up the stone steps to the first floor. As we stood behind an aquarium-glass window, we were shown a classroom where children were sitting in rows at small desks – all dressed in white, their gaze fixed on a chalkboard.

'This is our main classroom. The children are praying,' said the escort, translating for the steely-eyed woman. 'They are praying for our supreme leader Kim Il-sung.' He went on to explain that the children's white and grey living quarters were behind steel doors to the left.

'Why do such young children live here?' asked Mummy.

'The children come to us when they are four,' replied the escort. 'Their parents leave them to do service to the High Commander.'

My legs went weak at the thought of being separated from my parents.

'Do you think we could meet the children?' Mummy asked.

We watched as the children stood up in unison. At the command of the teacher, they walked over to us. They had snow-like skin and cheeks as red as apples. My mother, who never usually gushed over children, couldn't resist their cherubic looks and she reached out to touch one of the boys on the cheek. The boy jumped and grabbed my mother's leg, clinging on to her. She tried to console him with a kiss on the top of his head, but as he held on tighter, her eyes welled up.

'Will he get a sweetie because he's sad?' I asked our escort as he took the boy back to his classroom.

'No,' he replied, 'the children don't get sweets.'

Suddenly filled with anger, I ran downstairs, towards the car. My parents were shouting for me but, as tears rolled down my scrunched-up face, I ignored them. Outside it had begun to snow and the ground was already thickly carpeted. My face stung as the cold air froze my tears.

As my parents followed me, I could hear them apologising for my rudeness, asking me to come out and thank the steely-eyed woman for the visit. Indignant, I sat on the back seat of the car, pretending not to hear them until they said their goodbyes.

'Daddy, I am never going to school, ever,' I said with stern conviction.

On our last day in North Korea our official escort returned laden with gifts: multiple boxes of books, wine with snakes in the bottle and packets of local boiled sweets. All I could think of was how I was going to get rid of these gifts from a place I hated. I wanted to like the bright pink and green sweets, but my pride made me refuse them. Sweets were normally my weakness, but somehow these didn't appeal at all. I thought of the crying boy in the school and how he would never have the chance to try them.

The books were leather-bound volumes by Kim Il-sung, just like the ones I'd seen in the school, and our escort had all the books in the ship's library moved to make room for them. Some of the overspill books lay on the floor outside my room, and soon found their way onto my bedside table.

'Let's throw everything into the sea,' I suggested.

Daddy agreed that this was the best course of action as there was no space on the ship. A few days later, when we set sail on the high seas again, Mummy and I opened the small brass porthole in our bathroom, and I stood on a stool and began to fling the books out, one by one. I was so focused on getting rid of the books that I hadn't noticed how windy it was outside. As I turned to throw out the last book, a sudden gust forced the porthole shut, smashing it into my face and knocking me to the floor, leaving me with the metallic taste of blood in my mouth and a throbbing above my left eye. That night Mummy baked an angel food cake to comfort me.

I still have that scar of my eyebrow to remind me of that moment, but I now understand why I hated that school in North Korea so much. It wasn't because of the strict teacher, the young age of the children or the unwelcoming building; it was because I couldn't imagine being robbed of my mother's food, the comfort and sense of belonging it gave me during those years at sea, when I felt so cut off from other children's reality.

MEALS WITHOUT MEAT

Our final voyage took us to Kandla, on the Gulf of Kutch, in western India. The air reminded me of the times we'd spent in Karachi between voyages, except that here the cows roamed freely. On our way into town on the first day, the taxi driver stopped to buy fried crispy breads and fruit. I fondly imagined that these were to welcome us to India but was dismayed when he fed them to the cow that was blocking the road. Smoke rose from food stalls dotted around the pavements; people were sleeping on the streets, with whole families in torn fabric tents. There were pots balanced over small wooden fires, around which children ran, naked, dirty and untroubled. Our taxi driver was taking us to have dinner with the ship chandler's family, and I was told they had a daughter my age.

Once at the house, we were greeted by a shy-looking woman in a dull sari. There was a small red dot painted on her forehead. She bowed, asked us to take off our shoes and then led the way through a curtain of beads into a small, dimly lit room with stone floors. There was a strong smell of sandalwood in the air, which reminded me of the incense we burnt by my maternal grandfather's grave whenever

Months of cabin fever would be washed away with each sighting of land.

Amsterdam, 1977

we visited Karachi. My mother joined the ship chandler's wife in the kitchen, hoping to pick up recipes. I heard her gasping as she learnt how *hing* (asafoetida) added to the pan when cooking rice adds an intriguing flavour.

'We add *hing* to all our food,' said the ship chandler's wife. 'Since we can't use onions, ginger or garlic, it gives our food depth and savouriness.'

'We don't really use *hing* in Pakistan,' said Mummy. 'I think maybe the Gujarati community in Karachi use it. Why don't you use any onions, garlic and ginger? We couldn't live without them.'

'Because our religion doesn't allow it,' said the ship chandler's wife. '*Hing* added to hot oil changes in character and replicates the flavour of onion.'

Meanwhile, in the other room, their daughter Indra and I regarded each other with suspicion. But that awkwardness soon dissipated, and we started talking about books we had read. For the rest of the evening we were inseparable. At the dinner table, I announced that I wanted to spend the night there.

'But you don't have a change of clothes, or your new Gogi,' said Daddy. 'Why don't you come tomorrow and play with her?'

'I really want to stay, Daddy. Please.' I said, hoping my insistence might convince him. My new Gogi didn't smell comforting like my old one, and I knew I could sleep without him for one night. I couldn't miss this chance of a night spent with a new friend. Indra's mother put out food, filling the table with plum-hued beans, daal, rice, chapattis and knobbly vegetables. The dining room was filled with unfamiliar aromas; a strong earthy smell came from a rice dish that was placed in front of me.

I wouldn't take no for an answer, and Indra and I pleaded with Daddy until he agreed, just to shut us up. As we ate, he hoped I would change my mind, but then I said something that embarrassed him even more than my pushiness about staying. Just as the meal ended, I turned to Indra's mother and asked, 'But where is dinner?'

'Somi, that *was* dinner,' Mummy replied quickly, to shield Indra's mum from further embarrassment.

'That can't be dinner – where is the meat?' I said, with honest bewilderment. It was the first main meal I'd ever had that didn't include a meat dish. The crew on the ships we sailed with were mainly Pakistani, and meat featured heavily in the meals served on-board. Daddy always expected a meat dish, and Mummy found that she missed meat if she went without it for a few days, even though she loved vegetarian food. Sometimes I'd explore the ship's freezer stores, where hundreds of frozen carcasses hung from large metal hooks – these formed the basis of that daily mutton korma in the mess, and of the biryani, keema and korma that Mummy cooked for us. Until that day, I hadn't realised that there were people who chose never to eat meat.

After we moved back to Karachi, the idea of meat being central to a meal was reaffirmed. I never did forget my trip to Kandla, or the generous meat-free spread at Indra's home, nor did I forget the magic of pungent asafoetida (also known as 'devil's dung') – something I continued to use in my cooking, as did Mummy. All this sowed the seeds of an appreciation that food is all about the wealth of time taken to prepare it, and that there are families whose meals are complete without the need for meat.

When I was seven, Daddy announced that our days on the ship were coming to an end. Though I didn't know it then, my parents were worried for my future and wanted to give me some stability, with proper schooling and friends. I had grown tired of being on my own and I craved companionship; I was ready for a change. Daddy told us that we'd be living in a small village in England for a year before moving to Karachi.

A year in England meant a chance to study in school with other children, make friends and explore large, open spaces. From storybooks and our short trips to see my uncle in London, I knew the smells and scenery of England well. I had read every Enid Blyton book and imagined English villages to be idyllic and friendly, populated with girls in pinafores, laughing together and picking wild flowers. I was filled with excitement at the prospect of being one of those girls. I imagined the adventures I'd have with new friends, just like the Famous Five or Secret Seven I'd spent so much time reading about. For me, this marked the beginning of a life on land, a life I had craved for so long.

During my years of travelling the high seas, I had tasted the sweetest papaya in the Ivory Coast, discovered the unique taste of Singapore noodles at hawker stalls in the markets and picked fresh cinnamon in the spice gardens of Kandy. I had been exposed to a world of diverse flavours, but it was Mummy's free-spirited outlook on cooking that made me a non-conformist in life and in the kitchen. Most of all, I learnt never to follow recipes blindly, because I understood that if I let instinct guide me, I'd always learn a new way to tell the story of that recipe – and it would be *my* story.

Saffron black cardamom fudge

This recipe is based on my mother's fudge; the flavour of black cardamom becomes intense when heated, so don't be tempted to add more than a few seeds from the pod – you can use the rest in pullao or to make chai.

Prep time: 10–15 minutes
Cooking time: 15–20 minutes
Makes about 30–35 pieces

1 black cardamom pod, cracked open, 3–4 seeds extracted and ground
350 g (12 oz) sweetened condensed milk, or non-dairy alternative
150 ml (5 fl oz) whole (full-cream) milk, or non-dairy alternative
115 g (4 oz) unsalted butter
450 g (1 lb) demerara sugar
small pinch of saffron threads
1 tablespoon edible dried organic rose petals
1 tablespoon pistachio slivers

- Line a 20 cm (8 inch) square tin with baking paper and set aside.
- Put the cracked cardamom pod and the ground seeds into a non-stick or heavy-based saucepan with the condensed milk, milk, butter and sugar. Stir over medium heat until the butter has melted and the sugar has dissolved, then bring to a steady boil, stirring constantly.
- Let the mixture boil for about 3 minutes, or until the temperature reaches 115°C (239°F) on a sugar thermometer. (As we never had one on the ship, Mummy would drop a little of the bubbling mixture onto a cold plate – if it formed a soft ball and didn't stick to our fingers, it was ready!)
- Lightly crush the saffron between your fingertips. Add it to the pan and stir in with a wooden spoon, then take the pan off the heat and carefully fish out the cardamom pod.
- Let the fudge mixture sit for 4–5 minutes, then beat with the wooden spoon until it begins to come together into a ball and leaves the sides of the pan. If you like your fudge chewy, stop beating now; if you like it to be more melt-in-the-mouth, keep beating until it starts to get crumbly.
- Once the fudge has reached your desired consistency, press it into the tin, smoothing it with the back of the spoon. Sprinkle with the rose petals and pistachio slivers, pressing them into the fudge.
- Leave the fudge to cool and set – this will take about 1–1½ hours – before scoring it, then cut into pieces and store in a tin or jar for up to 2 weeks.

Chicken Odesa

A recipe remembered from my childhood, one of the first dishes I ever cooked. This can also be made with chicken mini fillets (tenderloins) – you'll need about ten of them. A green salad makes a nice accompaniment.

Prep time: 15 minutes
Cooking time: 12–15 minutes
Serves 4

4 skinless chicken breast fillets
100 g (3½ oz) salted butter, softened
1 large garlic clove, crushed
1 tablespoon chopped parsley, plus extra to serve
½ tablespoon chopped marjoram or thyme
4 tablespoons plain (all-purpose) flour
2 eggs
pinch of salt
150 g (2½ cups) fine breadcrumbs
3 tablespoons sunflower oil
lemon wedges, to serve

- Bash the chicken breasts inside a plastic bag or between two sheets of baking paper until they are only 2–3 mm (⅛ inch) thick.
- Mix the butter in a small bowl with the garlic and herbs, then spread liberally over both sides of the flattened chicken breasts.
- Take three shallow bowls and put the flour into the first one. In the second bowl, lightly beat the eggs with the salt. Put the breadcrumbs into the third bowl. Begin by dipping each chicken breast first into the flour, then into the egg and finally the breadcrumbs. Lay the coated chicken breasts on a plate, ready to cook.
- Heat the oil in a frying pan over medium-high heat. When it is hot, add the chicken breasts and cook for 6 minutes on each side, until golden brown and cooked through. Depending on the size of your pan, you may need to do this in batches.
- Scatter with the extra chopped parsley and serve with lemon wedges.

I learnt never to follow recipes blindly, because I understood that if I let instinct guide me, I'd always learn a new way to tell the story of that recipe – and it would be my story.

CHAPTER 2

The hope at hospitality's heart

Hospitality, to my mother, means the best table linen, starched and laid, and with no expense spared. This act of sharing with others isn't just at the core of my mother's personality but is also the basis of a cultural generosity that runs through her veins, as well as mine.

Winchester, 1980

THE CONSOLATION OF CUSTARD

I had grown up around grown-ups – either my parents or the crew on the ships we sailed in – and so by the time we settled down in one place, I was wiser and older than my years. Mummy taught me to appreciate different flavours, and Daddy was always around to teach me some maths or point me towards interesting books to read. But what I loved the most about my father was his storytelling. He told me stories of his days as a naval officer, how they used to wake up at 4.30 in the morning, play football and then have a massive breakfast; how he'd once made a 'curry' at the request of his cadet friends and blown their heads off with the amount of chilli he'd put in it. Daddy wasn't much of a cook, but his stories were what fuelled my imagination as a child.

Our bedtime stories would be about characters that he'd made up: a kangaroo called Greyfur and a boy called Springy Baba, who had shoes with springs on them so that he could jump to any country in the world and save endangered animals. Each night I'd look forward to Daddy telling me a new story about the adventures of Springy Baba. He'd tuck me into bed and then tell me a story, changing his voice to bring each character to life, and igniting my desire for travel, stories and magical places. Daddy's tales always included lessons about right and wrong, and the importance of integrity and standing up for those you believe in. When we stopped sailing, my bedtime stories were taken over by Mummy and she'd usually read to me. I missed Daddy's impromptu stories, but by then he had little time to tell me those regularly.

In the summer of 1980, we'd moved to South Wonston, a 'blink and you'll miss it' kind of village just outside Winchester. Everything was on a single road: the school, the post office, the church. All the identical tile-roofed houses were built with dark camel-coloured bricks; they had small front gardens, frosted-glass doors and a sense of quietness. Contrary to what I'd read in Enid Blyton books, it felt unwelcoming to me. I remember the first drive to our rented house in a cul-de-sac called Armstrong Close. It was late August, and it was meant to be a summer's day, yet the dark grey clouds were low enough to touch, muting the greens of the lush forest and farmland around the village, the air filled with the smell of manure and fresh hay.

The night before my first day at South Wonston Primary, I felt an unfamiliar combination of excitement and nerves; the smell of eggs made me feel ill, so Mummy made me a warm glass of milk with Ovaltine for breakfast. I had no idea what to expect, and the stories I'd read in Enid Blyton's Malory Towers books about how new kids at school were treated ran through my mind. The school was a low, grey building, with vast undulating hills behind it. I would later discover the pleasures that could be had rolling down those grassy slopes on a dry, sunny day. It was the one time I felt pure freedom in England, the energising scent of freshly cut grass and the bits of dried grass in my hair connecting me with nature.

In my first lesson the teacher called me up to the front of the classroom and introduced me. My face was burning, and I felt that all eyes were on me. She then asked me to sit next to a thin, sallow-looking boy. His straw-coloured eyes glared at me.

'Hi, I'm Sumayya,' I said.

'Don't you dare sit with me,' he fired back.

The tears burned behind my eyes. I just sat down and didn't look at him. I had come to terms with being alone on the ship, but feeling lonely in a space filled with children my own age was much harder.

The atmosphere at lunchtime was sterile and inhospitable. In the dining room, the food was behind glass screens and everything smelt of burnt toast, boiled potatoes and overcooked sausages – aromas of despair. I was used to the fragrance of exotic spices and fresh ingredients from different countries, with dishes laid out on large communal tables; I found small portions of food served on individual plates an alien concept. I was used to being fed until I felt as if I would burst, but at school there was no such thing as a second helping, and I was left unsatisfied by both the flavour and the experience of eating.

Throughout my first month of school meals, I felt as if I was invisible to the dinner ladies. Every day I'd have to ask them the same question, and every time I'd get the same response.

'Is this pork?' I'd ask. 'I'm not allowed to eat pork. Do you have something else for me?'

The dinner ladies would plop some lumpy mashed potato with toad in the hole or sausage onto my plate. I'd play with the food all through lunchtime, scared that I might draw attention to myself if I said anything about it, so I never did.

There was one time when the food made me feel sick to the pit of my stomach. Lunch was a soggy wilted pastry with dark brown pieces of meat inside it that smelt like dog food – I was sure it was off, and the gravy had spread over the mashed potato, so I couldn't even eat that. I later found out that this was the famous steak and kidney pie my father had always spoken of so fondly. I walked over to the dessert counter, hoping to find something more edible there. I felt a vague sense of familiarity as I looked down at the stainless-steel vat of hot, sweet yellow custard. There was cold tinned fruit on the side, with a few sought-after bright crimson cherries dancing about. Here was something I knew well – it was on the 'English menu' offering every week on the ships. The custard was always cold, yet inviting. Even though it was permeated with a synthetic vanilla scent and its dried-out skin would stick to the roof of my mouth, I loved eating it.

I asked for a bowl, sat in the corner of the lunch hall and, with each spoonful, I found consolation as the warm custard slid down my throat; it gave me hope that maybe, there might be small moments of familiarity in this very unfamiliar place.

COLD COW'S MILK

School days continued to be hard for me, even after we'd been in England for five months. I was too afraid to tell my parents how I felt. Each day I sat alone and tried to talk to the other children, only for them to walk away without including me in their groups.

On one wet morning, when the school grounds were waterlogged, we had indoor play. Morning play meant milk bottles. I looked forward to the cold, creamy milk in glass bottles with paper straws. Milk had never tasted as good as this before; it was different from the milk in cartons on the ships, which always had a papery taste. Early in the day, a man would bring the blue plastic crates into the classroom, and I'd gaze at them longingly, hoping to be the first to grab a bottle at playtime.

The teacher smiled and handed me one as she asked, 'Sumayya, have you made some new friends?'

'No, Miss. No one wants to talk to me,' I replied, while keeping my eye on the milk bottle in her hand.

'Why not? You're a lovely little girl!' she said.

I hesitated. I knew why in my heart but felt too scared to admit it. I wasn't the new girl anymore, there were newer children who'd joined the class since; somehow, they had all made friends. In my seven-year-old mind, I had tossed a few ideas around, but I could think of only one reason why I was still not making friends, and it wasn't because I hadn't tried. My family's travels had given me a sense of comfort and adventure, and nothing had been forced on me – not culture, tradition or religion. Though I didn't yet identify as Pakistani, I knew I was Muslim and that I shouldn't eat pork. I was never told that being this person made me different, or that I wouldn't fit in anywhere. But I knew now that this feeling of being different, an outsider, went beyond being the new child in the school.

'I think, Miss, it's because of the colour of my skin.' I grabbed the bottle from her hand and hid behind a bookshelf for the rest of playtime.

I think the teacher was as surprised as I was. She never said anything to me, and I couldn't face her for the rest of the day. I came back home that afternoon, lay face down on my bed, and cried uncontrollably for hours. That evening I came down to dinner and finally spoke to my parents.

'Daddy, I think we should just go back to the ship,' I said. 'At least there you were always around, and I made friends everywhere we went.'

'Don't worry, you'll make friends,' he said.

'I hate school and I hate England!' I said, with tears rolling down my cheeks.

CYCLE RIDES AND COLA SWEETS

For my eighth birthday, Daddy bought me a yellow bicycle with stabiliser wheels. He'd seen me after school, as I perched on the sofa and longingly watched the children on their bikes in Armstrong Close.

That afternoon I came back from school and threw my red Jack & Jill bag onto my tiny bed, with its freshly laundered Magic Roundabout bed sheets.
I wanted to be out before everyone else, so no one could laugh at my stabiliser wheels.

'Be careful, Somi, you don't know how to ride yet,' said Mummy, as I ran out the door, to the shed. Since I had told my parents how I was feeling, Mummy had been particularly overprotective.

'I'll be fine, Mummy. I have those stupid wheels on!' I replied, filled with dread at the idea of being judged for not knowing how to ride a bike.

I spent the afternoon falling and getting up, trying to hide from view behind the hedges and ignoring the familiar face of a girl at the window of one of the houses across the street. I'd seen her in school before, but I was lost in my efforts, my knees and elbows scraped and sore.

I felt a finger tap on my shoulder. When I turned around, there she was, on her own bike, with her bobbed blonde hair and a sweet smile.

'Would you like some help?' she asked.

I looked down at her back wheel. No stabilisers. 'Yes, please,' I replied, 'I have no idea what I'm doing.'

'My name is Dawn, I've seen you in class. It's not too hard – you just need someone to help.'

'I'm Sumayya.'

'I know,' said Dawn.

I was never told that being this person made me different, or that I wouldn't fit in anywhere. But I knew now that this feeling of being different, an outsider, went beyond being the new child in the school.

'I still have stabiliser wheels,' I said, embarrassed.

'Oh, don't worry, I had them until last week! Once you learn, you'll never need them again!' she said. 'Come on, I'll teach you now. Come over to the back garden, so no one has to see you.'

That was the day I learnt to ride a bike and made my first friend.

Dawn and I soon became inseparable, walking to school together in the morning and meeting up after school to do our homework. Being friends with Dawn meant I made other friends too. We would all go cycling on the farmland behind our house, and sometimes they would come over. My mother always kept the temperature in the house at 25 degrees, and after about ten minutes inside, every single child would strip down to their underwear. But they came to my house for the snacks: large bowls of crisps, tiny finger sandwiches with cucumber (lots of salt), strawberries and cream, and fairy cakes that she'd let us ice together. I never got anything when I went to any of their homes, except for Dawn's.

Every time I stayed at Dawn's past 4.30 p.m. her parents would cook me fish fingers. To me, fish meant the messy, bloody, smelling-of-the-sea things that my mum bought from street markets in the Ivory Coast and Turkey, or from the fish bazaar in Karachi with my Nani. These boneless, cookie-cutter-perfect pieces looked nothing like fish. They came out of a cardboard box, and tasted of it too. But I never said no to them, eating them with mealy steamed peas, while we made faces on our plates with Heinz ketchup.

As I began to discover the delights of pre-packaged food, cakes and sweets, life in England became a little easier for me. My parents gave me 50p pocket money each week, and Dawn taught me how to make that go a long way at the Pick 'n' Mix counter. We'd put large Cola Bottle jellies at the bottom of the paper bag, just two, because they were heavy, then Dolly Mixture (I only liked the ones with the pink middle) and Jelly Babies, then finally a mix of Parma Violets and Love Hearts – they were the lightest. If I didn't have enough money, Dawn would share her sweets. We'd hide behind trees and devour them before dinner; with each jaw-sucking tangy sweet that stuck to our teeth, we felt like we had spent our money well.

ENTERTAINING IN ENGLAND

Settling in hadn't been easy for my parents, either. The week we moved in, all three of us had gone to say hello to the next-door neighbours early one evening.

'We just moved in next door and wanted to say hi,' said Mummy, standing on the doorstep.

'We're busy – we're having our tea,' said the lady, closing the door as quickly as she'd opened it. My parents never went over again.

To Mummy, making friends in England meant feeding them, offering them food she made with love and patience. She did this by hosting coffee mornings and inviting all the neighbourhood ladies.

My birthday party gave her a great excuse to put on her best spread. On the day, Mummy was up at 6 a.m., moulding her shami kebab mixture around cocktail sticks, making chicken and tarragon sandwiches and extravagantly slathering her sponge cake with cream. She loved the flavour of the cream in England, so different from the buffalo cream in Pakistan; fascinated by the choice of whipping, double or single, she liked to use fresh cream for her cakes, rather than icing or buttercream.

The living room was decorated with pink and purple streamers. All the children from my class were invited and nearly everyone turned up. The snacks at my house were famous by now, as was the temperature inside: it was February, but my mother had set the heating to 30 degrees and everyone was dressed in summer clothes! We played pass-the-parcel and musical chairs and had lots of party poppers and whistles to annoy the grown-ups with. We were sweaty, with flushed cheeks, and I had never had more fun.

My mother, in her usual hospitable way, encouraged people to help themselves to the feast at the table. A few of the ladies couldn't resist commenting on the cake: 'Why would you use cream on a cake?' one of them asked. 'I don't think I'd eat a creamy cake.'

England, 1980

Mummy politely ignored these comments, but later complained to my father about how bad they made her feel.

'It's just these ladies in their small world,' Daddy said. 'They haven't seen the world as we have. I don't think they mean anything bad by it.'

That year in England offered me the chance to run free in fields, to learn to ride a bike, and to find my first true friend. After we moved back to Karachi, Dawn and I stayed friends, despite the distance. We wrote to each other regularly over the next few years and never lost touch; we met up every time I was in England, and she even came to Pakistan for my first wedding. Ours was a friendship born out of feeling lost and alone; she was the first person who accepted who I was and never asked any questions. But this was also the year I realised that I was different – because of the colour of my skin, my experiences and where I came from – and that feeling never left me, not even in Pakistan, the country that was meant to be my home and where I should have felt accepted.

Family shami kebabs

Both of my grandmothers and my mother cooked these (pictured overleaf), and this is a combination of all their recipes. Feel free to double the amounts: cooked shami kebabs freeze well and my mother's freezer is never without a batch. They can be served as a starter with drinks, or as a treat with afternoon tea, accompanied by chutney, pickle or ketchup – and chai, of course. They are also great with rice, daal and a pickle, alongside a main meal.

Preparation: 20 minutes + 30 minutes soaking
Cooking time: 1 hour 45 minutes
Makes about 15–20, enough to serve 6–8

4 cm (1½ inches) ginger, roughly chopped
1 egg, lightly beaten
2 tablespoons pomegranate seeds
3 tablespoons sunflower oil

For the coriander and mint chutney

100 g (3½ oz) coriander (cilantro) leaves with stems, but not roots
2 green chillies, deseeded if desired, roughly chopped – optional
15–20 mint leaves
salt, to taste
juice of ½ lemon

For the kebab mixture

175 g (6 oz) chana daal (split chickpeas) or yellow split peas
650 g (1 lb 7 oz) lean minced (ground) beef
1 onion, peeled and cut into quarters
4 garlic cloves, peeled but left whole
1 cinnamon stick
6 green cardamom pods, bruised
2 star anise
1 dried red chilli
1 bay leaf
1 tablespoon cumin seeds, roasted in a dry frying pan and ground
½ tablespoon coriander seeds, roasted in a dry frying pan and ground
10 black peppercorns, coarsely ground
1 tomato, cut into quarters
salt, to taste

- For the kebab mixture, soak the chana daal in a bowl of water for 30 minutes. Place all the remaining ingredients in a large saucepan with a lid. Pour in about 450 ml (16 fl oz) of water, just enough to cover everything. Cook over medium heat, stirring regularly, for 30–40 minutes, or until the water has evaporated completely – the mixture needs to be very dry.
- Meanwhile, make the chutney by blending all the ingredients in a blender or small food processor. The chutney needs to be thick enough to work as a stuffing for the kebabs, so don't be tempted to add any water to help with the blending.
- Once the kebab mixture is bone-dry, remove the cinnamon, cardamom pods, star anise, chilli and bay leaf.
- Transfer the kebab mixture to a food processor, along with the ginger, and blitz to a smooth paste. Add the egg and blitz again to combine.
- To make the shami kebabs, mould 2 tablespoons of the mixture into a ball about the size of a golf ball. Using your thumb, make a hollow in the centre and add about half a teaspoon of the chutney and a couple of pomegranate seeds, then form the mixture back around them, enclosing the stuffing completely. Gently flatten the kebab into a burger shape. Continue until all the mixture is used up.
- To cook the kebabs, heat the oil in a frying pan over medium heat and fry the kebabs in batches for 2–3 minutes on each side until well browned. Remove and drain on paper towels.
- Eat immediately, with any remaining chutney on the side, or freeze for up to 3 months, remembering to let them thaw before reheating thoroughly.

One of my favourite ways to eat these is by making the Karachi street food called bun kebab: a soft brioche bun is lightly fried in a little ghee and filled with a hot shami kebab, tamarind and coriander chutneys and salad.

Mummy’s Genoise sponge cake with fresh cream

This cake (pictured on previous page) is one my mother makes to this day. Based on a traditional Genoise cake, it is light and fluffy, and all it takes is a little patience and time.

Prep time: 20–30 minutes
Cooking time: 25–30 minutes
Serves 6–8

125 g (4½ oz) plain (all-purpose) flour
1 tablespoon cornflour (cornstarch)
pinch of salt
50 g (1¾ oz) unsalted butter
125 g (4½ oz) caster (superfine) sugar
4 eggs, at room temperature
½ teaspoon vanilla extract
handful of fresh raspberries or grated dark chocolate, to decorate
icing (confectioners’) sugar, for dusting – optional

For the filling and topping

250 ml (1 cup) whipping (pure) cream
5–6 tablespoons icing (confectioners’) sugar, to taste
½ teaspoon vanilla extract
1 teaspoon rose water
½ teaspoon gelatine powder, dissolved in 1 tablespoon hot water

To Mummy, making friends in England meant feeding them, offering them food she made with love and patience. She did this by hosting coffee mornings and inviting all the neighbourhood ladies.

- Preheat the oven to 180°C (350°F). Butter two 20 cm (8 inch) round cake tins and line them with baking paper.
- Sift the flour, cornflour and salt together. Set aside.
- Heat the butter until it has just melted, then leave to cool slightly.
- Quarter-fill a saucepan with just-boiled water, then set a heatproof bowl (ideally glass) over the pan so it sits just above the water without touching it. Add the sugar, eggs and vanilla to the bowl and, using handheld electric beaters, whisk for a good 3–5 minutes until the batter has a mousse-like consistency. Do this initially on low speed without moving the beaters around, then increase the speed and continue whisking until the batter is very pale and fluffy – when you lift out the beaters, a thick ribbon of batter should fall from them. Keep going until you achieve this, as it is extremely important for the lightness of the finished cake. Remove the bowl from the pan and whisk the batter for about 1–2 minutes, just until the bowl has cooled slightly.
- Now add the melted butter, carefully pouring it around the edges of the batter and taking care to leave behind any white sediment from the butter. Using a large metal spoon, gently fold the butter through in only two or three folds, lightly cutting through the batter in a figure-of-eight motion.
- Sift half of the flour mixture over the batter and gently fold it in using the same technique. Once it is incorporated, sift over the remaining flour mixture and gently fold that in too, being careful not to deflate the batter.
- Divide the batter evenly between the tins, then bake in the centre of the oven for 25–30 minutes, until the cakes are well risen and spring back when lightly pressed.
- Leave the cakes to cool in their tins for 5 minutes, then carefully loosen by running a thin-bladed knife around the edges. Place the cakes on a wire rack and leave to cool completely.
- Meanwhile, whip the cream and icing sugar to soft peaks, then add the vanilla and rose water. While whipping, drizzle in the gelatine mixture and keep whipping until the cream holds stiff peaks.
- Once the cakes are completely cooled, place one on a serving plate and smear some cream over it, then top with the other cake. Smear more cream on top of the cake and decorate with raspberries or chocolate, plus a dusting of icing sugar if you wish – this is all very rustic and there is no need for perfection.
- If not serving the cake right away, keep it in the fridge and eat within 24 hours.

A MENU TO IMPRESS
based on Mummy's entertaining
* Family shami kebabs page 38
* Yakhni chicken pullao page 166
* Chicken boti tikka, Bundoo Khan style page 146
* Mummy's wedding-style chicken korma page 228
* Mummy's Genoise sponge with fresh cream page 42

CHAPTER 3

Faith in the flavour of your hands

No two people ever replicate
a recipe exactly; knowing that
my hands can create unique
flavours gives me confidence in
my cooking, and in life generally.

Karachi, May 1981

COMPETING COOKING STYLES

Daddy had recently started his law business and money was tight, so on our return to Karachi, just a few months after my eighth birthday, we moved into the upstairs flat in Nani Mummy's (my maternal grandmother's) house. The flat was small and didn't have a separate bedroom for me, so I slept behind a screen in my parents' room, with no privacy and little room for my things.

My maternal grandparents had initially lived in Rawalpindi after partition in 1947, but moved to Karachi in the mid-1960s, when my Nana (maternal grandfather) took early retirement, after suffering a heart attack. Sadly, he didn't get to enjoy his new home for long as he passed away a few years later, leaving Nani Mummy a young widow. With characteristic grace and strength, she shouldered the burden of running a massive house all on her own, and the responsibility of marrying off her stepchildren as well as my mother and her brother. During those years, she'd rented out parts of the house – but now we were back home, she was happy to fill it with family again.

The house was just off the main airport road; embassies and schools fringed the side lanes. The houses on our street adjoined the *kachi abadi*, or shanty homes. Beyond our gate, I would watch barefoot children playing fearlessly near rubbish heaps and open gutters.

After heavy monsoon downpours, the canal often overflowed, bringing with it wafts of sewage through our windows. But we were shielded from the reality of our surroundings by a driveway lined with eucalyptus trees and a coconut tree that never bore any fruit, and high boundary walls covered with purple, white and red bougainvillea. Because Nana loved playing badminton with Nani Mummy, he had even built a tennis court, which was now our extended car park and Nani Mummy's vegetable plot. Here was where I spent my afternoons, discovering vegetables like *tori*, *teenday* and *loki* – local gourds that Nani Mummy grew and cooked simply with cumin or coriander seeds, to be eaten with just chapatti and fresh herb chutney.

Although we'd eat dinner in our flat, Mummy and I would have lunch with Nani Mummy. Frugal with her ingredients but generous with the portions, there would be multiple dishes, and meals were banquets, irrespective of whether there were other guests or not. Nani Mummy would lay the daily lunch trolley with four main dishes, rice and *achar* (pickles). I found a sense of comfort in everything she made and started eating with her more often.

Nani Mummy's hair was well-coiffed in a netted bun at the nape of her neck, and her ample body suited saris well. Her dark eyes seemed almost black behind her glasses, and she had perfectly shaped lips – made for lipstick, but feathered by age-lines now. The mango tree that stood in the middle of Nani Mummy's garden had, like her, lived gracefully through seasons of change. It was surrounded by *chikoo* (sapodilla) trees, which bore fruit that resembled round kiwi fruit in the summer, and guava trees, which were laden with luscious, pink-fleshed fruit in the winter.

I looked forward to the time when the mango tree's white blossoms formed tiny raw mangoes, with their promise of forbidden tartness. I'd cut the flesh into slivers and coat it with a masala of salt, chilli powder and lemon, then hide in the corner of the garden, devouring every jaw-aching morsel. Nani Mummy never approved: 'You have robbed them of their fate,' she'd declare in Urdu, 'I wanted to make some *achar*.'

Most of her food was basic Punjabi fare, like *tori gosht* (mutton with gourd) or *aloo gosht* (potatoes with meat). 'Punjabi food is rustic,' she explained. 'It's about slowly stewing spices with meat, and then adding vegetables to it. That's hearty village cooking – no point in cooking the hell out of meat the way your Dadi (paternal grandmother) does.'

There was a stark contrast between the food I ate at my two grandmothers' homes, and an undercurrent of competitiveness between their cooking styles. My Dadi's food was rich, each meat dish included onions cooked until they were as dark as night and at least ten whole spices. With her refined North Indian culinary heritage, she cooked with process and patience: she never mixed vegetables in a meat dish; vegetables were cooked on their own, with just as much care as the meat. She could not bear to cook any other way. Dadi also cooked her ingredients until they were really brown – in the early days of her marriage, Mummy was surprised at how caramelised her food was. On one occasion, Dadi even asked Mummy to re-fry the shami kebabs because they didn't look brown and cooked enough.

'If I cook them any further, they will be burnt,' Mummy protested.

But Dadi simply said, 'No, the darker the sides, the more the flavour.'

In comparison, Nani Mummy's food seemed almost peasant-like, with light spicing and wishy-washy gravy – always with meat and stewed vegetables mixed together. And her kebabs were always delicately light brown. But there was no less flavour in her food than in my Dadi's.

What I came to learn in each kitchen was that although they both used the same spices and ingredients, the flavours were different because of the story, heritage and method of their recipes. Dadi's family was from the Lucknow area, and they cooked Awadhi cuisine, the food of the nobles of India. Everything was made in the traditional *bhuna* way, where dishes were cooked until they were dry and the oil in them rose to the surface – this indicated that the spices were deeply infused into the main ingredient, giving it a haunting depth of flavour.

Nani Mummy's food was always fresh and quick, based on the cooking techniques of Punjabi farmers, who made meals from what the land gave them every season, using lots of butter and ghee.

Neither of them cut any corners with fresh produce and spices, but their food tasted different because it was cooked by different hands. Both my grandmothers maintained that cooking was a result of three components – ingredients, method and technique – and no one could replicate a recipe because no two people would ever cook a recipe in exactly the same way. After all, everyone has different hands, and hands bring food to life. They also both strongly believed that recipes shouldn't be written, but rather experienced and shared, following the oral tradition.

In the years after Mummy got married, she began to enjoy the results of Dadi's time-consuming methods, and as she gradually adopted many of the same cooking practices, her Punjabi roots went by the wayside. When I started to cook Pakistani food, I was surprised to see that I cooked like Dadi too. But the food I cooked to nurture myself during difficult times was always Nani Mummy's – dishes such as *aloo gosht*, with potatoes and meat swimming in a delicate, thin red sauce, sprinkled with home-made garam masala to add a fresh layer of spice.

AS COMFORTING AS CARDAMOM

Naturally, Mummy and Daddy wanted me to go to a good school – and Karachi Grammar School, my mother's alma mater, and the top English institution in the city, was their first choice. I had no idea what to expect from the entrance exam, and I don't think my parents did either.

On the day of the exam, we had to risk our lives to get to the school, as it was located in Old Karachi, a chaotic part of the city that was frequently subject to sectarian violence and curfews; the roads were deserted, with police vans parked up at every street corner. The city was especially sombre following the recent hijacking of a Pakistan International Airlines flight, and trouble was erupting everywhere.

Outside the school's open courtyard, policemen in grey shirts and khaki trousers swaggered around, guarding the main gate, loaded Kalashnikovs slung over their shoulders. Inside the sandstone building, girls and boys dressed in grey and white lined the corridors. Some of the children were sitting near the tuck shop, feasting on plates of chaat with spicy coriander tamarind chutney and crunchy *papri* snacks, and washing it down with excruciatingly sweet, bright-green Pakola ice-cream soda. I really wanted to be part of all this, but I felt anxious, like I didn't deserve to be here. Built during the British Raj, the school was a remnant of colonialism, and to attend it meant you were associated with that – the very walls exuded a sense of superiority.

With every minute I spent waiting outside the exam hall, I felt more and more nervous about the exam, and about myself. When I finally opened the maths exam paper, I felt a burning sickness pass through my body. As I read the words 'long division', my eyes began to sting – I had never done long division before.

'I've failed the entrance exam,' I said, as I walked in through Nani Mummy's back door, my head bursting with stress and the muggy summer heat. She was standing by her 1960s white gas cooker, and the kitchen was filled with the cooling astringency of cardamom.

'I'd better make you some *kheer* then,' she said.

Nani Mummy's *kheer* (rice pudding) was always soothing, even at the worst of times. She heated leftover cooked basmati rice with raw buffalo milk, cardamom and unrefined sugar. Most people used broken uncooked rice grains, but Nani Mummy mashed up cooked rice, which made her rice pudding mushier – but best of all, it cooked faster. As the milk came up to the boil, she added even more milk.

'Are you sure that's not too much milk?' I asked. 'It looks like a rice milkshake.'

'Have some faith, Somi,' she said.

'When will it be ready?' I asked.

'It's done when it feels right.' Nani Mummy replied.

'But how will I know it feels right? You're not even telling me any timings.'

'*Kheer* is about patience and faith,' she said, 'and the time it takes depends on many things, the rice and milk – each grain is different, each buffalo is unique.'

I watched, breathing in the sticky, sweet scent of hot milk. The flecks of cardamom danced around as the *kheer* thickened. When the pudding was chilled, it smelt like violets in a summer's garden. But I couldn't wait, so I took a hot spoonful and it singed the roof of my mouth: a strong taste, a mixture of pine and smoky mint, filled my senses. The sweet rice was balm to my heart, just like one of Nani Mummy's soft hugs, and it took my mind off everything, including what had happened at the school. No one could make *kheer* like Nani Mummy. It never crossed my mind that one day I'd have to make it on my own, and so I should memorise her recipe. I was sure she wasn't going anywhere.

Many years later, I tried to cook Nani Mummy's *kheer* without her. Despite following every step from memory and using all the same ingredients, the taste, smell and texture were so far removed from her *kheer*. I wished so much that I could call her and ask her what she did that made it so special. But by then it was too late to seek her guidance in exploring this visceral way of cooking, or to taste the flavour in her hands again. 'Cooking is a natural thing, you can feel it through your body, from your hands and your senses,' she would say. I needed to discover this on my own, by trusting myself and my memories.

PARATHAS AND SPICE MARKETS

I couldn't face Mummy and Daddy that night – the disappointment in their eyes would have been too much to bear. I stayed up chatting to Nani Mummy until we both fell asleep with the light on; her high-ceilinged bedroom smelt of a mix of calming *motia* (sambac jasmine) and the newspapers that were strewn across the bed and lodged between the pillows. On one side was a rosewood-framed sofa with an array of mismatched cushions that had lost shape; next to it stood a telephone table with a rotary dial phone. Her bed was two singles pressed together – the mattress was hard, and I could feel the springs in my back. Her cupboards were filled with chiffon saris and smelt of Yardley English Lavender drawer sheets. When being an only child felt stifling, overwhelming, and I wanted to escape the intensity of my parents' attention, I'd often spend the night with Nani Mummy.

The next morning, I woke to the sound of the cuckoo, and of my Nani praying. She was sitting on her prayer mat, mumbling in Arabic.

'Why do we pray in a language we don't speak?' I asked.

'It is the language of our religion; you'll soon understand the sentiments behind the words. I will teach you how to say *namaz* today,' Nani Mummy said, as she finished her prayer and blew it in my direction.

She brought over a plastic tray with tea and rusks, then stirred dried milk powder into a cup of richly brewed Lipton's Yellow Label. I watched the scattered freckles on her arms – some of them looked like tiny broken hearts. As we dipped our rusks into our tea, crumbs fell between the pillows, never to be brushed away.

I learnt nearly everything I know about Islam from Nani Mummy. She taught me the five *kalmas* prayers from the Quran by rote over cups of chai or after a lunch of keema-and-chutney-filled 'flying saucers'. Somehow all my religious lessons involved food: the eating of it, or the anticipation of it. On holy days I would go with Nani Mummy to the Sufi saint's shrine to feed the meat and daal porridge called *haleem* to the children that flocked there. Every year, on Nana's *barsi* (the anniversary of his death), after prayers we would cook semolina halva and distribute it to the entire family. But my favourite was any sort of rice dessert, especially the *firni* Nani Mummy made with ground rice for *milad*, the Prophet Muhammad's birthday (peace be upon him). I would always be the first to shove a spoon into the large bowl, hoping to find one of the lucky silver rings hidden inside – if you found a ring, your wishes would come true. I never did find one.

After our morning chai, Nani Mummy and I would make sweet parathas for breakfast, shaping them into squares.

'Why do you make your parathas square and not round?' I asked.

'Because square ones are special,' she explained. 'Besides, I'd rather spend time making the ghee that goes into them.'

I realised later that it was easier to make square parathas, requiring less precision. It was her ghee that took the time. Every day for a week, she'd collect cream from the raw buffalo milk that was delivered daily – by boiling and cooling it, then skimming off the cream. At the end of the week, she'd cook the cream for hours, until the solids separated out and the kitchen filled with a slightly animalistic hay-like aroma, which soon turned to mouth-watering butterscotch and toffee. The ghee would be strained into jars for storage, but it never lasted long in her house.

When Nani Mummy wanted to make parathas, she'd pour flour into a bowl and add water until it came together into a soft dough, adding a large pinch of pink salt and some ghee. As she kneaded the dough, the veins on the backs of her hands would stand out more than normal. I'd help her to roll the parathas, one by one, into thin flatbreads. There were so many variations – *laccha* (flaky), *aloo* (potato), *methi* (fenugreek) – but we always made sweet parathas. She'd slap a raw flatbread onto the *tawa* (a flat griddle pan), pressing it onto the hot metal with a scrunched-up tea towel to brown the bottom, as tiny bubbles formed on the top, then she'd flip it to cook the other side. As soon as the parathas were ready, she would smear on ghee and sprinkle them with *shakar* (raw sugar) until they glistened with specks of sugar. I would roll each paratha up into a sort of roly-poly: the *shakar* tasted like fudge, the home-made ghee tasted pure. She always made more than I should have been able to eat – but, in the end, I always managed to eat them all.

As with all leftovers, any surplus dough was never discarded. Anything cooked or unused would be wrapped in plastic and kept in the fridge or freezer. She would never throw anything away and I don't think she ever cared for 'best before' dates. 'If it smells ok and it isn't green, it is fine to eat,' she would say.

Except, that is, when it came to spices. Every month she would replenish her stock, particularly star anise, cinnamon and cumin, these being the spices she used the most. The best weren't to be found in supermarkets – most there would be stale, smelling more of wood than spice. She wouldn't even buy them from CSD, a supermarket for armed forces personnel where, as the widow of a former army employee, she was able to shop at discount prices. For spices, we would make the trip out to Empress Market.

In the heart of Old Karachi, Empress Market was a crumbling legacy of the Raj era, built to commemorate Queen Victoria. It was on a noisy road, where traffic came from all directions and no one respected the rules of the road. Minibuses decorated with garish truck art whizzed past and deafeningly loud rickshaws filled the air with exhaust fumes. Wooden carts laden with bargain fruit and vegetables were parked up around the market building, promising better prices – but for lesser quality. Above the main entrance was a large clock tower that hadn't worked since the 1940s. We would walk through one of the dimly lit corridors, flanked on either side by broken reed baskets and old crates piled high with vegetables, passing stalls full of spices and roots, and the lemon merchant with his wall-high displays of tiny lemons and fresh herbs. Our senses were assaulted with vibrant colour and the floral essence of coriander, mint and green chillies. At the back of the corridor was the spice merchant my Nani always went to – she was a creature of habit.

'*Asalam-al-lakkum*, Aunty, what can I get you today?' he greeted her. A stocky man with a shock of grey hair, he wore a dirty grey *shalwar kameez* (long tunic and trousers) and his pot belly stuck out noticeably.

'1 *pao* star anise, 1 *pao* cardamom and ½ *pao* cinnamon,' she ordered. (A *pao* is equivalent to about 250 g, or 9 oz.) 'And make sure you don't give me that cheap cinnamon you gave me last time; it smells of nothing. I will pick my own this time.'

With her nimble fingers, she grabbed a bag made of old newspaper and began to pick out the best pieces. The aroma of cinnamon rising from the pile of quills made me hungry for Nani Mummy's chickpea pullao. She checked each quill for size and shape, sniffing it to see if it was suitable, then giving a small nod as she popped it into the bag. As the most accomplished bargainer in our family, she didn't take kindly to being short-changed by market stall-keepers. 'I am not paying a hundred rupees an ounce, I am telling you right now,' Nani Mummy said. 'This broken star anise isn't worth that much; you'd better give them to me for fifty.'

The fruit market area was next to the spices and was where we would buy persimmons in summer or pomegranates in winter. But today we wanted prawns.

I found the fresh fish market area the hardest to deal with; the saline smell would punch you in the nose long before you even got close. The hall was filled with fishmongers sitting cross-legged on blue-tiled counters, their fish laid out on crushed ice. All the seafood in Karachi came from the Arabian Sea or the River Indus: there was kingfish, pomfret, red snapper, prawns and sometimes Sindhi hilsa. Each of the fishmongers would shout out prices, their voices echoing loudly, mingling together like a chant.

'Red snapper, fresh, 100 rupees a kilo,' shouted one.

'Red snapper, just out of the ocean, only 96 rupees today!' shouted another, louder and more competitive than the last.

Well-fed stray cats scrambled over the fish heads and bones that fell to the floor from the chopping benches. We walked over to Nani Mummy's favourite fishmonger to collect the prawns he kept aside for her each week. After they'd been weighed and packed, we hastily made our way out before our noses were filled with the intense fishiness of the place. The prawns were so fresh that it seemed as if they were still moving in the bag.

NANI MUMMY'S PRAWN KARAHI

Those prawns were cooked straight away. I still believe seafood should be cooked as soon as possible, so it retains the flavour of the ocean. When we got home, I was given the messy task of shelling and deveining them. The shells slipped off easily, but I held my breath as I pulled out the slimy gunk from the insides of the prawns. I couldn't help feeling that I was being given the dirty work.

'Why can't I learn how to cook them instead?' I asked.

'You are learning,' she said. 'Each step is part of the recipe, including buying and even peeling the prawns. Next time you'll know how to cook them without my help.'

Nani Mummy heated up a *karahi* pan, tossing in a couple of spoonfuls of ghee, a large five-finger pinch of cumin and a dash each of turmeric, chilli powder and salt.

'Add a little *ka*,' said Nani Mummy.

'How much is a little?' I asked.

'Smell it – imagine how much will taste right,' she replied.

When I shoved my fingers into the spice jar and took out about a teaspoon's worth, Nani Mummy raised one eyebrow. This was a test, the very first time I was asked to balance a spice. I had been entrusted with adding the make-or-break ingredient. Too little, and it would be drowned in the rich sauce, too much and it would overpower the delicate prawns. I sniffed the spice: it was intensely fragrant, like a cross between caraway seeds and fresh oregano. I knew *ajwain* (carom seeds) went well with seafood, but I also knew that seafood had a subtle flavour that shouldn't be masked. Finally, I took a tiny pinch of the small seeds and threw them in. Nani Mummy smiled. She then added grated tomatoes and chopped green chillies and let everything soften until the sauce was half-juicy, half-dry. She took time over this, stirring patiently until the sauce was thick and filled with the sweetness of sun-drenched tomatoes, balanced by the sharp heat of fresh green chillies. This was the one recipe she never made with a watery sauce. 'You must wait for the tomato water to dry,' she said. 'The sauce gets too slimy otherwise.'

And that was nearly it. She added the prawns, quickly tossing them in the glistening sauce until they turned pink, their faint fishiness replaced with the headiness of the spicy sauce. I chopped coriander and more green chilli for the garnish and squeezed in some lemon juice. Spooned onto a large sharing platter, the pinkness of the prawns complemented the shades in the deep red tomato sauce, begging to be eaten immediately. We'd bought some roti from the local tandoor on the way home and, as I licked the jaw-aching lemony sauce of the prawns off my fingers, Nani Mummy berated me: 'What a dirty habit – well-brought-up young ladies never lick their fingers!'

Mummy and Daddy had booked me in to sit another school entrance exam the next day, and I was dreading the prospect, but being at the market and cooking with Nani Mummy had been a welcome distraction. I ate slowly, suppressing my nerves.

I finally got into a nearby school. A newly opened one called Foundation Public School, it promised an excellent level of education. My class was a mixed bunch, and initially I felt that I had nothing in common with them; no one understood my accent or appreciated my experiences. I was the tallest girl in the class, and I hid behind my braces. I was missing Dawn, and in many ways I felt more alone than I had when we first arrived in England or in all those years at sea. I found it hard to keep up and looked forward to getting home. I would throw my bag down on the bed and head out to the garden to pick vegetables or go shopping for ingredients that would form dinner that night.

I came to realise that learning didn't happen just in the classroom, but in the markets and bazaars Nani Mummy took me to, and in the kitchen with her and Mummy. I learnt how to select the best-quality spices and soon became unfazed by raw meat or fish. Trusting my senses didn't come easily to me, but the more I believed in myself, the more things improved. Although I didn't fully appreciate the confidence that 'the flavour in my hands' offered me until much later, I did quickly realise that being around food made me feel different – both the cooking of it and the lessons I learnt from it. It was this education that offered me refuge as I began to find my place in our new home.

Trusting my senses didn't come easily to me, but the more I believed in myself, the more things improved.

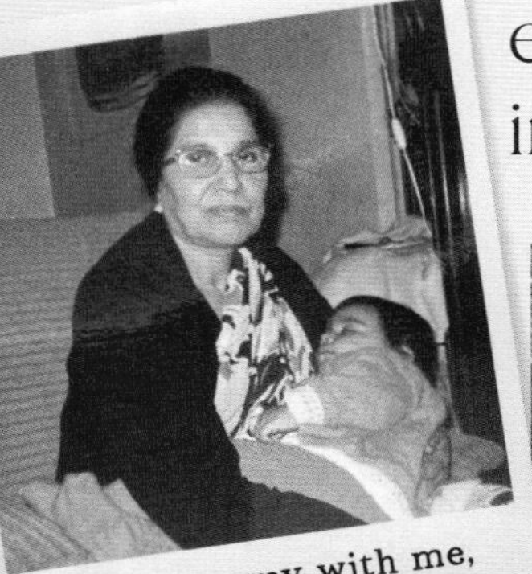

Nani Mummy with me, aged 1

Nani Mummy's prawn karahi

This goes beautifully with Bitter lemon, mustard seed and garlic pullao (recipe on page 273), though it's equally delicious with sourdough as a quick lunch.

Prep time: 10 minutes
Cooking time: 15–20 minutes
Serves 4

2 tablespoons ghee (or 1 tablespoon unsalted butter and 1 tablespoon sunflower oil)
1 heaped teaspoon cumin seeds
½ teaspoon nigella seeds (*kalonji*)
½ teaspoon carom seeds (*ajwain*) – optional
1 cm (½ inch) ginger, finely grated
4 large ripe tomatoes, coarsely grated, skins discarded
2 tablespoons concentrated tomato puree (tomato paste)
¼ teaspoon turmeric powder
½ teaspoon Kashmiri chilli powder (or other chilli powder or paprika)
salt, to taste
450 g (1 lb) shelled, deveined fresh raw prawns

To garnish

juice of ½ lemon
2.5 cm (1 inch) ginger, cut into fine strips
2 tablespoons chopped coriander (cilantro) leaves
1 green chilli, deseeded and finely chopped

- Place a wok or frying pan over medium-high heat and add the ghee. When it is hot, add the cumin, nigella and carom seeds (if using) and fry until fragrant, about 1 minute.
- Next add the ginger and fry for 10–15 seconds, until fragrant, then stir in the tomatoes. Lower the heat slightly, add a splash of water and keep stirring until it starts to simmer. Add the tomato puree, turmeric, chilli powder and salt.
- Keep cooking until the sauce thickens and the oil begins to rise to the surface, about 7–9 minutes. Once this happens, add the prawns and cook, stirring, until the prawns turn pink, about 3–4 minutes. Be careful not to overcook the prawns, or they will go rubbery.
- Turn the heat off, add the garnishes and cover, then leave to infuse for a minute or so before serving.

Based on my maternal grandmother's recipe, this is best made with fresh raw prawns, rather than already cooked ones.

Nani Mummy's firni

I find the greatest comfort in making and eating this sweet, silky rice dessert that my grandmother used to make for me. Use freshly ground cardamom for intensity and freshness of flavour.

Prep time: 10 minutes
Cooking time: 15 minutes
Serves 4–6

60 g (2¼ oz) ground rice
500 ml (2 cups) whole (full-cream) milk, oat milk or rice milk
2–3 tablespoons caster (superfine) sugar, to taste
200 ml (7 fl oz) sweetened condensed milk, or non-dairy alternative
3–4 green cardamom pods, cracked open, seeds extracted and ground – you need ½ teaspoon ground cardamom
pinch of saffron threads
½ teaspoon screwpine extract (*kewra*) or rose water
1 tablespoon chopped pistachios
1 tablespoon edible dried organic rose petals or buds
1 tablespoon edible silver leaf – optional

- In a bowl, soak the ground rice in 200 ml (7 fl oz) of water for about 10 minutes.
- In a large saucepan, bring the milk to the boil over medium heat. As soon as it is boiling, reduce the heat and simmer for 10 minutes, or until thick.
- Add the sugar, condensed milk and the ground rice, along with any soaking water that's left, and return to the boil. Let the milk boil for another 5–7 minutes, stirring constantly to prevent it from burning.
- When it has the consistency of thick custard, stir in the cardamom, then turn off the heat and stir in the saffron and the screwpine extract or rose water. Allow to cool for a few minutes before pouring into terracotta or glass bowls and topping with chopped pistachios.
- Chill in the refrigerator for at least 1 hour before serving, scattered with rose petals and the silver leaf, if using.

'Cooking is a natural thing, you can feel it through your body, from your hands and your senses,' Nani Mummy would say. I needed to discover this on my own, by trusting myself and my memories.

CHAPTER 4

Feed your guests, and feed them well

In Pakistan, nurturing friendships and family centres on our relationship with food. The most deeply etched sentiment is that you'd give up your own food to a guest. Feeding others is a way of sharing more than just a meal; it is a representation of your gratitude for their presence in your life, and creating elaborate, laborious meals is the most generous gift of all.

Karachi, May 1984

THE FORBIDDEN KULFI

'*Kulfi-wala, kulfi-wala!*' The chanting outside my bedroom window snapped me out of my heat-induced coma. The kulfi seller's shrill voice pierced my ears. What I'd do to have just one street-side kulfi, to let it melt away that lethargy of humidity. These ivory ice creams softened the dense Karachi coastal air, a pleasure I was denied. They were made using raw milk – and possibly 'gutter water' with 'a hundred different germs', according to my parents – but their denial only made me want one even more.

I watched from afar as children from across the street ran to the *kulfi-wala*. He'd park his wooden cart outside our house for the rest of the afternoon and passers-by would flock to him, seeking a moment's respite from the heat. The kulfi, so faint and slender that it seemed to disappear almost as soon as it emerged from its stainless-steel mould, was dipped into pistachio powder. Balanced precariously on its bamboo stick, it dripped screwpine-infused melted cream and powdered nuts, making a sticky, delicious mess.

The kulfi pops were kept frozen in a large steel tin with blocks of ice, covered with a dirty jute cloth that was teaming with ants and flies – this probably added to Mummy's reservations. I watched the other children longingly, feeling sorry for myself that my parents forbade me such a simple joy. Mummy made her own kulfi at home, to make up for it. She told me stories of its travel from Persia to the Mughal kitchens, and now to our streets. She explained that kulfi is more than just an ice cream to Pakistanis, being both a celebration of simplicity of flavour and a reminder of opulence.

'The secret of making real kulfi isn't in the street version,' she tried to convince me. 'The texture comes from nuts or breadcrumbs, slowly cooked in milk until it's thickened and rich,' she said.

'That's boring. It'll take ages,' I said.

'Nothing good comes quickly, Somi. You think the man on the street takes such time to make kulfi?' she said. 'He's looking to make a quick buck. That kulfi is nothing but dirty frozen milk.'

Mummy made her kulfi by boiling buffalo milk until it thickened, scraping the bottom of the pan to avoid it burning, then adding condensed milk, followed by buffalo cream. The delicate perfume of milk and cardamom filled the air, and each step took time. It was cooked for what felt like hours, until it had all reduced down to half of what it was. Then she would add saffron, ground pistachios and almonds (or sometimes breadcrumbs), heating them through before sweetening the kulfi.

'The saffron or rose water goes in right at the end to give it a rich flavour, like the Mughal version,' Mummy said. 'If you add them any earlier, their aroma disappears.'

I'd roll my eyes, knowing that by the time the kulfi was ready, I'd no longer crave it.

The kulfi was poured into small, unglazed terracotta urn-shaped moulds called *matka* that would sit in a basin of salt and crushed ice, and the whole lot would go into the freezer.

'Why is salt mixed with the ice, Mummy?'

'Because the salt will quicken the freezing, and so there won't be any ice crystals in the kulfi.'

After a couple of hours, the kulfi would be ready. I'd grumble that we could have just bought one from the street-side seller and taken a gamble on the germs, rather than have to wait for nearly a whole day, but I'd forget all that as soon as it came out of the freezer. The terracotta moulds would be cold to the touch, with no beads of condensation. Peeling back the circle of paper from the top of the kulfi, to reveal tiny speckles of pistachio and saffron on its surface, was magical.

Home-made kulfi didn't melt into a liquid like ice cream; its melted texture was more like cake batter, delicate and fluffy. As the spoon reached the bottom of the *matka*, fragments of unglazed terracotta would be scraped off and break down into the kulfi, their earthiness mingling with the sweet taste of the cream. I relished this moment; I was certain that a kulfi on a stick could never have the same flavour.

It was in these small moments that I realised my life wasn't like that of many other people who lived in Pakistan. I was protected from the perils of the outside world, which was chaotic, dirty and unsafe – yet I grew up around it, with no visual filters. It felt confusing to me that there were these two sides to Pakistan, and I wasn't sure whether I was on the right one. Surely kulfi on the street would be worth trying just once, taking the risk of getting sick, just to experience what everyone else did.

NAUREEN'S ROLL-UPS

After two years at my new school, I began to get good grades, and I finally felt like I had found my way with education. I was top of the class in every subject, and my parents couldn't have been prouder. That summer, as a treat, we went to Greece and Turkey on holiday, and returned just in time for the start of term. I was excited about the new school year, and I couldn't wait to get back to my streak of good grades and attention from teachers and classmates alike. But that year, Naureen joined my class and everything changed.

Naureen had a black bob with a wavy fringe, and a different accent. Her family had just moved back to Karachi from Houston. She seemed shy, with an air of calmness about her. I wanted to talk to her, to reach out to another person who sounded different, like I did. I saw a little of myself in her: that quiet, shy girl in South Wonston, and the way I had felt in Karachi at first. She had that lost look in her eyes that I used to have – but although I was more confident now, somehow I was nervous around her, and I didn't speak to her until the end of that school year.

The day before school ended for the summer, we got our report cards for the year. Quietly confident of topping the class again, I was taken aback by the announcement from our class teacher: 'I'm excited to say that our new student Naureen has come first this year!'

My heart sunk, I felt robbed of my rightful title. Something inside me clicked, and I knew that I had to befriend her. I began a friendship based on competition and a little curiosity, but the friendship blossomed. We'd study together at her house, but by the end of the day we'd be listening to Laura Branigan's *Self Control* on full volume, singing at the top of our voices and dancing on the bed.

Every time I'd go there, she'd be waiting for me at the door with a packet of Betty Crocker fruit roll-ups and a jug of Kool-Aid on a tray. I had never eaten or drunk anything that tasted less of fruit than a grape roll-up and a watermelon Kool-Aid.

'These are the treats I grew up with in Houston,' she explained.

'They taste so disgusting that they're actually irresistible!' I said, peeling the sticky, glistening sweet off its plastic wrapper. She gave me a few to take home, and I wondered how long her stash would last.

Naureen loved stationery as much as I did, and we traded Hello Kitty stickers and pencils. She also had something much sought after in Karachi: the Scratch 'n' Sniff stickers you could only get in America – cookies 'n' cream, strawberry shortcake and grape jelly, with their saccharin-sweet, synthetic flavours that would leave a whiff of envy on my fingers long after I had left her house. I longed for these stickers that smelt of food, with their almost otherworldly reputation. I wanted to share something equally special with her, something she'd never tasted before, so I took it upon myself to learn how to make the Pakistani version of fruit roll-ups, *aam papar* (mango fruit leather). Even though I'd never made it on my own, I'd helped Nani Mummy make it every summer, so I had a rough idea.

The whole of Karachi smelt of mangoes in June. Every fruit stall in the city was piled high with different varieties: Sindhri and Langra mangoes were fragrant, large and yellow with pointy ends, and they tasted of honey; Anwar Rathore were small and greenish yellow, with a floral fragrance, almost like rhubarb. Squeezable, green-hued Chaunsa mangoes were fun to eat – you'd squish up the flesh, still in its skin, and then suck the molten lumpy pulp through a hole you made in the skin at one end of the fruit.

Naureen and I chose an assortment of mangoes from the stalls outside her house, and I began by carefully peeling a Sindhri mango, cutting every bit of flesh from the stone and then mashing it with a fork, adding salt, sugar, chilli powder and a pinch of roasted cumin. I'd cook the bright-orange mango pulp until it was soft and mushy before pressing it into a baking tray to make a half-centimetre-deep layer, then I'd leave it out in the sun all day to dry. After a day's sun-baking, the mango pulp would turn ochre, shining as if it had sucked up the sun's rays and was reflecting them back at us. The *aam papar* was sharp at first bite, and the spice in it scratched the back of our throats. It stuck to our teeth as it dissolved slowly, the taste reminding me of Sun-Maid raisins. When there was only one *aam papar* left, I hesitated, then offered it to Naureen, with my Nani's voice ringing in my head and telling me to share my last bite with my friend, no matter how much I craved it.

As much as I adored Naureen's roll-ups, with their fake fruit flavour, my version, made from the bounty of a Karachi summer, changed her idea of what fruit leather could be. We spent the rest of the holidays climbing mango trees and picking the juiciest fruits to make our treat again.

Naureen continued to beat me in exams, but it never got in the way of our friendship, and I resigned myself to the fact that I might never be top of the class again.

THE PATIENCE OF TURNIP KEBABS

Every Sunday, I'd go with Mummy and Daddy to my paternal grandparents' house. Dada and Dadi lived in Nazimabad, an area of Karachi where many of the Muhajirs (Muslim immigrants from India) settled following partition in 1947. This was some distance from where we lived, and the traffic between our place and theirs was notorious. We'd encounter buses driving at high speed and motorbikes with burst exhausts that rattled our brains. Although children and grandparents crossed the wide roads with no fear, there was no sense of road rules or pedestrian priority, and Mummy would close her eyes as Daddy navigated his way through this barrage of chaos.

'I've sailed ships through violent storms, we'll be fine,' he'd reassure my mother.

At Dadi's house, food would be central to the visit. We'd all sit at a long rectangular table and eat together. Meals were always at the table in our home too, but it was usually only the three of us, and there was something celebratory about sitting at a dining table with eight people (three of us, Dada and Dadi and three of my aunts who were living there at the time), that made the simplest Sunday meal an event.

We'd walk into the house and my Dada would be sitting by the television in his room, giving his relentless running commentary on the Urdu drama he was watching, his comments and opinions on the characters were as annoying as they were funny. I'd join him because it would give me an excuse for staying away from the kitchen, where I would be made to wash vegetables or plates.

Before long, Dadi would find me and tell me to come and help. Her kitchen had walls brushed with white limewash that had faded in patches, and the counter was made of concrete with light blue tiles on the top. A large burner fuelled by gas canisters sat in front of a large window that overlooked a garden full of herbs and flowers. I remember the flame on that burner being ferocious, and the whistling steam from the pressure cooker terrified me.

'*Beta* (child), pressure cookers make my life easier,' Dadi would say. 'Remember I have to cook for five people every day.'

But pressure cookers have never been my tool of choice in the kitchen. Even years later, I refuse to use a pressure cooker. To me, they make food taste rushed, leaving the flavour one-dimensional and basic, rather than allowing spices to express their flavour in all its complexity as they would if they were slow-cooked.

I wonder now why Dadi even bothered to use a pressure cooker when her style of cooking was mindful and meditative: all her food was so intricate and labour intensive that one more time-consuming step wouldn't have mattered. One such recipe was her turnip kebabs, made from steamed turnip, spices and herbs – they would take hours to make, but would disappear in five minutes when they came to the table. I never specifically learnt the recipe, but somehow picked it up through osmosis. When I eventually tried to make it decades later, it came to me as if I was turning the pages of a familiar storybook, each line remembered and retraced. The smells, stories and voices of the women of my family in the kitchen came flooding back.

'Peel the turnip until you can see no skin,' Dadi would say to Mummy, as Mummy made a mental note of it all (the top-shaped turnips we got from the markets were notoriously difficult to peel). 'After peeling, steam it until it's soft and the water runs dry, as if the moisture has been sucked in like a sponge.'

Next she'd take out the steaming turnip and let it cool, then crush it and squeeze out every single drop of moisture. This was crucial, because if any moisture remained, the kebab would fall apart in the pan. My task was to chop the coriander, mint and dill, while my aunts would toast cumin and coriander seeds and mix them with *anardana* (ground dried pomegranate seeds). Then we stirred everything together in a bowl with the turnip. Dadi would finish off the seasoning with some fresh ginger and salt. Taking it in turns, we formed the mixture into flat patties, ready to be dipped into beaten egg and fried. As they cooked, the kitchen came alive with the scent of the deep, sweet caramelisation of the turnips in the pan and a grassy freshness from the ginger, green chilli and herbs.

Turnip kebabs were always served with daal, rice and coriander chutney, which Dadi would make on her stone *sil batta* (mortar and pestle). There would be a meat dish to accompany it too, as no meal was considered complete without either lamb korma or chicken *saalan* (a thin, gravy-based stew).

My first few attempts to make Dadi's turnip kebabs were a failure – I just couldn't get all the moisture out. I'd get frustrated and angry, but Mummy would remind me what it meant to make them, what all cooking meant: it meant falling and then getting up and trying again, each time learning a little more about yourself. It meant never expecting perfection, but realising that cooking was about process, patience and perseverance.

Though I didn't know it then, it was this ethos of cooking that I tapped into when I began recreating my childhood meals later in life: I didn't need to know a recipe, merely recalling the flavours, smells and textures was enough to help me recreate it. In those everyday lessons I learnt that the effort taken to cook and share with generosity was as essential a component of any dish as the ingredients used. Sharing food means more than just sharing a meal.

Dadi's turnip kebabs

*This is based on my mother's handwritten recipe, as dictated to her by my paternal grandmother. Making these (pictured overleaf), and the patience they demand, takes me right back to my Dadi's home. The turnips you need here are the top-shaped, white-fleshed ones, rather than orange-fleshed swede (rutabaga). You should be able to find the dried pomegranate (*anardana*) at most Asian supermarkets or online, or you can substitute lemon juice – and if you're cooking for vegans, use cornflour instead of egg to bind the mixture. Eat the kebabs warm, with lemon wedges, coriander chutney (recipe on page 187), daal and rice.*

Prep time: 1 hour + overnight soaking
Cooking time: 30 minutes
Makes about 10 kebabs, enough to serve 5–6

3 tablespoons sunflower oil
3 tablespoons cornflour (cornstarch) or 1 beaten egg
lemon wedges, to serve

For the kebab mixture

50 g (¼ cup) chana daal (split chickpeas)
2 dried red chillies
3 turnips (not swede/rutabaga), peeled and cut into quarters
1 large potato, peeled, boiled and mashed
1 teaspoon cumin seeds, roasted in a dry frying pan and ground
1 teaspoon coriander seeds, roasted in a dry frying pan and ground
1 tablespoon ground dried pomegranate seeds (*anardana*) or juice of ½ lemon
¾ teaspoon garam masala
2–3 spring onions (scallions), including green parts, finely chopped
1 green chilli, deseeded and finely chopped
handful of coriander (cilantro) leaves, finely chopped
2.5 cm (1 inch) ginger, finely chopped
10 mint leaves, finely chopped
handful of dill leaves, finely chopped
salt, to taste

- For the kebab mixture, soak the chana daal overnight in a bowl of water. The next day, drain the daal, then place in a saucepan with the dried chillies. Add just enough fresh water to cover and boil for 15 minutes, or until dry and cooked. Drain and set aside.
- Put the turnip into another saucepan with 100 ml (3½ fl oz) of water, cover with a lid and cook over medium heat until all the water has gone. Check to see if the turnip is cooked: the tip of knife should slide in easily; if not, add another 25 ml (¾ fl oz) of water. Keep cooking until the turnip is done – this should take about 25–30 minutes altogether. Mash the turnip, then wrap in muslin (cheesecloth) and use your hands to squeeze out any excess liquid until it is completely dry.
- Place the mashed turnip in a bowl, then add the mashed potato, cooked chana daal and all the remaining ingredients for the kebab mixture. Mix and knead until everything is well combined.
- Mould about 2 tablespoons of the mixture into a ball, then flatten into a burger shape. Place on a plate and repeat until all the mixture is used up. The kebabs can be cooked straight away or frozen for up to 3 months and cooked directly from frozen.
- When you're ready to cook the kebabs, heat the oil in a frying pan over medium heat. Spread out the cornflour or egg on a plate. Working in batches, dip the kebabs into the cornflour or egg, lightly coating them all over, then place in the hot oil and cook for 3–4 minutes on each side, or until nicely browned. Serve with lemon wedges.

Mummy reminded me what it meant to make these kebabs, what all cooking meant: it meant falling and then getting up and trying again, each time learning a little more about yourself.

Street-side kulfi, Mummy's style

You can find kulfi moulds at some Asian shops and kitchenware suppliers but making the cones with baking paper is a lovely thing to do – it gives the kulfi (pictured on previous page) the tapered shape I remember from the kulfi vendors on the streets of Karachi.

Prep time: 15 minutes + overnight freezing
Cooking time: 5–6 minutes
Serves 6–8

5–6 green cardamom pods, cracked open, seeds extracted and ground
1 x 397 g (14 oz) tin of sweetened condensed milk
500 ml (2 cups) whole (full-cream) milk
4 tablespoons ricotta
5 tablespoons dried whole (full-cream) milk powder
1 tablespoon cornflour (cornstarch)
large pinch of saffron threads
1½ tablespoons pistachios, finely ground using a pestle and mortar – you need 2 tablespoons ground pistachios
1 tablespoon ground almonds (almond meal)
honey or sugar, to taste – optional
poppy seeds, to decorate

Mummy told me stories of how kulfi travelled from Persia to the Mughal kitchens, and now to our streets. She explained that it is more than just an ice cream to Pakistanis, being both a celebration of simplicity of flavour and a reminder of opulence.

- Place the cardamom, condensed milk, milk, ricotta, milk powder and cornflour in a blender or food processor and blend until combined. Pour the mixture into a saucepan and heat over low heat, stirring regularly. Keep stirring and cooking until the mixture thickens, about 15–20 minutes.
- Stir in the saffron, half of the ground pistachios and half of the ground almonds. Let them warm through, then take the pan off the heat.
- When the mixture has cooled slightly, taste it and adjust the sweetness by adding honey or sugar, if necessary, then leave to cool to room temperature.
- Pour the cooled mixture into kulfi moulds, then seal and freeze overnight. You could also use cones made from baking paper to make kulfi on a stick: stand each cone upright in a small glass (or a cream horn mould, if you have one) and pour in the mixture to the top of the cone. Let them semi-freeze for an hour or two before inserting a lolly (popsicle) stick into each one.
- When ready to serve, if using moulds, dip them into warm water to help ease out the kulfi. If using paper cones, gently peel the paper away to reveal your kulfi on a stick. Roll the kulfi through the poppy seeds and the remaining ground pistachios and almonds to decorate, then eat immediately.

CHAPTER 5

Cooking on meatless days

Coming of age in 1980s Pakistan feels restrictive. I begin to realise what it means to be a Muslim girl in Pakistani society, and it feels as if I always fall short of expectations. Spending weekends with my maternal grandmother to escape, I discover the wonder and colour of bazaars, and learn how to pick the best ingredients.

Karachi, 1984–1985

MEATLESS DAYS AND SUNDAY MARKETS

On weekends, I'd pull on my shorts, jump on my bicycle, and head out to see an older cousin who lived a few streets away. The midday sun would leave the pavement steaming, the heat would make the tyres on my bike smell acrid. I loved riding my bike, because it meant I wasn't reliant on my parents driving me, but when I turned twelve and got my period, everything changed. I was no longer allowed to wear my shorts when going out, and I wasn't allowed to cycle on my own as much. It seemed as if all the rules had changed.

Life was changing in Pakistan more widely too. When General Muhammed Zia-ul-Haq took power in 1977, deposing Zulfikar Ali Bhutto as prime minister, he vowed that he would hold elections within ninety days of becoming president, but these never eventuated. In response, all the political parties launched a national Movement for the Restoration of Democracy (MRD) in 1981, but Zia-ul-Haq took a hardline stance, and as a result the country was virtually in a state of siege. Soldiers patrolled the streets and barbed wire fences spanned intersections to prevent protesters from gathering.

This controlled calm lasted until February 1985, when a general election was finally held on a non-party basis, and Zia subsequently nominated a member of the National Assembly as prime minister. The new arrangement didn't last long, however, and the strife Zia caused only ended when his plane blew up in August 1988, and he died in the explosion.

Since we'd settled in Karachi in 1981, I'd only known the city in this state of uneasy peace, interrupted by spells of sporadic political disruption. If unrest flared up, life became even more restrictive, and we couldn't drive around as freely. If we were stopped by Kalashnikov-wielding officers, they'd knock on our car window and question us. All of this had been part of the fabric of Karachi life since we'd moved back – but as a young woman now, both my home life and the world around me felt equally stifling.

Whenever violence erupted, shops and schools closed for weeks at a time and we'd be stuck at home every day. I'd be expected to help serve tea to visitors, and to listen to lectures from my parents about how I mustn't talk back to them in front of their friends. With schools shut, I had no friends to hang out with, and so I needed to find a distraction. Sometimes I'd play with my younger cousins, who lived next door, but this would soon bore me. I longed for company my own age.

Nani Mummy lived just downstairs from us, and going to her place in the afternoons and at weekends was my greatest escape. I'd walk through the gate, into her plentiful fruit and vegetable garden. In the summer, I'd pluck mangoes that hung ripe and heavy in the tree, or some bananas, their herbal grassiness rubbing onto my fingertips as I peeled them, so Nani Mummy could made a banana chaat snack with chaat masala and lemon.

Not only was she the one who patiently listened to me, but she also had the ability to turn the most mundane task into an adventure. We'd do some gardening or cook together, and she'd always make dessert at the end of every meal. Sometimes it would be *firni* rice pudding, and other times *zarda*, sweet saffron rice. Her *zarda* was the most beautiful dessert I had ever eaten. She'd soak basmati rice for an hour and make a saffron-infused sugar syrup. Next she'd heat ghee in a pan and infuse it with cloves and cardamom pods before adding the soaked rice, sugar syrup and some water. Once the rice had absorbed all the liquid and the rice was cooked through, she'd top it with roasted nuts and coconut and pieces of green and pink candied pumpkin. As we sat in the shade of her verandah to eat it, she'd just listen, smile and nod at me while I hurled out my complaints about my parents.

Every Sunday we'd go to the weekend bazaar that took place on an empty plot near an area of the city called Defence Housing Authority (DHA), where most of the land had been reclaimed from the Arabian Sea. In the light blue Fiat that Nani Mummy had shipped over from London when she moved back (she had lived in London with my uncle for some years), the drive took an hour, and getting there early was important so we could get the best produce. Sometimes Mummy would come with us, but I always liked the times I went alone with Nani Mummy, because she would talk to me, and I didn't have to share her with my mother.

Each week, the vendors would set up their makeshift shops under the large red, green and yellow *shamyana* marquees, selling everything from cookware and books to fresh chicken and vegetables. As soon as you got out of the car, you'd be surrounded by young boys with baskets who wanted to carry your groceries around for a few rupees.

In Karachi, Tuesdays and Wednesdays were meatless days, when no meat could be bought or sold anywhere in the city, so these Sunday shopping trips would also mean we'd buy enough meat to last us through the week. Even though people ate chicken, it was red meat that really satisfied the Pakistani soul, and I never understood why, in a country where red meat was on the table every day in affluent homes, this restriction had been put in place. Many years later, I discovered that it

Nani Mummy lived just downstairs from us, and going to her place in the afternoons and at weekends was my greatest escape.

was originally enforced by the Ayub Khan government in the 1960s to help preserve the dwindling numbers of livestock and keep the price of meat affordable. The law wasn't ever revoked and people had got into the habit of stocking up ahead of meatless days.

So our first priority was to go to the *gosht-wala* (meat-seller). There were chickens crammed into rusty pens and butchered legs of lamb hanging from metal hooks at the makeshift stall; blood dripped from the sides of the vinyl-sheet-covered table, the smell of chicken droppings, feathers and blood mingled with the metallic aroma of animal carcasses.

'Give me 1 kilo mutton boti (chunks) and 1½ kilo chops,' ordered Nani Mummy.

The *gosht-wala* sharpened his knife on a steel and chopped the meat on a tree-stump chopping board that was etched with score marks and covered in blood. Even at such a young age, I was oblivious to these confronting sights and smells. The meat was popped into a large plastic tub that Nani Mummy brought with her to avoid using unnecessary plastic bags.

Next we'd move on to the *sabzi* (vegetable) and *phall* (fruit) areas. A couple of dozen stalls sold vegetable and fruit, and it was always seasonal: if it was winter, pomegranates, peaches and cherries would be piled high; in summer, guavas and mangoes of every variety would be plentiful. Large jute sacks filled with shiny vegetables glistened in the rays of sunlight that found their way through the sides of the marquee. I'd reach out to grab a guava or some of my favourite berries and Nani Mummy would gently slap my hand to stop me from 'stealing' – but the shopkeepers never seemed to mind, as long as we bought a kilo of whatever I had tasted.

I'd be given the task of buying herbs, which I enjoyed. Their perfume cut through the putrid animal smells and the earthiness of the dirt all around us. In our house, we'd usually get through a bunch a day, so I'd pick out at least six bunches of the freshest coriander, mint, dill, green chillies and tiny lemons. I'd go to one particular stallholder because sometimes he had starfruit for sale, cut into slices: each looked like a perfectly formed star, and he'd sprinkle a slice with chilli powder and salt and hand it to me for free, with a smile.

Markets brought my senses to life. There was something about the urgency in the shouts of the vendors that rose above the noise of animals, car horns and prospective shoppers haggling prices. Picking each ingredient with your hands, or finding new shops selling better-quality produce, felt like a part of the cooking process and it brought more meaning to a meal. My mother and Nani Mummy never settled for less than perfect produce, checking whether every leaf on a bunch of coriander was unblemished, and if a tomato was from cold storage or fresh from the farm – there were small lessons in every visit to the market. At the Sunday market, a man sold multi-coloured chicks from a cardboard box punched with air holes. I'd see their tiny red, pink and green heads bobbing in and out of the holes and it would make me angry that he could be so cruel as to dip the chicks into food dye so that children would be drawn to them. I'd plead with Nani Mummy to buy them all, just so we could release them from their captivity, but of course the poor things were so traumatised that they only ever survived a few days after we got them home. The back of the markets had kitchen equipment, vintage and second-hand books, and this is where I spent the most time, adding to my precious library of Hardy Boys and Nancy Drew novels.

Of the many vegetables we bought at the bazaar, I loved *toori*, a slender gourd that cooked quickly. *Toori ki sabzi* was one of the first Pakistani recipes I remember being cooked at home. My mother would slice the gourds into discs and salt them to draw out excess liquid. Meanwhile, she'd fry cumin and mustard seeds with ginger, garlic and lots of sweet tomatoes, cooking this base until the oil rose to the surface. When she added the *toori*, it would slowly release its juices and soften to become a delicious mush that was best eaten with freshly made chapattis.

Mummy's side of the family was Punjabi and most of the vegetable dishes included meat or daal, but she'd always ask, 'Why can't vegetables just be vegetables?' She developed a fascination with cooking vegetables on their own – something she learnt from Dadi, who was from Uttar Pradesh, where vegetable dishes were simple, and any meat dishes were slow-cooked separately. The secret of infusing layers of spice into vegetables was what Mummy kept trying to perfect, through experimentation, researching Indian recipes and learning from others; and, in turn, my love for vegetarian food comes from her.

Many years later, I came to realise that cooking vegetables in this way was a mindful experience, much more so than cooking meat. From the garden or the markets to our kitchen, each process was slow and intentional. Although I also learnt how to cook meat well, it was this primal connection with food grown in the earth that brought me peace and a sense of calm at a time when I needed it most.

TURMERIC AND KAJAL

The other place I'd go to shop with Nani Mummy was Saddar, which had been the city centre before partition. Many of the long-standing shops, like Singer sewing machines and family-run jewellers, as well as the wholesale markets, were found in this area. This was where we'd go if we needed a new washing machine or an obscure herbal remedy. It was chaotic; the roads were filled with reckless drivers and triple-parked cars.

Bohri Bazaar, one of the oldest open-air marketplaces in the city, was here too. Nani Mummy was set in her ways of shopping in the older parts of Karachi, and she loved going to the same market she'd gone to with my grandfather. Since only dire emergencies would persuade my mother to go to Saddar, it was me who always got dragged along to keep Nani Mummy company.

As we entered the bazaar, our senses would be assaulted with a cocktail of sweat, herbal balms and spices. With little more than a flimsy cloth to shade their displays from the sun, shops and stalls sold everything from colourful plastic *lota* bidet jugs to stainless-steel plates and bowls. Nani Mummy would sometimes walk in front of me and get distracted by a display, and I'd lag behind, kicking leaves with my shoe and wishing we could move on to explore more of the market.

Men would stare at me as they walked by. Even though I was barely thirteen, that didn't stop them from undressing me with their eyes. On one occasion, when a man brushed past me, his arms swinging loosely, I felt his hand linger on my bottom for what felt like minutes but probably was only a fraction of a second. I had a sense of embarrassment, almost as if it were my fault for allowing myself to be touched, but I never said anything to my family.

'You need to realise you're a woman now, and no longer a child,' Mummy insisted. 'Start by dressing like one.' I was told to wear more 'conservative' clothes, to not run around in the markets and other public places without a *dupatta* (long scarf), and to ensure that it covered my chest. The way the soft, elegant, three-and-a-half-metre length of *dupatta* fabric fell when it draped across my shoulders made me feel like a princess. At the same time, I resented being told that I had to wear one as soon as I got breasts, to avoid men looking at me in a 'funny' way – it wasn't as if a *dupatta* stopped them anyway.

Although the Bohri Bazaar trips could be distressing, there were things I'd enjoy: eating a plate of *dahi bara* lentil dumplings with loads of turmeric in them, served with tamarind and spiced yoghurt; or buying the only make-up I was allowed to use, Hashmi's kajal – and sometimes Mummy would let me use the kajal she'd made at home. At least I'd leave with the earthiness of turmeric on my breath and dark kohl around my eyes. And Nani Mummy always promised me a chaat snack plate. Sometimes we'd even indulge in a bottle of Coke, Pakola ice-cream soda or my favourite sweet, slightly fizzy Apple Sidra soft drink that I wasn't allowed to drink at home.

The constant scrutiny of my parents, controlling my behaviour as I came of age, meant that my life was changing and my freedom was being restricted. I found refuge in small things, like eating street food with my Nani Mummy and cooking vegetable dishes with my mother. But I had begun to see a side of my homeland's culture I definitely didn't like. My home was such a safe space, and my father showed respect to women, but I was discovering that not all men were like that. Maybe in my heart of hearts, I understood my parents' concerns and the restrictions they imposed on me, but it didn't make it any easier to live with them.

Bohri Bazaar lentil dumplings with spicy tamarind and yoghurt

*This recipe (pictured overleaf) is based on my mother's lentil fritters, with all the toppings from the Bohri Bazaar version. You should be able to find urid daal, carom seeds (*ajwain*), tamarind sauce, chaat masala,* sev *and* papri *in Asian shops or online.*

Preparation 30 minutes + overnight soaking
Cooking time: 25 minutes
Serves 6–8

200 g (1 cup) urid daal
2 teaspoons cumin seeds, roasted in a dry frying pan
1 teaspoon chilli powder
salt, to taste
pinch of carom seeds (*ajwain*)
400 ml (14 fl oz) sunflower oil

For the yoghurt topping

300 g (10½ oz) full-fat Greek-style yoghurt
1 teaspoon caster (superfine) sugar
¼ teaspoon crushed garlic
1 teaspoon dried mint
salt, to taste

To garnish

1 small red onion, finely chopped (to soften the strong onion aroma, soak in water for 10 minutes, drain and dry on paper towel)
2–3 tablespoons ready-made tamarind sauce
1 teaspoon chaat masala
½ teaspoon chilli powder
1 teaspoon cumin seeds, roasted in a dry frying pan and ground
1 green chilli, deseeded and finely chopped
1 cm (½ inch) ginger, cut into fine strips
7–8 mint sprigs, leaves picked and chopped
handful of coriander (cilantro) leaves, chopped
4 tablespoons *sev* (crisp, savoury noodles made with chickpea flour)
handful of *papri* (crunchy discs made with wheat flour), crushed

- To make the dumplings, put the daal into a bowl of water and leave in a warm place overnight. The next day, the soaked daal should have a fermented smell and the water should appear bubbly; if not, leave it a little longer.
- Drain the daal, reserving the soaking water. Put the daal into a food processor with the cumin seeds, chilli powder and salt and blend to a fine paste. The texture should resemble thick hummus: if the batter is very thick, add 1 teaspoon of the reserved soaking water. Add the carom seeds and mix well, then set aside for 10 minutes.
- Heat the oil in a wok or heavy-based saucepan until it reaches 180°C (350°F) on a deep-frying thermometer, or until a cube of bread sizzles in 30 seconds, then reduce the heat to very low. (The idea is not to have the oil so hot that it will burn the outside of the fritter before the inside is cooked.) Have a bowl of cool water nearby.
- Working in batches of 3–4 at a time, drop teaspoonfuls of the batter into the hot oil (a teaspoon is enough, as the dumplings will double in size as they cook and you are looking to create a flattish, round fritter). Keep the fritters moving in the hot oil so they cook evenly – if you carefully make a small hole in each fritter with the tip of a knife, they will cook faster too.
- As soon as the fritters are nicely browned on the outside and cooked through, lift them out and immediately drop into the bowl of water. Leave them for 2 minutes, then remove and use your hands to gently squeeze out the excess water.
- When all the dumplings are ready, arrange them in a serving dish. For the yoghurt topping, whisk all the ingredients together. Pour onto the dumplings, then garnish with the red onion, tamarind sauce, chaat masala, chilli powder, ground cumin, chilli, ginger, mint, coriander, *sev* and *papri*. Serve at room temperature.

Home-made kajal (kohl)

This beauty recipe is not for the faint-hearted! It's messy and time-consuming, but the result is a natural, pure eye kohl (pictured on previous page). If you do decide to give it a go, remember that the kohl will have been made in a non-sterile environment and doesn't contain any preservatives, so keep it in a cool, dry place, always wash your hands before using it, and use it within a few months.

250 ml (1 cup) pure, cold-pressed organic castor oil
15–20 cm (6–8 inches) pure cotton-wool pleat
2 teaspoons pure, organic ghee, chilled

You will also need:

an unglazed ceramic *diya* (Indian-style lamp) or a small ceramic bowl
a small silver plate or large silver serving spoon (or a fine-mesh stainless-steel sieve)
a small, clean, soft bristle make-up brush
a couple of unused matches

As silver is meant to be good for the eyes, silver utensils are traditionally used: an almond is pierced with a silver fork and lit, while a silver spoon held over it collects the soot from the burning almond – but that takes ages, and many, many almonds!

- Start by cleaning your work surface and washing and drying your hands thoroughly.
- Pour the castor oil into a small bowl.
- Pull the cotton pleat in half – you only need to use half a cotton pleat each time. Take one half and, with wet hands, roll it into a tight 2–3 mm (⅛ inch) thick wick. Add the wick to the oil, ensuring it is completely submerged, then leave in a cool, dry place overnight.
- The next day, take out the saturated wick and place it in your *diya* or ceramic bowl with about 2.5 cm (1 inch) of the wick standing upright, as it would in a candle, and the rest of it braced against one side of the *diya* or bowl.
- Holding your plate, spoon or sieve about 15 cm (6 inches) above the wick, carefully light the wick and wait for the soot to be deposited on the plate, spoon or sieve as the oil burns. Keep an eye on the wick: you'll need to keep pulling it upwards so that 2.5 cm (1 inch) is still sticking out.
- Once you have used up all the wick, blow it out and leave your soot-covered plate, spoon or sieve to cool.
- Using the make-up brush, carefully sweep the soot into a clean small bowl. Be warned: this is *very* messy!
- Now take a pea-sized amount of ghee from the fridge and, working really fast, pop it into the soot and use your fingers – with a gentle touch – to combine the ghee and soot until it is completely incorporated. Quickly roll the kajal onto the wooden end of a match and press to compact it around the matchstick. Repeat with more ghee and another matchstick if there is still some soot left in the bowl.
- Place the soot-covered matchstick/s in a small box (an empty matchbox works well) and leave to dry for a week. The kajal will be super-soft at first, but will become firmer as it dries.

CHAPTER 6

Green chillies on the side

I discover that our food isn't about chilli heat, but about balancing spices and flavours. I learn how to make the spices sing at first bite by layering each spice and being deliberate with every step, rather than taking shortcuts.

Karachi, 1985

SUN-BAKED CURRY LEAVES

If there is one aroma that brings up mixed emotions for me even now, it is the oily perfume of curry leaves warmed by the monsoon sun.

The leaves of the curry leaf tree that stood proudly at the entrance of my Dada and Dadi's home helped bring flavour to Dadi's green chillies stuffed with dried pomegranate and my aunts' raw green mango chutney: these accompaniments were filled with taste sensations that gave life to simple meals of daal and rice.

As a teenager, I cared less for going over to their house every single weekend for Sunday lunch. It felt like an obligation, when all I wanted to do was talk on the phone to my friends, or sometimes a boy I had a crush on. My father was strict about phone use, so I looked for any excuse to get the house to myself.

On the pretext of exams or tests I had to study for, my parents would reluctantly allow me to stay home. They'd let Nani Mummy know I was going to be on my own – but the minute they left, studying rarely happened. I'd pick up the phone and keep talking until I heard them in the driveway; sometimes, I'd put on my Fleetwood Mac and Joan Jett mix tapes, turn up the volume and dance without fear of judgement. I was shy on the dance floor at parties, so this would be my time to let go. I was also embarrassed about my musical choices, as everyone I knew liked songs in the Billboard Top 50, but I enjoyed country and rock.

When my parents returned, they'd smell of a cocktail of dark, intoxicating spices and curry leaves, and I'd feel a pang of regret at missing my Dadi's cooking.

As I began to develop my own interests, helping in the kitchen started to bore me. Grudgingly, I would pick curry leaves for my Dadi and bring them to her so she could make daal or her potato *bhujia*. I took for granted the beauty of the leaves' heady aroma and the bounty the tree offered. Although the tree itself was small, it had an abundance of tiny stems, each bearing about ten leaves.

I'd pick the leaves off the stems and the lingering scent would be embedded in my hands for the rest of the day. I'd compulsively smell my hands: at first the scent was almost like bitter limes, but it soon mellowed into a fragrance like bergamot. Curry leaves came to represent an uneasy mix of my teenage desire for freedom from chores and a yearning for Dadi's comfort food.

Much of what I know of my Dadi's life comes from the stories she told me during the leisurely afternoons we spent curled up on her bed with cups of chai. She'd light up a cigarette and roll up a paan (a betel leaf filled with betel nut, screwpine extract and cardamom) to chew. Smoking and chewing paan wasn't something many women from her era did, yet Dadi did so with grace, confidence and a sense of free-spiritedness.

Born in the mid-1920s, my Dadi was one of four children, and grew up in Azamgarh, Uttar Pradesh. She was beautiful, with delicate features and a slender frame. She tied her salt-and-pepper hair in a loose, low bun, using no nets or hairspray to secure it, just a simple black hair pin. I'd watch her sometimes as she did her hair; she'd scrunch up her nose as she slipped the pin into her bun. She never used make-up and preferred to wear a light chiffon sari or cotton *shalwar kameez*.

When she was fifteen, her marriage was arranged to my Dada, who was fifteen years older than her. They had eight children, and my father was the eldest. Although it was customary in those days for women not to be educated, Dadi wouldn't stand for that, and she was one of the only women in her family who learnt to read and write. She forced her parents to find her a tutor, and was taught from behind a curtain, because of the segregation demanded by purdah.

Nothing stopped her from living the life she wanted, and even with Dada, she got exactly that: a home of her own, with total autonomy in the running of the house and kitchen. Dada handed over his pay cheque to her and she kept a record of everything, spending money carefully so that the household ran like clockwork. Dadi, in turn, supported Dada in every decision he made.

When partition happened, in 1947, Dada was a civil servant posted in Calcutta, and when he was transferred to Rawalpindi, in the newly created Pakistan, Dadi accompanied him without hesitation, even though it meant leaving her life and family behind in India.

Initially settling in Rawalpindi, my grandparents began building a house in Karachi, then the capital of Pakistan, eventually moving there in 1965, by which time my father was stationed at the naval headquarters in the city.

Many migrants settled in Karachi after partition, and the specific areas they made their home would come to reflect their culture. Dada and Dadi's house was in the suburb of Nazimabad, where there was a substantial Muslim community from different parts of India. While they might have been bound together by religion, these people were culturally diverse, and separate Hyderabadi communities grew up, as well as Hindu and Christian areas.

Dadi and I would go to the open-air market close to her house, but the concentration of Indian Muslims in the area meant that the experience was quite different from my shopping trips with Nani Mummy. The differences lay in the details: the way the butcher cut the meat, and the way Dadi bargained with the shopkeepers in her strongly accented 'U.P.' (Uttar Pradeshi) Urdu that sounded so unlike my Nani's Punjabi lilt. At Haddi market there were a few butchers, many fresh produce stalls and one large dry-goods shop where everything was sold loose. We'd go in and ask for five kilos of chana daal or basmati rice, and the shopkeeper would use a stainless-steel scoop to weigh the rice on an old-fashioned scale with a bowl on one side and weights on the other before tipping it into a brown-paper bag.

Whereas most women of her status would send a young boy servant to do the mundane shopping, Dadi felt a sense of purpose in doing the weekly shopping for herself – but she also did it because she was finicky about the quality of her ingredients. Both of my grandmothers and my mother always insisted on this careful selection of their ingredients and taught me to do the same.

In Pakistan, most affluent households had servants to help cook, clean and maintain the home, but Dadi never wanted domestic cooks to help her. The kitchen was her domain. It wasn't just that Dadi loved cooking, it was that she held the fort in her home, through running the kitchen and taking charge of the groceries and household finances. That was her strength and her freedom; without making waves, silently, she needed to be a decision maker. Growing up around my Dadi, I not only learnt about the alchemy of spices and the magic that slow-cooking them brought into life, I also learnt that I had inherited her free spirit.

THE SILVER PAANDAN

When I picture my Dadi now, I see her mouth stained a perpetual shade of brick red. The paan mouth-freshener she had after every meal was filled with many flavours and textures, but it was the red *kattha* paste that left its indelible mark.

On Sunday evenings, after our meal, Dadi would sit down on her bed, and everyone would join her and Dada in their bedroom. That was where the television was, and we'd all sit on chairs and the floor to watch an Urdu drama after the nine o'clock news, usually *Tanhaiyaan*. We'd wait all week to catch up on this series about two sisters who lost everything when their parents died in a car accident. Everyone was gripped by its bold theme; it was also the first Pakistani drama to portray strong female characters, and I felt a real affinity with the lead character, who fought to regain their family home.

This was the time when Dadi would bring out her antique *paandan*, a rectangular box for storing betel nut and other paan ingredients. To Dadi, this was more precious than jewellery, as it represented something she enjoyed doing, and Dada made sure she didn't leave it behind when they moved to Pakistan, even though it was heavy. Made of solid silver, with intricately carved floral designs, a latch and hook (which never had a lock), it looked like a small a treasure chest. It had been given to her by her mother as part of her *jaheez* (dowry); no bride in Pakistan got married without a *jaheez*, including kitchenware, clothes, jewellery and make-up, to take to her new home – usually her in-laws' house.

Holding it by its handle, Dadi would carry over her *paandan*, its perfectly polished silver gleaming in the striplight above her bed. Inside were nine small compartments and a single large one, each containing a flavouring she liked to add to her paan: silver-coated cardamom seeds, brown shavings of betel nut, fennel seeds coated in multi-coloured sugar, a tiny bottle of *kewra* (screwpine extract), a paste of white slaked lime called *chuna*, and another of reddish-brown *kattha*, made from the bark of acacia trees. Although I never quite understood why Dadi chewed paan, I was intrigued by the process.

'Dadi, can I have a paan?' I once asked her.

'No, Somi, you're too young, and it's not good for you anyway,' she answered.

'Then why do you have it, Dadi, if it's not good for you?'

'Because I'm an old woman, I can enjoy things that aren't good for me – but also because I rarely listen to anyone about most things!'

Beneath the first layer of the *paandan* was single large compartment containing heart-shaped betel leaves wrapped in a moist muslin cloth. Dadi smiled and made a 'shushing' gesture, pressing her finger to her lips, as she made me my first tiny paan. She took one of the shiny betel leaves and filled it with just the cardamom and fennel seeds. No one was watching, and so I popped it into my mouth. As I chewed, the leaf's peppery oils filled my mouth, the astringency of the cardamom and the sweetness of the fennel balancing out this spicy explosion. I smiled at Dadi as she made herself her 'special' paan, the one with chewing tobacco in it, and 'shushed' her back.

SENSORY SUNDAYS

The women from my father's side of the family cooked collaboratively, as if they were a single unit. Dadi was the head cook, giving her daughters – my phuppos (paternal aunts) – tasks that came together to create the meal. Even for a feast, I don't think she ever announced a menu or gave a step-by-step breakdown of what was to be cooked; everyone in the kitchen just knew what she needed and calmly did their part. I never got to cook anything, but would be given the job of picking herbs or curry leaves. And in those moments, I learnt more than I realised.

'Somi, go outside and pick some *dhania* (coriander) and *pudina* (mint) leaves,' she would say. 'I need your help making the chutney.' Coriander and mint were the two main ingredients, but green chilli was the soul that brought the chutney to life.

Dadi never grew chillies, as she believed that a chilli plant grown in the garden would lead to arguments between husband and wife. Her own marriage clearly benefitted – my paternal grandparents lived to enjoy their golden anniversary and beyond, and my father told me he couldn't remember a single day when they fought. To this day, even though I grow my own herbs, I still refrain from growing a chilli plant anywhere near my house – married or not, no one wants to risk discord at home!

After I had picked all the herbs, Dadi would wash them and take them to her outside kitchen, next to the lime-washed boundary wall. Among the plants there would be common house lizards and, on hot days, a multitude of flies and an army of tiny red ants walking in a line, trying to find their next prey – the ants were nasty, with a sharp bite that stung and left a red, itchy dot on your skin that lasted for days. On the concrete floor, Dadi had an old *sil batta*, a sort of flat mortar and pestle with a large rectangular stone and a smaller cylindrical stone that was used to crush and grind pastes. You'd add splashes of water and keep rolling the cylindrical stone over the rectangular one until you had a smooth paste. This laborious task would take time, patience and strength, but it was the way she always made her coriander and mint chutney. Only in her older years did she succumb to the convenience of an electric blender, and even then with reluctance.

Many chutney recipes arrived in Pakistan with Muslim Indian immigrants, who brought with them their unique cooking techniques. Coriander chutney was commonplace in our kitchen, but Dadi's was special and she used it in different ways. One of my favourites was inside delicate shami kebabs: fried patties made from minced beef boiled with chana daal and spices, usually smoky cardamom, star anise and cinnamon, then ground to a paste with fresh ginger. Traditionally the grinding was done on the *sil batta*, but modern cooks tend to use a blender or food processor. This recipe for shami kebabs supposedly originated in the royal kitchens of the Mughal emperors, and my Dadi's version had been passed down the family for generations. Her signature recipe involved placing a little of her coriander chutney and a couple of pomegranate seeds in the centre of each patty, so that when you'd bite into the shami kebab you'd get an explosion of fresh herbs, with the unexpected tartness of pomegranate.

'Why are there green chillies on the plate?' I asked Guddo Phuppo.

'It's so that you can add as much heat to your food as you like,' she explained.

This was a peculiarity I only came across on the dining table at my Dadi's house: long finger chillies, plated up and presented like a side salad with every meal. All my phuppos and my grandparents would munch on a chilli with each bite of food.

I was particularly close to my youngest phuppo, Guddo, and she was always up for a chat, unlike the others, who were constantly studying, intent on becoming doctors and engineers. Like me, Guddo loved to dance on her own, listening to Tina Charles and the Bee Gees. She was slim and her curly dark brown hair sat neatly at her shoulder; she wore pretty colours such as peach and turquoise, and I admired her dress sense, as well as her ability to laugh away her troubles. Her smile lit up her face and she laughed with her whole body.

She taught me to eat rice in the traditional way, with my hand. Although some of my father's family ate like this, it wasn't something my parents ever did, and it took some skill. Guddo Phuppo showed me how to bring the rice together between the fingers and thumb of my dominant hand, compacting it into a sort of triangle (*nawala*), before mixing it with some curry or daal and then elegantly placing it in my mouth. Maybe it was just the novelty or maybe it created a sensory connection to our food, but I soon found that it made the food taste better. As my friendship with Guddo blossomed, my reluctance to go to Dadi's house for Sunday lunch every week faded.

We would talk about my school friends, rivalries and crushes, and we'd laugh about how boring the 'grown-ups' were, even though she was fifteen years my senior. I always felt like I could speak honestly to her, and over the years I trusted her with my deepest secrets. Whenever I went to see my grandparents, we'd spend time chatting about music and the latest movies, and watching TV shows on pirated VHS tapes that the grown-ups didn't like, such as *Miami Vice* and *Knight Rider*. She'd take me shopping for outfits and we'd buy matching ones.

The older I got, the more the age difference was bridged, and she became my closest confidante in my family.

DADI'S VERMICELLI DESSERT

Eid was the best time at Dada and Dadi's house, and it wasn't just about the food. Being an only child meant that I got the most Eidee (present money). In my most polite voice, I'd greet my aunts and uncles with '*As-salam-alaikum, Eid Mubarak* (peace be with you, have a blessed Eid)', then I'd have to quietly accept sweaty kisses and hugs. I'd grab the kitsch envelopes with bright pink, green and red roses and leaves printed on shiny paper and move on to the next relative with a fake smile plastered on my face. Out of all the cousins, I'd be the 'richest' at the end of the day.

We'd arrive early in the morning, and the air would already be filled with the heady aromas of the lunch cooking, from the spicy richness of mutton korma and biryani to the sweet nuttiness of chana daal halva and *seviyan* vermicelli dessert. I was usually too busy collecting my packets of Eidee to pay any attention to how Dadi made her vermicelli dessert, but one Eid when I was sitting in the living room, counting my rupee notes and munching on *seviyan*, I picked up on a conversation between her and my mother.

'You need one part crushed *seviyan* to sixteen parts sugar,' Dadi explained to my mother.

'What? Sixteen parts? That's a bit excessive!' replied Mummy.

'If you infuse the syrup with saffron, right at the end, you'll never realise how much sugar there is; this is done to preserve it.'

I was surprised by what I heard, because eating Dadi's *seviyan* dessert you'd never think it contained that much sugar: the infusion of cardamom and cloves was heady, and the vermicelli was cooked down until it glistened with the sugar syrup, but it didn't taste overly sweet.

Dadi went on to explain to my mother that this version, called *qawwami seviyan*, came from the region of India she grew up in, and it was a family recipe that had been passed down to her. *Seviyan* was made differently in Pakistan, she told us, and she wasn't sure she liked the watered-down version they made.

'There's no set recipe, you just make it,' said Dadi. 'I'll have to show you.'

She opened the wooden door to her larder cabinet and opened a jute sack of raw sugar crystals and using her hands she counted sixteen handfuls, then she asked me to crush a packet of the roasted vermicelli. Heating up a few tablespoons of ghee, she added cloves and cardamom, and when they began to splutter, she added the crushed vermicelli, filling the kitchen with the warmth of spices and the grassy, buttery smell of ghee. She asked me to melt the sugar with a splash of water until it became *ek taar ka sheera* – the point at which a little sugar syrup dropped onto a plate could be pulled into a strand between the fingers (*ek taar* means 'one string') – so that the syrup would thicken the dessert but not set rock-hard. Next she added the saffron and let it infuse, then carefully poured the syrup over the vermicelli. As the bubbles spluttered and smoke rose from the pan, she stirred vigorously and the crackling subsided as the dessert came together. Dadi poured it out onto a serving dish and decorated it with silver leaf, crushed pistachios and almonds.

Mummy wrote out Dadi's method and tips on a page torn from one of my aunt's notebooks, scribbling down steps in the process rather than any measurements. I don't think she ever looked at the piece of paper again, but she made it from memory at Eid each year.

Unlike my father's side of the family, I never did adopt the habit of munching green chillies with every meal, but I did inherit a love of slow, mindful and intricate cooking. I learnt how to manage heat by adding fresh chilli later in the cooking process. These are lessons my Dadi and my mother taught me, but it wasn't until many years later that I realised how much knowledge I had amassed at their side, in and around the kitchen, picking curry leaves or herbs.

One day, many decades later, when Mummy and I were looking through old recipes, she found that scrap of paper with the *seviyan* recipe on it. We both laughed, agreeing that we didn't see the point in keeping recipes when neither of us ever used them. The instructions were as vague as the skills I picked up in the kitchen from the women of my family. But no matter how haphazard their instructions were, their lack of measurements or exact timings, nothing stopped me from being able to recreate those dishes. Somehow, I was always able to create food that tasted of home. Perhaps I learnt from just being around women who saw cooking as an act of freedom and creativity, without rules – this helped me to view food as an instinctive extension of myself, and eventually helped me to find my voice.

Potatoes with curry leaves and turmeric

A recipe I created from the need for more uses for a glut of curry leaves, this was inspired by childhood trips to my Dadi's home. I usually eat this rustic dish with chapattis or parathas.

Prep time: 10 minutes
Cooking time: 15–20 minutes
Serves 4

500 g (1 lb 2 oz) small baby potatoes
1 teaspoon turmeric powder
½–1 teaspoon salt, to taste
3 tablespoons sunflower oil
½ teaspoon brown mustard seeds
1 teaspoon cumin seeds
¼ teaspoon nigella seeds (*kalonji*)
3 dried long red chillies
10–11 fresh curry leaves
3–4 teaspoons full-fat Greek-style yoghurt

To garnish

handful of coriander (cilantro) leaves, finely chopped
1 tablespoon chopped dill
1 green finger chilli, chopped – optional, for more heat
½ lime

- Boil the potatoes until cooked through, but not overdone and falling apart. Drain well, then toss them with the turmeric and salt.
- Put the oil into a saucepan and place over medium heat. When it is hot, add the mustard, cumin and nigella seeds and stir until they begin to pop. Add the red chillies and stir for a few seconds, then add the fresh curry leaves – stand back, as they will splutter a lot!
- Once the curry leaves turn shiny, add the potatoes and fry until they are coated in all the spices. Lower the heat, then stir the yoghurt into the potatoes and turn off the heat.
- Sprinkle with the coriander, dill and green chilli (if using), then cover until you're ready to serve. This dish is best eaten fresh, with a squeeze of lime juice – either hot or warm, but not reheated.

Fennel paan masala sweets

I created this recipe in memory of my Dadi's habit of chewing paan, a herbal mouth freshener, after meals. In many ways, it was her 'dessert', so I felt it would be fitting to make a sweet with the flavours of paan. Mukhwas *is a pre-made paan masala with sugar-coated fennel seeds and salted sesame seeds that can be bought at Asian shops or online, as can the rose jam and matcha powder.*

Prep time: 15 minutes
Cooking time: 10 minutes
Makes 15–20 pieces

- 1 teaspoon ghee
- 4–6 green cardamom pods, cracked open, seeds extracted and finely ground
- 1 x 397 g (14 oz) tin of sweetened condensed milk
- 3–4 tablespoons unsweetened desiccated coconut
- 2 digestive (wheatmeal) biscuits, finely crushed
- 1 tablespoon matcha (green tea) powder
- 2 tablespoons *mukhwas*, plus extra to decorate
- 2 teaspoons rose water
- 1 teaspoon rose jam – optional
- edible silver leaf, for decoration – optional

- In a non-stick frying pan, heat the ghee over medium heat. When it is hot, add the cardamom and fry until fragrant, about 10–15 seconds, keeping it moving in the pan.
- Add the condensed milk and cook, stirring constantly until it starts to thicken. Stir in the coconut, then turn off the heat.
- Now add all the remaining ingredients except the silver leaf and mix until it all comes together and pulls away from the sides of the pan, then let it cool for a few minutes.
- When it is cool enough to handle, roll teaspoonfuls of the mixture between the palms of your hands to make small balls. Press in a little more mukhwas to decorate – and, if desired, add a tiny piece of silver leaf to each ball too.
- If not serving them straightaway, keep the sweets refrigerated, but bring to room temperature 30 minutes before eating.

Seviyan ladoo (roasted vermicelli truffles with coconut and cardamom)

Although inspired by Dadi's sweet vermicelli dessert, this version is made into slightly untraditional vermicelli truffles. Be careful to get the right kind of vermicelli for these: seviyan *is a special roasted wheat vermicelli that's used for desserts, and it can be found in Asian shops.*

Prep time: 10 minutes
Cooking time: 10 minutes
Makes 15–20

- 2 tablespoons ghee
- 3–4 green cardamom pods, cracked open, seeds extracted and ground – you need ½ teaspoon ground cardamom
- 1 x 200 g (7 oz) packet of roasted vermicelli (*seviyan*), finely crushed by hand
- 1 x 397 g (14 oz) tin of sweetened condensed milk
- 3 tablespoons unsweetened desiccated coconut, plus 2 tablespoons extra for coating
- 2–3 tablespoons crushed pistachios

- Heat the ghee in a wok or deep frying pan over medium heat. When it is hot, add the cardamom and crushed vermicelli and cook, stirring, until the vermicelli is light brown, about 2–3 minutes.
- Pour in the sweetened condensed milk and stir until incorporated. Add the desiccated coconut and cook, stirring constantly, until it has been absorbed and the mixture comes together into a ball. Turn off the heat and leave to cool.
- Meanwhile, put the crushed pistachios into a shallow bowl.
- When the mixture is cool enough to handle, take out tablespoonfuls and shape into balls, then roll in the extra desiccated coconut and the crushed pistachios.
- If not serving straightaway, keep in the refrigerator and eat within 2 days.

As the bubbles spluttered and smoke rose from the pan, Dadi stirred vigorously and the crackling subsided as the dessert came together.

AN EVERYDAY MENU

inspired by Dadi's cooking

CHAPTER 7

Chaat isn't a starter

I search for any chance to spend time with my first love, and indulge in forbidden plates of street-food chaat – with its piquant promise, it brings tiny moments of escapism.

Karachi, January 1986–1987

CRAVING CREATIVITY

In Pakistan there were two kinds of schools: those where every subject was taught in Urdu, with English as a second language, and you'd study for a matriculation certificate; and those affiliated to the University of Cambridge where students could sit O- and A-level exams – such as St Michael's, where I'd recently moved to from Foundation Public School. At these schools, classes were in English, and Urdu was the second language. While I grew up being able to speak Urdu fluently, because of my obsession with English literature, I treated it as a bothersome subject that I had to pass. Whenever I couldn't find the right Urdu vocabulary, I'd just slot in English words, like most affluent Pakistanis did, and speaking this hybrid language left little need to master the language for its own sake. Many years later I would regret not paying more attention to Urdu, leaving me with a superficial knowledge of my own mother tongue; I also missed out on its beauty, its literature and poetry.

Most Pakistani parents created an intense pressure to do well academically; it was as if the grades their child got defined their own social status. Such pressure wasn't something that would motivate me to study, though. School was becoming difficult and studying cast a dark shadow over my heart. It was time to choose my O-level subjects, and I had no idea what I was good at. I just knew that English and history made me feel happier. By the time I was in my early teens, I had developed an insatiable appetite for books and had read many of the classics. Thomas Hardy's *Tess of the d'Urbervilles* was my favourite, and I devoured all the books by the Brontë sisters and Jane Austen, but it was Somerset Maugham's writing that intrigued me the most. History was a form of escapism for me – I'd even developed historical crushes on the likes of Alexander the Great and Napoleon and fantasised about travelling back in time to meet them. My mind was filled with wild ideas, stories and a desire to find something I loved, and I just knew it wasn't maths or science.

I wanted to find a way to study abroad, but Daddy reminded me often enough that this would only be possible if I studied 'important' subjects like maths and science, not frivolous ones that offered a 'creative' career. I knew I was privileged and that not many children in Pakistan had the opportunities I did; most girls of my age were either forced into arranged marriages or made to work. There was such a disparity between those who expected their children to go to colleges abroad and those who couldn't even afford to send their children to school, but at the time I took for granted how lucky I was that my father wanted me to be educated.

‘Daddy, I’d really like to study history and literature for my degree in London,’ I said.

‘History and literature are wonderful subjects, but you should be thinking about a degree that can help you find a lucrative career,’ he said. His voice was kind, but his stern, determined expression made it clear that I didn’t really have much choice.

‘But history or literature would mean I could teach!’

‘Somi, teachers make very little money. I think reading is important, you know how much I read. But think of your future.’

At the age of thirteen, I struggled to prioritise stability over the subjects I loved.

FIRST LOVE

The following term, some new students joined St Michael’s School. They were the first batch of A-level students, and there was much excitement among the girls at the prospect of new boys to drool over.

One of the newly appointed prefects caught my eye. He was tall and wiry, with a wispy moustache that sat right under his Grecian nose, and his eyes were a light shade of amber. His swagger suggested a subdued confidence, and there was something about the way he turned and looked at me, the intensity of his gaze, that made me feel self-conscious, yet flattered. For the next few weeks all I could think about were his eyes and how I really wanted to know his name.

I ended up finding out his name in an unexpected way. Every week, my friends and I would go to a fast-food chain near school, called Mr. Burger, in the Clifton area of Karachi. We all wanted to mimic the teenagers we saw in 1980s American films, idly hanging out in burger joints – and this was the only such place in town, so we’d sit round the low tables and gossip over burgers, slushies and fries.

‘You know who owns Mr. Burger, right?’ asked Arzu, a Turkish girl who’d moved to Karachi with her parents for a year. She was tall and pretty, and boys loved her – not least because she kissed them, apparently.

‘No idea. Should I know?’ I asked, as I took a bite of the soggy fries.

‘Well, you’re the one who’s not stopped searching for him for the past month.’

‘Oh my goodness, you mean the boy with the stringy moustache?’

‘Yep. His name’s Danesh. His family owns Mr. Burger. Sometimes he’s here, I’ve seen him.’

Summer holidays came and went, and I spent most of the time preoccupied by thoughts about Danesh. I longed to go to Mr. Burger to see if I could catch a glimpse of him, but Clifton was some distance from our house, and no one in our family was interested in going there with me.

It wasn't until the next term that I saw him again, and that was in school. He was standing by the tuck shop, and Arzu was all over him. He didn't see me, but I seethed with jealousy and betrayal.

Then, on the last day of term, Danesh passed me in the hall and slipped a piece of paper into my hand. With my heart pounding, I opened it to discover that he liked me and wanted me to call him over the break: 'Make sure you ask for my sister if my parents pick up – I'll explain why later – but you're so pretty and I can't wait to get to know you.'

Winter in Karachi was the best time of the year. The sun was still strong during the day, but the evenings brought with them the briny comfort of cool marine air.

Usually, coming back to school in January, at the start of the new academic year, filled me with dread. The building itself resembled a prison block, with metal grilles on the windows that looked like jail bars, and the grounds were just bare earth, dusty and parched.

But this year was different.

What Danesh and I had already felt special, even just from the few conversations we'd had over the holidays. I could tell that this was more than just a friendship, and I couldn't wait to get to know him better.

I found my way to my new classroom and met up with the friends I hadn't seen over the holidays.

Arzu quizzed me: 'You know Danesh is seeing someone else now?'

'Really? I didn't know,' I replied.

'He's half-Scottish,' said Asma. 'That's why he has those golden eyes and fair skin. Isn't he a dream?'

I pretended I hadn't heard.

'Yeah, I kissed him last term,' Arzu went on, a smug look crossing her face.

'You still like him?' Asma asked, poking my waist affectionately.

My face was expressionless.

'And you think he's going to like you?' continued Arzu.

I finally spoke up: 'What's that supposed to mean?'

'Well, it means he's got his pick of the pretty girls,' said Asma, who was beginning to get on my nerves now. They both were.

'We'll see about that!' I muttered under my breath as I walked away.

I could hardly breathe. It was mid-March and already the intense heat was energy-sapping. It was bearable with air-conditioning, but there were no such luxuries in school; all we had was a single, barely moving ceiling fan. From the window near my desk, I tried to catch the occasional breeze, which felt cool against the beads of sweat on my upper lip. I couldn't wait for breaktime, when Danesh and I would meet.

We'd been secretive about our relationship, but I was desperate to tell the world. After a few weeks of arguing about whether it was worth telling people who might interfere, Danesh succumbed, and we decided not to hide our relationship any longer. An air of quiet confidence came over me as I walked next to Danesh, flirting during and after school, and other girls looked on with envy.

Danesh and I would meet on the bleachers at breaktime, to share our lunch and dwell in each other's gaze for those twenty minutes. When we lined up to go back to class he'd wink at me from his prefect post by the stairs, then I'd sneak out just before the teacher came to class and we'd go up to the prohibited rooftop, where we'd step over the cement bags that blocked the doorway and steal kisses.

But I hadn't noticed that we were being watched by more than just the jealous girls in school.

A few weeks later, I noticed that there were some new rules plastered on the noticeboards. Large, laminated notices stated: 'Boys and girls cannot chat in the common room' and 'Girls and boys are not to loiter together on staircases'. Although St Michael's was ostensibly a Catholic school, set up by the heads of two single-sex schools, it was meant to be co-ed, so this seemed very strange.

Then, one afternoon, the head girl called me out of class: 'Sumayya Usmani, Mrs Smith would like to see you.'

What had I done? I was never late to school or missed a day. I was decent at most subjects, except maths and science, and Mrs Smith, the headmistress, had already had that conversation with me. I was trying to avoid the obvious – this was clearly something to do with Danesh and me. We had been spending more time together in school, and there was a strange feeling in the air. Each time I spoke to Danesh or sat with him outside I knew people were talking, I'd heard whispers from friends and other students. Being blatant about having a pre-marital relationship in Pakistan was sort of illicit, but somehow I thought people wouldn't think much of it. We were only teenagers.

'Sumayya, come in. We need to talk about your behaviour.'

'Yes, Miss.' I could barely speak.

'It's clear you know what this is about,' said Mrs Smith. 'I've been watching you and some of the A-level boys. This sort of behaviour won't be accepted in this school.'

Mrs Smith was a short, ample woman, who wore her tops a size or two small. She had well-worn kitten heels on her feet and a perpetual scowl on her face. She wore loud, cheap perfume and a garish shade of red lipstick, applied just short of her lipline. As I tried to hold my nerve, I became transfixed by a couple of ingrown hairs on her chin that had begun to curl their way out and begged to be tweezed.

'Well, Sumayya, you've forced me to do something,' she continued. 'I'm going to ban the A-level boys from talking to you O-level girls – and if I catch you, you'll all be suspended.'

Could she really do that? *What the fuck?* I wanted to shout. Instead, I bit back sudden scorching tears. I don't remember if she said anything else; all I could do was nod my head and ask to be excused. I never thought our actions would lead to such big changes – changes that would affect everyone at school. This was the punishment we got for flaunting our relationship. It wasn't as if we could go out on real dates; I was pretty certain Daddy wouldn't be comfortable with me chatting to a boy on the phone, let alone going out anywhere. School was the only place we could meet.

FIRST DATES

But Danesh and I found ways around it all. We wrote notes and passed them to each other while walking to class; we met after school or bunked classes; but our favourite thing was having plates of chaat at Boat Basin, opposite the school. Chaat was that in-between meal, not a starter or a main course, but that tease of your tastebuds, just enough to satisfy cravings of spice.

When you got to the strip of roadside restaurants and their outdoor stalls, the stench of the mangrove swamp, mingled with the aromas of barbecuing tikkas and sizzling beef burgers, would hit you hard in the face. We'd buy cold, piquant chaat from the makeshift rickety wooden carts laden with baskets and stainless-steel urns of ingredients. Not the most hygienic set-up, admittedly, but the *chaat-wala*, in his shabby *shalwar kameez*, would always assure us: 'Don't worry ma'am, I'll make it fresh.' He'd pile a plate with spicy chickpeas, boiled potatoes and garlic yoghurt – plus lots of tamarind chutney, at my request, and a final sprinkle of chaat masala and fresh coriander. Danesh preferred Karachi kebab rolls, greasy parathas filled with fiercely spiced strips of chicken or beef, coriander chutney, raita and raw red onions, tightly wrapped in greaseproof paper. He called chaat a 'girly' snack and always ordered a couple of kebab rolls for himself instead, laughing that his metabolism would melt away the calories.

We'd get our snacks as takeaways and hide behind the school building to eat it together, sitting cross-legged on the ground, side by side. It was socially unacceptable for unmarried couples to sit together in public, but the thrill of sneaking out to eat chaat made us feel free.

'Have some, *jungli*,' he'd say, smiling mischievously as he shoved a kebab roll at me and I recoiled from the smell of raw onions.

He always called me *jungli*, *pagal* or Usmani – rather unique terms of endearment, calling your girlfriend 'crazy', 'wild' or by her surname, but it made my heart melt.

While trying to eat chaat elegantly, I'd look into his eyes, thinking about how I would love him forever. Danesh, with his reckless, rule-breaking ways, and his flightiness that mirrored mine. He made me feel at ease.

Chaat became our way of finding escape, stealing moments that were so hard to come by. Sometimes he would pick me up in his car on the day he would be off from classes and he'd have some takeaway chaat on the back seat, ready for us to eat together by the beach. Sometimes we'd be stopped by the police, asking us if we were married, but Danesh would step out of the car and offer them a small bribe to let us off.

Sea View beach was where couples came on clandestine dates and the police were quick to take advantage of the situation. For me, this just added to the thrill – but I also knew that I was doing everything that was forbidden in my culture, in my country, and by my parents. I was dating a boy, sneaking out and eating roadside chaat. My mother forbade me from eating street food because of the risk of typhoid contamination from the dirty water that was sometimes used to cook the food or wash utensils. And Daddy didn't think a girl my age should be going around with boys, or it would affect my reputation.

But somehow, our love flourished in those stolen moments, forbidden glances and secret love letters. Listening to Foreigner songs and watching *Sixteen Candles*, I'd daydream, imagining how life would be perfect once we were married and could get away from people telling us what to do.

We found more inventive ways to meet, seeing each other at birthday parties or at mutual friend's houses, and finding ways of speaking on the phone for longer.

When my family took me to Dada and Dadi's house on Sundays, the women would go to the kitchen. In the past, I had obligingly followed them, but now I had other plans – I used this time while the women were busy to phone Danesh. Dada's home office had two doors, one that led to my grandparents' room, and another that opened into the living room. On his desk there was a green rotary phone.

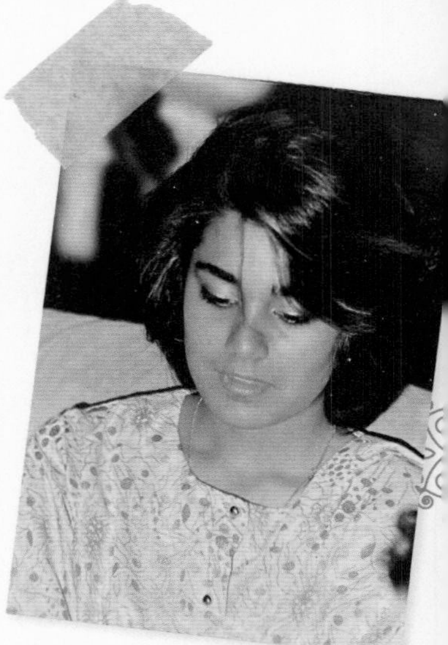

We had to coordinate our clandestine calls carefully, and usually planned times to speak in advance, through notes or quick whispers in school: 'Call me at one on Sunday, ask for my sister and she will give the phone to me.' That way his parents didn't know it was me calling. I don't think his Scottish mother would have minded, but his father was a traditional sort of Pakistani man who wouldn't have accepted his son talking to some girl from school, and especially not one he was sneaking around with.

'Can I just go and do some homework at Dada's desk, please?' I'd ask, innocently. Checking that none of the grown-ups were about, I'd pick up the phone. One time, I was so preoccupied with making the cut-off time, my face flushed with excitement, that I hadn't realised that Guddo Phuppo was standing right by the other entrance to the room, watching me.

'So, who is he?' she asked.

'Err, what?! I'm not talking to a boy!' I snapped back defensively, the colour draining fast from my face.

Guddo Phuppo would understand, I thought. I realised I had a chance to come clean, to be honest about my feelings, and maybe make it all feel more real.

'Fine. His name is Danesh, and he spells it D-A-N-E-S-H and not D-A-N-I-S-H,' I said, trying to make a case for how cool I thought he was.

'Oh, I love that he spells it differently. I already like him!'

She even told me she would give her son the same name, if she had one, and then she smiled, her pretty curls bouncing as she turned and left the room, mumbling something about keeping guard so I could talk to him. In that moment I had found validation that no parental disapproval, strict head teachers or nagging friends could take away from me. I had a grown-up who believed I had the right to be in love.

I came back to the kitchen after my call and helped lay the table with guilt-fuelled diligence, and a smile plastered on my face.

'What's so funny, Somi?' asked Mummy.

'Oh, nothing – I just love Dadi's food so much.'

FALSA BERRIES AND KALA NAMAK

'*Falsay-wala! falsay-wala!*' A shrill chant could be heard on most early summer afternoons. The *falsay-wala* sold nothing else but falsa berries and small bags of chilli masala for sprinkling over them.

Falsas, found only in Sindh province, were a little larger than blackcurrants. They had the darkest purple skin, and when ripe you could squish them between your fingers, exposing their surprisingly pale insides and their ever-present round seed that was so large it made no sense to spit it out. Besides, I enjoyed the satisfying noise it made when you crunched into it, even if it did give you jaw-ache.

Mummy hated falsas and never bought them, but Nani Mummy would buy some every day in summer, either for me to eat or to make falsa squash with, which we would freeze so we could enjoy it later in the year when falsas weren't around. The man who sold them in our neighbourhood walked around in the scorching sun all day with a bamboo pole slung across his shoulder, mountains of berries balanced in baskets tied to either end. By midday, they'd be sun-ripe and juicy. He'd weigh them out on a hand-held scale, and always included a tiny brown paper bag of chilli powder and *kala namak* (black salt) – its sulphuric smell would overpower the kitchen, but its intensity added umami to the sun-sweetened berries.

Back in her kitchen, we'd pick the softest ones, wash them, add the chilli masala and place a plate on top of the bowl. We'd shake them up and down to soften them even more, making them juicy and letting the masala cover every squished berry. Sometimes Nani Mummy would have a bowl of falsas ready in the fridge when I came home from school, and the cool air from the noisy air-conditioning unit on the wall above her bed, together with her gentle voice telling me about her day, would lull me into an after-school siesta. In the heat of the day, Nani Mummy and I would spend hours in her garden together, tending to her petunias, snapdragons and begonias, and picking *motia* (sambac jasmine) buds to put in a bowl of water to bloom, filling her room with the sweet smell of spring turning to summer.

At home, I wasn't sure how long I could keep pretending that I wasn't in love. I think Mummy knew there was someone I was interested in, but Daddy was in denial. I knew that if I told my parents about Danesh, Daddy would tell me to end it immediately.

I'd find any excuse to avoid doing my homework with Daddy, as I struggled with the maths and science he wanted me to study. Instead I'd think of a reason to go to Nani Mummy's house, where I'd curl up on her bed and watch *WWF Superstars of Wrestling* with her, or re-watch *The Breakfast Club* on video, eating falsa berries, with a crunching that could be heard even above the noise of the air-conditioner. I longed to escape from the restrictions and expectations I could feel brewing all around me, but I had only just turned fourteen.

Boat Basin chaat plate

This is a recipe based on the chaat I used to sneak out and eat on dates with Danesh when I was a teenager. You can find the chaat masala spice blend and crispy sev *noodles in Asian shops or online.*

Prep time: 15 minutes
Cooking time: 15 minutes
Serves 2–4

2–3 large potatoes, peeled and cubed
2 teaspoons sunflower oil
1 teaspoon cumin seeds
1 teaspoon finely chopped ginger
¼ teaspoon turmeric powder
1 teaspoon chaat masala
salt, to taste
1 green chilli, finely chopped
2 tablespoons chopped coriander (cilantro) leaves
3–4 tablespoons *sev* (crisp, savoury noodles made with chickpea flour)
2 tablespoons pomegranate seeds
juice of 1 lime

For the yoghurt topping

100 g (⅓ cup) full-fat Greek-style yoghurt, whipped until smooth
½ teaspoon crushed garlic
1 tablespoon chopped mint
salt, to taste

- Boil the potatoes until they are cooked through but still firm. Drain and leave to cool.
- In a frying pan, heat the oil over medium heat. When it is hot, add the cumin seeds and stir until fragrant and light brown, then add the ginger and fry for about 10–12 seconds, or until aromatic – be careful not to let it burn.
- Now add the potatoes and fry until lightly brown and crispy around the edges, then add the turmeric, chaat masala and salt and mix well. Take the pan off the heat, then stir in the green chilli and half of the coriander leaves. Spoon into a serving dish.
- For the yoghurt topping, mix all the ingredients together. Top the potatoes with this, then scatter over the remaining coriander leaves and *sev*. Finish with the pomegranate seeds and lime juice. Eat immediately.

CHAPTER 8

Pickled lemons and perfect phulkas

When Nani Mummy becomes ill, I discover that food has the power to heal mind and body. I also come to realise that food is matrilineal, offering a moment of closeness and recognition between Mummy, Nani Mummy and me.

Karachi, March 1986

RAINFALL RITUALS AND DOOTH PATTI

No other lemon could ever come close to a *desi* lemon. I call them *desi* because the word means 'of the homeland' and I've never seen them anywhere else. Pakistani lemons are small, round and bright yellow. Their delicate skin has little zest, but what they lack in zest they make up for in taste. This golf ball of a lemon would slip off the chopping board if you weren't careful – but, as you slice into it, you're assailed with the scent of summer.

Nani Mummy's lemon tree, at the beginning of spring, looked as if it had nothing but shiny leaves, but these leaves guarded white blossoms. When the petals fell to the ground, they'd leave behind tiny green dots that would grow into fruit that, at first, looked like limes. Slowly the sun would turn them yellow and they'd be ready for picking; Nani Mummy made sure we checked on them every day and picked them as soon as they were ripe.

Sometimes we'd run out of recipes to use up all those lemons. I'd make cheesecake, Nani Mummy would make her *achar* (pickle) and Mummy would make a pitcher of *nimbu pani* lemonade, blending whole lemons with raw sugar, fresh mint, black salt, roasted cumin, black pepper and ice. But my favourite was making salted lemons with Nani Mummy. There was something special about this simple way of preserving the season, time and moment without disturbing the purity of the lemons' flavour. Nani Mummy would use a sterilised jar, wash a dozen lemons, pop them into the jar, and then she'd pour in several spoonfuls of pink salt before screwing on the lid. It was my job to shake the jar around and ensure everything got well mixed. We'd then leave the jar on the windowsill for about a month, giving it a shake every day.

Soon the gritty salt would melt and the surface of the lemons would glisten; the salt would draw out moisture from the lemons and half the jar would be filled with a murky juice. After about a month in the jar, they'd be ready to taste. As we opened it, a hissing noise would escape the jar, and Nani Mummy would laugh, saying it was the friendly bacteria saying hello.

The lemons smelt like vinegar, jaw-achingly tart; their skin still looked intact but would give way under the back of a fork, oozing juice. They looked mushy and tasted somewhere between bitter and sweet. I'd chop them into bite-sized pieces and devour them with a bowl of daal and rice. Sometimes we'd leave the jars on the windowsill for months; as the seasons changed, they'd turn from a pale yellow to a dark shade of ochre and would taste even more bitter.

August brought with it the monsoons. The sea breeze was heavy, and the ground yearned for a downpour as the skies turned overcast. So many people around the world crave sunny skies, but in Karachi, essentially a desert climate, grey clouds, brimming with an imminent shower, drew people out of their homes and onto the streets. The excited chatter of children filled the air, as they stood outside, longing for the first raindrop. In our garden, the usual stillness was replaced with the rustling of leaves, and the bougainvillea on our boundary wall danced in the wind; just before the air turned humid and cooler, you could almost see steam rising from the raw earth.

In the kitchen, we'd be getting ready for our 'rainfall rituals'. Monsoons were synonymous with chai and pakoras on the verandah. Nani Mummy and Mummy would put the *dooth patti* chai on the stove. *Dooth patti* translates to 'milk and tea leaves', and that's exactly what it was. One mug of raw milk and a heaped teaspoon of loose tea for each person was simmered slowly with about half a dozen cardamom pods. Once it came to the boil, Nani Mummy would add about half a mug of cold milk and the chai was kept at a simmer until it was thick and frothy, another ten minutes or so. Meanwhile, I'd slice potatoes thinly and Mummy would make the batter for the pakoras: a three-to-two ratio of chickpea flour to rice flour, spiced with cumin seeds, black salt, chaat masala and fresh herbs.

Outside, the rain would trickle down from the sides of the porch like a beaded curtain, and the grown-ups would sip their tea, watching from under the shelter of the verandah, while my cousins Sabrina, Natasha, baby Zain and I danced as the heavens opened. We'd return with our clothes soaking and slippers sliding. When the rain stopped, the air was filled with the ethereal scent of petrichor, the distinctive smell that still reminds me most of home. Maybe it was because of the sheer joy the rain brought into my childhood, better than an amusement park or fairground.

As much as the rain was a blessing amid the heat, I also loved the unusual fruit that ripened in the warmth. Collecting jamuns (Java plums) from the tree at my great-grandfather's house was one of my favourite summer pastimes. As you bit into one of the purple plums, their tannins had an astringent effect on the palate, but that odd sweet-bitter drying element made them compulsive to eat, and I'd gorge on them until I felt sick. Nani Mummy refused to grow jamuns in her garden, because the trees were lofty and unwieldly, and because she hated the way the fallen berries stained the ground permanently.

Abajaan ('father dearest'), Nani Mummy's father and my great-grandfather, lived only a few streets away and we went to visit him a lot. He was nearly a hundred, but he was sharp-witted and loved to chat. Nani Mummy would take me with her, with promises of letting me pick jamuns. I had mixed feelings about going there, as I'd get bored while the grown-ups talked, plus I dreaded the slobbery kiss Abajaan would give me. He'd fumble out of bed and walk over to his 'cupboard' of concrete shelves with a pair of rosewood doors hinged onto them. Inside lay his many small treasures: Urdu digests, papers from the civil service job he'd left years ago, and brown paper bags with oily marks on them, filled with *boondi* sweets he'd bought. These rainbow-coloured drops were made from flour, sugar and bicarbonate of soda and they needed to be eaten fresh, but Abajaan kept them for weeks; I think he only changed the bag about three times a year.

I liked him, though. He was kind and still had a twinkle in his eye; he would offer me *boondi* and plant a big kiss on my cheek after handing them over. When he talked about his civil service days he always told the same story, about when he was ninety and was wondering why his pension had stopped coming through. He'd made his way to the pension office, only to find out that they'd assumed he was dead. I'll never forget how much we laughed when he told us the first time, and then every time he retold it we'd laugh not at the story, but at the way he'd stand up on his frail feet and act it out, shuffling around the room and shouting out the words he'd said to the pension's administrator: 'I'm still ALIVE! I'm still alive!'

BIG CHANGES

Naively, I thought that if Nani Mummy's father was alive, there was no chance she'd go soon; I had all the time in the world with her. Nani Mummy seemed so healthy and full of life – I don't think I'd ever seen her with so much as a cold. I never thought of her as a big woman, but I suppose she was. I always thought of her as soft and pillowy. I loved the delicate saris she wore, and if I'd had a fight with my parents or was frustrated about my studies, I'd lay my head on her cushiony tummy and fall asleep with tears in my eyes. No one noticed that her tummy had been looking a little bigger than normal, and I don't think she even realised it herself.

Danesh and I were still stealing fleeting conversations, and Daddy had recently confronted me after he'd caught me seeing Danesh outside school. As a protective father, he felt Danesh was a bad influence and would corrupt his innocent daughter; he forbade me from speaking to him. My parents watched my every move and knew all my tricks to deceive them, but sometimes I'd long to hear Danesh's voice, if only for a few minutes, and I would sneak out to Nani Mummy's place to call him. On hot afternoons, the monotonous buzzing of the air conditioner would lull Nani Mummy to sleep and I would grab my chance.

I watched as Nani Mummy fell into a deep nap. Her lips parted to let out tiny snoring gasps – this meant she wouldn't wake up in a hurry. I pulled the rotary phone that lived on the table next to the sofa into the front room. The phone cord was just about long enough, but I had to tinker with the wires at the joints in the cord (which would send a tingling shock through my fingertips) so it wouldn't disconnect. I'd pick up the receiver and dial the number, but the door wouldn't close completely. The rotary dial made such a racket that I was afraid it would wake her up; peeping through the door after dialling each number, I'd make sure it hadn't disturbed her sleep. Finally, I'd get Danesh on the phone, and if he was alone, we'd talk for hours. One time, lost in conversation, with butterflies in my tummy and no doubt a ridiculous giddy look on my face, I noticed the hem of a chiffon sari in my line of sight. There Nani Mummy was, standing with her hands on her hips, one well-coiffed eyebrow raised, looking right at me.

'Who are you talking to? I know it's a boy, so don't bother lying to me,' she said.

I hastily got off the phone. She didn't seem angry at all, so I didn't bother denying it. 'Yes, Nani Mummy, it's a boy.'

'Someone you might marry?' she asked, smiling.

'I would like to one day, but Daddy hates him.'

'You leave your Daddy to me,' she laughed. 'Is he nice to you?'

'Nani Mummy, he treats me like a *shehzadi* (princess).' I gave a little princess twirl as I smiled, feeling relief in my stress-knotted tummy.

'Well, if he's that good, I think you'd better learn how to make chapattis properly!'

We headed to the kitchen and, just like that, she was on my side. I was only a teenager; marriage shouldn't have been the only thing on my mind, but I couldn't think of any other way I could be with him. We'd talked about how we could make it happen one day: we'd wait for him to start working and then hopefully everyone would be on our side.

Nani Mummy measured out the chapatti flour using her hands; she never weighed anything. In went a large pinch of salt, and then she got me to pour lukewarm water over the flour while she kneaded it into a soft dough. When it was fluffy and even, she set it aside.

'The dough is ready now, come and learn how to make the perfect *phulkas*.' (*Phulkas* are small, puffed-up chapattis that are an art to make.)

She rolled the dough into balls, then dusted some flour onto a round wooden board that was roughly the same circumference as a rolled-out chapatti. She flattened the dough ball onto the board then, taking her rolling pin, she floured it and, with a flick of her wrists and hands, rolled out the dough into a thin flatbread in no time, rotating it gently as she did so.

It looked so simple, but when I gave it a go, it stuck fast to the board! I watched as she heated up her *tawa* griddle pan, keeping the heat low, and popped the chapatti onto it. Using a tea towel, she pressed down on the chapatti and swivelled it around the pan to ensure it cooked through. Then she lit another flame on the hob and, grabbing a pair of tongs, she flung the chapatti directly onto the flame, where it puffed up into a ball. I let out a gasp.

'I'll never be able to do that!'

'Yes, you will. Just try and I'll help – you can do anything, my Popplu.' (Popplu was her pet name for me, one she'd come up with; Nani Mummy was always making up cute names for her loved ones.)

With practice, because of her belief in my ability, I found I could make perfect *phulkas* – the first skill every Pakistani housewife needed – and I was only fourteen.

Sometimes we'd visit Nani Mummy's friend Mrs Ashfaq, who hosted *milad* celebrations to mark the Prophet Muhammad's birthday (PBUH). The women would spend the afternoon sprinkling rose water over us, and saying prayers that were meant to bless the spirit of the Prophet Muhammed (PBUH). I'd watch in awe as some of them got emotional, praying loudly and asking for divine help with ailing mothers or husbands. But what was even more fascinating to me was the way their tears seemed to disappear almost instantly when lunch was served.

When we got home after one of these afternoons, Nani Mummy looked tired, more so than usual. She asked if I would let her take a nap, which was odd for her as she was usually full of energy in the early evenings. I left her that day and went home. I didn't see her for a few days as I was busy with my studies.

One day soon afterwards, Mummy told me that Nani Mummy had just come back from the hospital.

'Why was she there? There's nothing wrong with her,' I said.

'Somi, sit down, I need to tell you something.' My mother's face was expressionless, but her voice was trembling.

'The doctor has found a lump the size of a football in one of her ovaries.'

'That's not possible…' I said. My heart skipped a beat, and I felt the sting of bitter tears. Life was never going to be the same again.

I began to realise that we shared a bond of flavour; that food was our way of expressing love and nurturing each other.

WARM KHICHRI

After she'd had a hysterectomy to remove the cancer, I spent a few nights a week at the hospital with Nani Mummy. Most days she was so sick from the chemo that she could barely talk. She hated the hospital food, so my aunt brought her parathas and daal, and my mother made her chickpea pullao and raita. She couldn't taste anything properly, though. 'It all tastes of metal,' she said.

Nani Mummy never spoke about the illness. She just smiled her way through it, but her spirit wasn't the same. She was trying to be strong, never once naming the disease and shrugging off the pain and vomiting, but she couldn't enjoy food like she used to, and I could see that upset her.

Whenever I'd been ill as a child, I'd crave khichri. Most of my friends dreaded this sloppy mix of overcooked rice and moong daal, but Mummy and Nani Mummy made it not only with love and patience but with ingredients that elevated it. Khichri was meant to be just rice and moong daal cooked until soft, making it easier to digest, but my mother and grandmother added red onions softened in butter with cumin, slivers of garlic and a pinch of black salt, infusing the kitchen with the heartening scent of khichri. It was as though that in itself could heal me, no matter what I was suffering from: a cold, mumps or chicken pox. There was magic in each spoonful; it slid into your tummy, bringing life to your body and soul.

Mummy always said that the butter added all the strength and goodness, whereas most people made it bland. And neither of them would ever overcook rice, not even for khichri. 'It doesn't have to be overcooked to be healing and good for you,' Nani Mummy would say.

I'd never watched my grandmother or mother cook khichri, but I had smelt every stage of it being made. As I watched Nani Mummy throw up everything she ate, I thought that maybe khichri's healing magic might be able to nurse her back to health, as it had done for me so many times.

Each night I stayed in the hospital with her, I'd cry. After she fell asleep, I'd go for a walk in the lush gardens that surrounded Karachi's Aga Khan Hospital. This was a moment of freedom for me, freedom from pretending to smile, or holding the bucket for her and trying not to gag as she vomited. I'd walk, cry and pray hard that her cancer would go away.

Mummy didn't shed a tear, a stoic side of her I'd never seen before. I realised what inner strength and courage it must have taken for her to remain strong for Nani Mummy, but I still couldn't understand why my mother didn't just break down, like I did, and how she managed to be so matter-of-fact about it all.

'Mummy, aren't you sad about Nani Mummy?' I asked.

'Of course I am. But I don't like to show my feelings,' she said. 'It doesn't mean I feel them any less deeply.'

'But I can't stop crying, I'm so worried about her,' I said. I missed the Nani Mummy I knew so much – the hours of laughing, gardening and cooking with her.

'Well, you can see how strong she is, right? She's taught me that dealing with the reality of things gives us the strength to find solutions.'

'Mummy, do you think we can make khichri for Nani Mummy?' I asked. 'Maybe it could heal her, just as it always heals me?'

In the kitchen at home, my mother left me all the ingredients for khichri. I insisted on making it myself. I wasn't sure of each step, but I spent time smelling each ingredient. Using my hands, I measured out a three-to-one ratio of basmati rice and moong daal, then I weighed it just to make sure – and, to my delight, my estimation was nearly spot on. I smiled as I realised that I'd inherited my mother's talent for guessing weight by sight. I put the rice and daal in water to soak. I sliced a small red onion and a garlic clove; I remembered Nani Mummy once telling me that the garlic must be sliced very finely so that it cooks quickly, or it will taste uncooked in the khichri. After the rice and daal had been soaking for an hour, I put them on to boil, adding a generous pinch of salt. I checked the rice every now and then as I was nervous about overcooking it.

When the rice and daal were perfectly cooked, I took the pan off the stove, covered it and left it to one side while I heated some ghee in another pan, added cumin seeds and, when they spluttered, added the sliced onions and let them soften. Finally I popped in the garlic slices and allowed them to get slightly brown around the edges, nothing more. I quickly poured this *tarka* (tempering) over the cooked khichri, stirring it gently, so as not to break the fluffy grains of cooked rice. I was pleased; I knew it looked right, and it smelt just like the khichri Mummy and Nani Mummy used to make. I packed it into a Thermos box and took it to the hospital.

As I handed the Thermos over to Nani Mummy, she smiled weakly.

'Popplu, it smells perfect,' she said, as her smile grew bigger.

'I tried to make it just like yours and Mummy's,' I said.

'She did it all by herself,' Mummy beamed.

'Ah, *meri bachi* (my child), I'm so proud of you.'

Nani Mummy's nearly black eyes welled up and she took her glasses off to wipe away her tears. She always got emotional about small things, even just watching sentimental shows on TV. Though such displays of emotion often embarrassed my teenage self, I loved this side of her. She ate slowly, closing her eyes, as if she was savouring each moment, each bite. Then she opened them, and told me about her little tricks to make khichri even better, and I made a mental note of them all.

'And now you will be well, just like I am when you make it for me,' I said.

Nani Mummy smiled again as she finished it all. And for the first time in weeks, she didn't get sick that night.

Soon, Nani Mummy returned from the hospital. The doctor said she would be tested weekly to see if the chemo had destroyed the rest of the cancer cells. I stayed by her side as much as I could, taking care of her. Sabrina, Natasha and Zain would come over and play with me, and we'd watch re-runs of *Tom and Jerry*, laughing together while we stuffed our faces with popcorn and pomegranate.

Sometimes I wasn't so nice to Nani Mummy, though, and she didn't deserve it. When I think back about those times now, I'm filled with regret and I wish I could apologise for hurting her. Maybe it was my teenage hormones, or I was going through more than I knew how to handle – but if she asked me to go with her to see her friends or go shopping when all I wanted to do was watch movies or talk on the phone, I'd get snappy and talk back, saying how I hated doing things with her, when I really didn't.

I'd also still use her phone sometimes to call Danesh, and in many ways spending time with her gave me a convenient excuse to be out of the house and near a phone. I felt guilty about taking advantage of her illness to talk to my boyfriend, but I did it anyway; I knew she was aware I was on the phone even when she was napping, but she never stopped me.

I'd try to contain my moods, and if I slipped up, I'd quickly try to make it up to her by making Lipton tea with powdered milk, just the way she liked it, and we'd dunk rusks in our tea and sit and chat for a while.

A few weeks later, we found out that Nani Mummy was in remission.

'Nani Mummy, my khichri healed you!' I said one evening, when my mother and I were having dinner with her.

'Yes, Somi, it really did,' she said. 'You have healing magic and flavour in your hands,' she said, touching my cheek gently with her soft, wrinkled hands, and my mother smiled too.

'Just like you and Mummy do,' I said.

It was in those days while she recuperated that I felt closer to Nani Mummy and my mother than I ever had before. For the first time, I also became conscious that one day, no matter how hard I tried, or how much khichri I made, Nani Mummy might not get better. I began to realise that we shared a bond of flavour; that food was our way of expressing love and nurturing each other – and that maybe there really was magic in my hands, a power that had carried through the generations.

Nani Mummy's preserved lemons

*My Nani Mummy would make these every year, and they always remind me of her; I even found a jar with my name written on it after she died. She would use small, round Pakistani (*desi*) lemons – about the size of golf balls, they are sharp and very aromatic – and pink salt. This unrefined salt is mined in the foothills of the Himalayas, and can be found in health-food shops or online.*

Prep time: 15–20 minutes + at least 2 weeks pickling time
Makes 1 x 1 litre (4 cup) jar, or 2 x 500 ml (2 cup) jars

- 12 small *desi* lemons or 6 regular lemons
- 4 tablespoons Himalayan pink salt
- 1–2 red chillies – optional

- Sterilise your jar by rinsing it out with boiling water, then set it aside to dry.
- If using small *desi* lemons, just leave them whole and combine them with the salt in a bowl. If using regular lemons, cut them into quarters before combining with the salt.
- Toss well and transfer to the jar, adding a chilli or two if you like, then seal and leave in a cool, dark place for 2 weeks. Shake the jar every day to move the lemons around – the salt will cause them to release liquid.
- After 2 weeks the lemons should be sufficiently preserved; however, the longer you leave them the more intensely pickled they'll become.
- Once the jar has been opened, store it in the fridge, where the lemons will keep well for up to a year, as long as you don't use a metal utensil to remove them from the jar and you ensure that it is tightly sealed again afterwards.

There was something special about this simple way of preserving the season, time and moment without disturbing the purity of the lemons' flavour.

Khichri

This is the soothing dish I cooked for Nani Mummy when she was in hospital, and that she and Mummy cooked for me when I was unwell. It brought me back to life then, and it still does now.

Prep time: 10–12 minutes + 30 minutes soaking
Cooking time: 15–20 minutes
Serves 4–6

115 g (½ cup) moong daal (split mung beans)
250 g (1¼ cups) basmati rice
salt, to taste
1 tablespoon ghee (or 1 tablespoon unsalted butter mixed with 1 teaspoon sunflower oil)
1 teaspoon cumin seeds
1 small red onion, cut into rings
1 garlic clove, thinly sliced
Greek-style yoghurt, to serve

- Mix the moong daal and rice together in a large sieve and rinse well, then put them into a bowl and pour in enough water to cover. Let them soak for 30 minutes–1 hour (the longer they are soaked, the quicker they will cook).
- Drain the rice and daal, tip into a large saucepan and pour in about 250 ml (1 cup) of water, just enough to cover. Add the salt and bring to the boil, then reduce the heat and simmer until the daal and rice are cooked and any excess water has evaporated, about 10–12 minutes. The rice shouldn't be mushy and the daal should still have a little bite. Take off the heat, cover and set aside.
- In a small frying pan, heat the ghee over medium heat. When it is hot, add the cumin seeds and fry for 30 seconds until they splutter, then add the onion and fry for a further 2–3 minutes, or until soft. Add the garlic and fry until it is slightly brown around the edges (be careful not to let it burn).
- Pour the contents of the frying pan over the rice and daal and stir well. Serve with yoghurt on the side.

CHAPTER 9

Benazir and Bundoo Khan

I realise that my independent spirit doesn't fit in with the restrictiveness of Pakistani society. As I become aware of the political and social changes around me, I find that, in my world, love, music and food are all interlinked.

Karachi, April 1986

A NEW HOPE

'You should study Law, then you could go into politics, because what the country needs is a strong leader.' Daddy often said this to me. In Pakistan, many politicians had been ex-lawyers, and I think this was a career path my father would have been happy to support, if it had been my dream.

Law was my father's second career and he was passionate about it. Having managed to set up his own firm at forty-one and make a success of it within a few years, he was the only maritime lawyer in Karachi at the time, and his hope was that I would take over the firm one day. He never forced me to think about Law as a career, but his powers of persuasion and occasional hints began to weave their way into my mind. My father wanted me to have the same opportunities as a son might have, and I wanted to make him proud.

'There is nothing a man can do that a woman can't do,' he'd say.

My father's tenacity in making sure I had opportunities not only gave me the ability to stand up for myself on many occasions, it also fuelled the anger I felt towards other men in Pakistan. *How dare these men think that I'm not capable of what they are, just because I'm a woman?* I thought.

At home, the disparity between women and men was not especially evident, and I was surrounded by strong female role models. I'd grown up watching Nani Mummy managing on her own, and I saw her as firm and confident; no one could ever take her for a ride. Even though my mother was the opposite in some ways – timid and underconfident in the wider world – at home she was opinionated, and my father consulted her about every big decision. Their relationship was based on an understanding and respect for each other's strengths.

But outside my home, I noticed how men walked freely on the streets, and rode motorbikes and drove cars, whereas when women drove cars and rode motorbikes, men sneered at them and shouted vulgarities. On the one hand, men in Pakistan had respect for their sisters and mothers, and showed courtesy to women in public by letting them go ahead of them in queues, but on the flip side women weren't always permitted to make decisions for themselves or run their own businesses.

Though there were no laws to stop women from doing these things, it was simply tradition and culture that dissuaded them. In a world of black and white, this left Pakistani women in a place of grey. Most women just turned a blind eye, but the level of hypocrisy made me angry and I refused to accept this as my fate.

The one place that truly 'belonged' to women was the kitchen and, even though I hated the idea of being a 'typical' Pakistani woman, it was this shift in the balance of power in the home, centred on the kitchen, that might well have laid the foundation for my interest in cooking.

Since he assumed power, Zia-ul-Haq had overseen a campaign of Islamisation, passing laws designed to exclude women from public life. Now everyone in Pakistan was talking about a woman who seemed to offer new hope for freedom from the restrictive society he had created.

Benazir Bhutto, aged thirty-three at the time, was the daughter of Zulfikar Ali Bhutto, the Pakistan People's Party (PPP) prime minister who had been overthrown in the 1977 coup and subsequently executed. With her return from self-imposed exile in London, many people hoped she might be the one who could see the country out of dictatorship, and there was also the prospect that she might improve the plight of Pakistani women.

Because Daddy had lived in Pakistan in the 1970s and witnessed the effects of the Bhutto government's nationalisation programme, he had reservations about the Bhutto family. For me, the idea of this woman who spoke of change, democracy and female leadership aligned with my ideas of independence; I may not have known much about her political agenda, but her words were enough at that time.

In April 1986, Benazir landed in Pakistan, and everyone in Karachi was excited about her return and the revival of the PPP. The province of Sindh was a party stronghold, and black, red and green flags were flying across its capital city; there were PPP slogans emblazoned on banners and party-related songs playing everywhere. A particularly catchy song that I loved went '*jeay, jeay*, Bhutto, Benazir' (long live the legacy of Zulfikar Bhutto and Benazir Bhutto), sung in Sindhi, and I'd turn it up loud on my cassette player and dance to it, ignoring my father's protests.

Benazir was going to be driven from the airport to the Mazar-e-Quaid mausoleum, the final resting place of Muhammad Ali Jinnah, founder of Pakistan, and I wanted to watch the procession from the roof. Like most houses in Pakistan, ours had a flat roof with easy access. If the electricity went, we'd sit out under the stars and enjoy the cool breeze; sometimes we'd have parties there and other times Nani Mummy would go up to watch the birds or just look lovingly down at her garden. The house was near the airport, and when my Nana built it, there was barren land all around so you had a direct view of the runways, and he and Nani Mummy would take their afternoon chai up to the roof to watch the planes taking off and landing.

'Daddy, Mummy and I are going up to the roof to wave at Benazir!' I said.

'Sure, but you know I don't approve of all this political party support?'

'She's a woman and she may change things for us all!' I went dancing out of the room and onto the roof with my PPP flags.

When I got to the roof, I saw the streets packed with thousands of PPP supporters, cheering and shouting slogans. In the distance, I could see a four-wheel-drive and there was Benazir standing and waving at the crowd out of its sun-roof. Music was blaring from loudspeakers, people were dancing and jostling each other just to catch a glimpse of her.

The atmosphere felt different from anything I'd known in Karachi before – there was a sense of excitement and hope in the air.

The next day in school, everyone was talking about it. As teenagers we didn't know what it all meant, but we understood that change was sure to come.

'You do know I support MQM, don't you?' said Danesh.

'What? Why? I like Benazir because she's a woman who will give us a real democracy.'

'My father's family are Muhajirs. They migrated from India to Pakistan, so MQM supports us,' he said.

'Oh, well my dad's family is the same, they are migrants too. But do we have to support the same party?'

'Well, I'd like you to.'

'Ok – if you really want me to,' I said.

'I do,' he said.

MQM stood for the Muhajir Qaumi Movement, a political party established by Altaf Hussain to protect the interests of migrants from India, and it had a strong following in many areas of Karachi where Muhajirs had made their home.

Although I knew little about MQM, I was always ready to please Danesh. I didn't really know what politics was all about, but I did know that I wanted to impress him and emulate anything he did – so, just like that, I changed my political inclination. Looking back now, I'm surprised at how easily I gave in to Danesh's demands of me, often going against my liberal upbringing and all the things I believed were wrong with the country I was living in. As a rebellious teenager in a conservative society, I was confused about my place in the world.

WEEKEND WANDERINGS

On weekends, when Mummy didn't want to cook, we would go to Bundoo Khan, a local barbecue place, where spiced smoke rose from the coals as a row of men ferociously fanned the grills laden with skewers of meat glistening in the fluorescent light. A line of waiters would usher us towards the white plastic tables and chairs in the makeshift outdoor seating area. Sometimes we would sit inside if the mosquitoes were bad, but the real excitement was outside. A laminated menu would soon appear at our table, which we'd read under the faint light of the moon and the bulbs dotted above our heads.

We'd always order the same things – chicken tikka for me, chicken boti for Mummy and mutton seekh kebabs, boti tikkas and lamb chops for Daddy and anyone else who was with us – often Nani Mummy and my mamo (maternal uncle) and his family.

Food was served quickly, with piles of tandoori naans, parathas and deep-fried puris, the ubiquitous fresh chutney, either tamarind or coriander, and a plate of sliced red onions, lemons and green chillies, called 'salad'. The chicken tikka was always spicy and made my tummy rumble the minute I saw it – I'd pull off pieces of the chicken meat, roll it up in hot naan and reach for the chutney. 'Don't eat the chutney!' Mummy would say. 'It's probably made using dirty water and it will make you sick.' Mummy was never a fan of street food; she much preferred sitting inside in the air-conditioning, away from the bugs, rather than perching outside in the humid smoky air.

While my uncle and my father discussed politics, I listened quietly, trying not to wade in with my own opinions or questions, as Mummy had been warning me recently not to interrupt when the grown-ups were talking. I couldn't follow much of what they were saying. They discussed how Benazir was probably seeking to avenge her father's death; I wanted to find out about MQM and its leader, Altaf Hussain, but I didn't dare ask or they'd wonder why my adolescent political allegiances had shifted from Benazir, and I didn't want to admit that it was because I wanted to make Danesh happy. I returned home with my hair, skin and clothes reeking of coal smoke and spice, and my mind full of questions.

That weekend, we went to my Dada and Dadi's house and I overheard my parents discussing politics again. It was all anyone seemed to be doing, as people were worried that local skirmishes might provoke Zia to curb the demonstrations. From what I caught of the conversation, it was clear that Dada supported MQM and I really wanted to ask him more, but I felt like my questions would be dismissed as childish.

CHANA DAAL HALVA AND BAKHARKHANI TEARS

Each Sunday Nani Mummy and I went out to buy some goodies to have with our chai: *zeera* (cumin) biscuits and *bakharkhani* – a salty-sweet, flaky, puff-pastry-like biscuit of sorts that we'd crush and soak and soften in milk to eat like a porridge.

In Karachi, Irani bakeries sold the best pastries, biscuits and pineapple cream cake; they were originally set up by people fleeing Iran, and the name had stuck, even though many of them were no longer run by Iranis. We'd always go to one in the Muhammad Ali Society commercial area and we'd get stuck behind the queues of people waiting for fresh tandoori naans from the Irani restaurant next door.

One Sunday, after we got back and were sitting on Nani Mummy's bed with our chai and brown-paper bags from the bakery, the phone rang.

'Somi, come home,' I heard my mother's voice say.

'Why? I'm just having chai with Nani Mummy; I'll come later.'

'Dadi isn't well, and Daddy says we need to see her now,' Mummy said.

Fear shot through my heart as I put the phone down – my other grandmother was sick and my mind was swirling with visions of sickness, hospitals and the fear of losing someone I loved.

The next few months were difficult, with daily visits to the hospital again, as my Dadi's oesophageal cancer was serious, and in my heart I was convinced it must have been a result of her smoking and the betel nut she chewed in her daily paan. I remember mentioning this to my father and my aunts, but they refused to acknowledge it, perhaps because it was too painful to accept that an ordinary Pakistani pastime was the cause of her suffering.

After weeks in hospital, she returned home, and the next Sunday we went to see her and she ushered me into her room. '*Beta* (child), sit, I want to talk to you.' Her weak fingers pointed to the chair by her bedside. Dadi was always slim; I never understood how she was able to produce eight children and remain so slender, but now her shoulders looked a little more hunched than usual as she sat up on her bed.

'Remember the chana daal halva I used to make?' she said.

'Yes, Dadi, but I don't care about that just now. How are you feeling?'

'Yes, Somi, I'm ok. But I want to tell you about it, because if something happens to me, I don't want it gone with me.'

'You're not going anywhere!' I protested.

But Dadi went on to tell me how she'd soak chana daal overnight to soften and expand the grain, and then in the morning she'd boil it in milk in a pressure cooker for two whistles.

'But I hate the pressure cooker,' I said. 'It scares me – how can I cook chana daal without one?'

'You can boil it for about forty-five minutes and keep pressing the daal against the side of your pan to check if it's soft enough,' she explained.

She then told me how to cook a sugar syrup to *ek taar* ('one string') consistency, the same way she did for her *seviyan* vermicelli dessert. 'Make sure you add cloves and green cardamom, then take them out once they have done their work.'

'The hard work starts next,' she said. 'You need to grind the cooked daal; we used to do it by hand on the *sil batta*, but now I use a food processor. Then heat some ghee in a pan and add the ground daal. Let it sizzle and keep stirring it so it doesn't stick.' She told me to keep it moving and if it stuck, to add more ghee. I remembered from when she'd made it before that it smelt both sweet and nutty, and the slightly singed flecks that appeared on the surface of the ochre chana daal looked like tiny ants.

'As you stir the daal, it will get a little darker, and this is when you pour over the sugar syrup with a pinch of saffron strands,' said Dadi. 'The air will fill with saffron smoke, it will be floral and heady, then the paste will become less stiff and easier to stir; it will glisten, and the spicy smell will become mellow and delicate.'

Then she told me to take it out of the pan and put it into a dish to cool before rolling small spoonfuls of the halva into balls and decorating them with silver leaf, ready to eat.

'Did you know that when Dada and I came to Pakistan, I brought a container of chana halva, ladoo sweets and gulab jamun with me?' asked Dadi. 'Dada told me we had to pack quickly and leave all the food behind, but I had just made some chana halva and gulab jamun so I packed them up in a jar, hoping they wouldn't get squashed or leak on the way.' She continued to tell me how she took the long journey from Jaunpur in India by train and bus, and when she finally made it to Rawalpindi she unpacked her sweets and ate them, thinking of how she had made those same sweets in a home that now represented her old life and ate them in a new place as she began her new life.

I could sense that Dadi wanted to spend whatever time she had left getting to know me better, telling me her forgotten stories of migration, food, and her love for her family, and I tried to appreciate the time I had with her.

Many years later, when I wanted to cook her chana daal halva, I tried to remember how she told me to make it. Mine tasted a little like hers, but I wished I could ask her what made her halva so special. I tried to recall the elegant, accurate way she spoke in Urdu and, as I closed my eyes, I could see her nimble fingers taking a pinch of saffron, grinding it between her fingertips and adding it to the halva, filling the room with its earthy scent.

My first-year O-level exams were looming, and I would soon have to decide on my A-level subjects. Daddy was still hoping I'd stick with maths, but I was so apprehensive about maths exams that I begged Daddy to speak to Mrs Smith about dropping it, even though it was meant to be a compulsory subject. In return, I accepted his trade-off to consider law as an A-level subject when the time came.

A week before the exams, I met Danesh after school for chaat at our usual Boat Basin place and immediately noticed that he was looking distracted.

'What's wrong with you?' I asked.

'Nothing, really,' he said, 'but we do need to talk.'

'What's happened?'

'You know how my uncle lives in America? Well, he's asked me to study at university there, in Connecticut. It's such a great opportunity, and besides my father wants me to go.'

'Oh, right – how long are you going for?'

'The degree is four years, so I will be leaving right after my A-level exams in May,' he said.

'What about us?' I asked.

'What about us? I mean, we can still have a long-distance relationship, and I'll come back for you in four years. I'll be back during holidays, and I'll write to you every week and call you on the weekends, I promise. But you must promise me that you won't go abroad to study,' he went on.

I tried to take it all in. At the time I didn't hear the uncertainty in his voice, and I didn't even think of how ridiculous his request was for me to stay in Karachi while he went off to America. My pride told me to keep smiling, but inside my heart was breaking. My tears welled up as he paid the bill, but I didn't want him to see how much his plans hurt me, so I just told him that I was happy for him and I'd do as he asked. Many years later, I would wonder why I readily agreed to give up so many opportunities for him.

I got home that afternoon, threw my bag down in my room and ran to see Nani Mummy. She was on the phone, so I went into the kitchen and opened the rosewood cabinet where she kept her pickles and biscuits and pulled out the jar of slightly soggy *bakharkhani*. As I broke off small pieces and hastily ate them, tears streamed down my face and onto the pastry, making it saltier and soggier.

'Use a plate, Somi,' said Nani Mummy from her bedroom, as she saw the flakes of pastry fall to the floor. But then she caught sight of my red eyes and tear-stained face. She gasped, hung up and ran over to me.

'Whatever's happened, don't worry,' she said. 'I'm here, everything will be ok.'

I cried on her shoulder, soaking her sari, as I held on to her for what felt like hours.

My Dadi was sick, my Nani was better – but the cancer could come back – and my first love was going away. I was losing all the people I loved, and I couldn't stop any of it. I tried not to lose hope, though, and I spent as much time as I could with Dadi; I'd wasted so many years not listening to her stories and I wanted to make up for lost time. I also kept telling myself that if I did as Danesh wanted, and waited for him in Karachi, he'd come back for me.

In a world of black and white, cultural norms left Pakistani women in a place of grey.

Chicken boti tikka, Bundoo Khan style

Family weekend trips to our favourite open-air barbecue restaurant meant we'd get to eat boti tikka with flatbreads and tamarind chutney – as the grown-up chat bored me, that was the only reason I'd willingly go along. For this recipe (pictured overleaf), you'll need some bamboo skewers to thread the cubes of chicken on; remember to soak them for at least half an hour so they don't get singed in the oven. Serve with naan or basmati rice.

Prep time: 25 minutes + marinating time, from 1 hour to overnight
Cooking time: 25–30 minutes
Serves 4–6

½ teaspoon chilli powder
½ teaspoon crushed black peppercorns
¼ teaspoon turmeric powder
1 teaspoon cumin seeds, roasted in a dry frying pan and ground
1 teaspoon coriander seeds, roasted in a dry frying pan and ground
½ teaspoon garam masala
½ teaspoon unsmoked paprika
3 garlic cloves, crushed
2.5 cm (1 inch) ginger, finely grated
salt, to taste
juice of 1 lemon
4 skinless chicken breast fillets, cut into 2 cm (¾ inch) cubes
2–3 tablespoons sunflower oil

For the tamarind chutney

100 g (3½ oz) dried tamarind – about half a block
4–5 tablespoons dark brown sugar
1 teaspoon salt
1 teaspoon cumin seeds, roasted in a dry frying pan
½ teaspoon crushed black peppercorns
½ teaspoon chilli powder

- In a large bowl, mix the spices, garlic, ginger and salt with the lemon juice. Add the chicken and leave in the fridge to marinate for at least 1 hour, or as long as overnight.
- In the meantime, soak about 6 bamboo skewers in water and make the chutney. Put the tamarind into a small saucepan with 150 ml (5 fl oz) of water, the sugar, salt and spices. Bring to the boil and stir until the block of tamarind breaks up and the sugar and salt have dissolved, about 10–15 minutes. Strain through a fine-mesh sieve into a bowl, discarding the tamarind seeds and cumin seeds. Set the chutney aside while you cook the chicken.
- Preheat the oven to 180°C (350°F) and line a baking tray with baking paper. Thread about 4 chicken pieces onto each bamboo skewer, then place on the baking tray. Brush the chicken with oil and cook for 20–25 minutes in the oven, or until the chicken is brown around the edges and cooked through.
- Serve hot, with the bowl of chutney alongside.

The chicken tikka was always spicy and made my tummy rumble the minute I saw it. I'd pull off pieces of the chicken meat, roll it up in hot naan and reach for the chutney.

Sweet chana daal halva

This is a recipe noted down on a scrap of old diary paper by my mother, as dictated to her by Dadi, and then given a little of Mummy's own flair. 'Daal sweet?', you might ask, puzzled – but try it before you judge it (pictured on previous page).

Prep time: 15 minutes + overnight soaking
Cooking time: 45–50 minutes
Serves 8–10

200 g (1 cup) chana daal (split chickpeas)
1 litre (4 cups) whole (full-cream) milk, plus 1 tablespoon hot milk extra
generous pinch of saffron threads
4 tablespoons ghee
2–4 green cardamom pods, cracked open and seeds extracted
4–6 cloves
220 g (1 cup) caster (superfine) sugar

To garnish

handful of slivered pistachios
handful of slivered almonds
a little edible gold or silver leaf

Whenever I make this halva, I recall the elegant, accurate way Dadi spoke in Urdu and, as I close my eyes, I can see her nimble fingers taking a pinch of saffron and grinding it between her fingertips, filling the room with its earthy scent.

- Soak the chana daal overnight in a bowl of water.
- The next day, drain the daal and tip into a saucepan. Add the milk and bring to the boil, then simmer for 25–30 minutes, stirring constantly, until the daal is tender and the milk has been absorbed – the mixture should be quite dry.
- Scrape the mixture into a food processor and blitz thoroughly until you have a smooth, dry paste. Set aside.
- Crush the saffron threads between your fingers, then place in a small bowl with the hot milk and leave to soak for 10–12 minutes.
- Heat the ghee in the rinsed-out saucepan, add the cardamom seeds and cloves and cook over medium heat until fragrant, then remove the cloves. Add the daal paste, turn the heat down to medium-low and fry for 8–9 minutes or until the mixture is golden brown in colour and smells very nutty. Make sure you keep stirring constantly so it doesn't catch and burn. When it's ready, take off the heat, cover and set aside.
- Put the sugar and 60 ml (¼ cup) of water into a small saucepan and stir over medium heat until the sugar has completely dissolved and you have a thin sugar syrup. Pour the syrup over the daal mixture, then cook over low heat, stirring constantly, for a few minutes until well combined.
- Working quickly, add the saffron milk and stir briskly so the daal mixture doesn't cool or harden, then remove from the heat and pour into a shallow dish or baking tray. Allow to cool slightly, then either score into diamond shapes with a knife or use your hands to roll small pieces into balls or logs.
- Decorate with the nuts and silver or gold leaf, then eat at room temperature. Stored in an airtight container, this halva will keep for about 3–5 days in a cool, dry place.

CHAPTER 10

Cooking Mummy's pullao

I learn the art of cooking pullao, and rice generally. I come to understand that an unhappy state of mind can be a reason for failing in cooking. Food is about love and nurturing – they are almost essential ingredients, and if either are missing, food will never taste good. I also learn that cooking is about identity and individuality.

Karachi, 1987

MUMMY'S LOST DREAMS

Mummy wasn't like most well-to-do Pakistani women, in that she didn't have a domestic cook in her kitchen or servants running the home. The only help she'd tolerate was a young woman who came over to clean the house each morning, but even then the poor girl couldn't seem to do anything right as far as my mother was concerned.

Despite doing most of the housework and all the cooking, not a hair on Mummy's head was ever out of place. She dressed impeccably and had a way of making the simplest outfit look glamorous. With a perfect hourglass figure, she took the time to exercise and do yoga regularly and follow a strict beauty routine. She wore well-fitting trousers or long skirts, and her flouncy blouses would be in complementary hues; the pure silk *shalwar kameez* she wore always had exactly the length of *kameez* that was in fashion at the time. Any out-of-fashion clothes were relegated to the back of the wardrobe, ready and waiting for the time when they'd be back in vogue. She brought her entire look together with make-up – her almond-shaped eyes lined perfectly in kajal, with a 1960s-style feline flick, and her lips stained in a classic Chanel red.

Every week Mummy and I would go to Tariq Road, where a bustling street market and large shopping centres were packed with shops selling bolts of colourful silk, chiffon and cotton lawn for making into a *shalwar kameez*. The air was filled with the aroma of clean cotton, smooth silk and sweaty shopkeepers. Each shop would lure you in by pulling rolls of beautiful fabric off their shelves and throwing it open before you. Seats would be placed in front of the counters so you could sit in comfort, and they'd order soft drinks or chai for you; eighty-watt bulbs hung overhead, and the heat from the bulbs made you sweat even more. Sometimes the shopkeepers would comically model lengths of material on themselves to demonstrate how well it draped, showing off with a catwalk stride.

Mummy would scour the shops for the perfect fabric, settling on a colour scheme and matching all three pieces of a new outfit: *shalwar*, *dupatta* and *kameez*. If any of them didn't quite match, we'd go to the dyer with a length of white chiffon, which he'd dye to match.

But in stark contrast to the confidence with which my mother presented herself, socially she was shy and withdrawn.

'Why are you always so quiet, Mummy?' I asked her once.

‘Because I’m shy, most people think I am proud, but I don’t feel confident enough to start conversations,’ she said.

‘But you always talk a lot at home!’

‘Yes, I’m less self-conscious when I’m talking to people I know, but when I’m in a new place with new faces I’m scared to begin conversations. I worry about what people might think of me.’

Mummy told me that she was prepared to do whatever it took to help me grow into a confident young woman. Whenever Daddy was being over-protective, especially when I wanted to try something with an element of risk, like horse-riding or gymnastics, she’d argue my case to him, explaining how important it was for me to take part in activities that brought me out of my shell. Many years later, she told me how delighted she was that I could stand up in a room and speak to a crowd of strangers; it’s what she always wanted me to be like – fearless and confident.

Some of my mother’s shyness could be attributed to the way her father raised her. A traditional man in many ways, he nevertheless believed that his daughter should be educated, and he was open to the idea of her finding her own husband, as she did. Mummy studied nutrition and home economics in Karachi; and, as the family was living in Rawalpindi at the time, she was even allowed to stay at the college housing there. When she finished college, she was offered a job as a nutritionist for Pakistan International Airlines catering, but her father told her she couldn’t work; she never asked again.

‘I wish I’d pushed your Nana about taking that job,’ she told me. ‘I’d have been good at it. I was passionate about nutrition, as it was a new way of thinking in those days – to plan meals thoughtfully – but Nana didn’t think it was right for a woman from my background to work.’

Mummy was also a wonderful artist but lacked the self-confidence and motivation to pursue her oil painting professionally. Instead, after she got married to Daddy, she applied her talents in other ways, like keeping her home beautiful and cooking; it was as if she treated cooking as an art, and anything she cooked sung with complexity of flavour. She never compromised on presentation or ingredients, and she never stopped learning new ways of cooking.

Ever since Danesh had told me he’d be moving to America I’d been distracted, and I hadn’t done well in my exams. None of my friends understood, either because they didn't have boyfriends or theirs weren't leaving the country, and I couldn't talk to anyone in the family except Guddo Phuppo, and she was busy with her teacher-training exams. This was my first heartbreak, and although I didn't know how I was meant to feel, I think I felt worse because he didn't break up with me cleanly but left me clinging on to the hope of a future that seemed impossible.

Seeking consolation in sweet treats – something I'd found a comfort ever since my mother made me that cardamom fudge in our cabin at sea – I found myself craving cheesecake. There weren't many Western-style bakeries in Karachi then, and those there were only took orders for special occasions, so I began making cheesecakes on my own, using a recipe in Mummy's tattered copy of *Good Housekeeping Cookery Book*. I made the base with melted butter and digestive (wheatmeal) biscuits and let it set in the fridge. As we couldn't buy cream cheese, I hung yoghurt overnight in cheesecloth; the next day I whipped the strained yoghurt with cream, vanilla and gelatine, and made my own icing sugar by hand-grinding regular sugar, as I'd seen Mummy do. The cheesecake was nothing special but it fulfilled its purpose. I think perhaps I didn't use enough gelatine or wasn't patient enough to wait for it to set properly, and if I left the cheesecake out of the fridge for any length of time, it would melt and go rancid in the heat.

Even though it was the summer holidays, I didn't feel like seeing my friends, preferring to wallow in my own misery. I'd take huge slices of cheesecake, sit on the sofa and watch *Pretty in Pink* over and over, or lock myself in my room and listen to Madonna's 'Crazy for You' or Foreigner's 'Waiting for a Girl Like You' – which was 'our' song – while swallowing mouthfuls of tear-salted cheesecake. Mummy had noticed that I wasn't myself, but I didn't feel like talking to her because I knew she'd tell me to get over it. Or worse, she'd tell Daddy what had happened, and then I'd get a joint lecture about what an 'idiotic boy' Danesh was and how I should forget him.

A WEEKEND PULLAO

The spiced air that pervaded the whole house was a smell that was synonymous with weekends in my home. We rarely had anything lavish to start the day, like the traditional Pakistani *halva puri*; my parents weren't keen on this heavy breakfast of sweet semolina halva, spicy potatoes, chickpea masala and deep-fried puri breads. Mostly we'd just have cornflakes, or toast with butter and jam, but occasionally Daddy would cook his famous omelette – the only thing he really knew how to cook. He'd beat four eggs with an abundance of chilli powder, turmeric, green chillies, fresh coriander and anything else he could find. Next he'd fry cumin seeds with thinly sliced potato and chopped garlic in oil and butter until they were nearly burnt, then add the eggs and cook the omelette until it was charred and overdone. But somehow it was delicious: there was something about the slightly acrid garlic, near-burnt potatoes and the overall intensity of flavour that we liked. He took so much pride in making it, and he'd always laugh about how we complained about him burning the eggs and making them too spicy, yet he'd have to share his omelette three ways every time.

One Sunday morning that summer I woke to the familiar earthiness of chicken cooking with spices. My mother liked to cook lunch early because it freed up the rest of her afternoon.

'Can I have some?' I asked.

'You can come and help me cook it first!' my mother replied.

'Mummy, I really don't feel like it,' I said. I was feeling sorry for myself and the last thing I wanted to do was get up and help in the kitchen.

In the upstairs part of my Nani's house, our kitchen was built on an extension of the patio, and to make it feel more modern, Mummy had it fitted with the latest cooker and off-white Formica counter tops. This meant that the faintest splash of turmeric-infused korma or even a sprinkle of chilli powder would make her bring out the bleach, but the stains were usually immovable no matter how much you scrubbed. I never understood why she'd insisted on off-white in a kitchen where most of the food was cooked with colourful ingredients that stained!

'Oh, come on – once you start you'll feel like it.'

'What's on the stove?' I asked.

'That's the *yakhni* for the pullao – the stock that spices the entire dish.'

Traditionally mutton was used for pullao as the meat broke down as it slowly cooked in the stock to become soft, stringy fragments, but I always preferred chicken because it didn't get stuck between my teeth like mutton did. My mother's *yakhni* stock was made by boiling up some chicken on the bone with quartered red onions (with the skin left on), garlic, ginger and whole spices, including cinnamon, star anise, cloves, coriander and cumin seeds, bay leaves, black and green cardamom.

As the stock simmered away, every now and then she skimmed the froth off the surface and topped it up with more water. The stock got murkier and more intense as the kitchen filled with the heady, haunting aroma of dark spices, almost like a rich, musky incense. The stock was ready when shiny dots of fat from the meat bobbed up to the surface; it would be deeply infused with spices, the chicken soft and tender.

While the chicken and stock cooked, she rinsed basmati rice a few times to get rid of as much starch as possible, then left it to soak for an hour. She explained that this would make the cooked rice fluffier and stop the grains from sticking together.

'Now we need to make the base of the pullao before we add the rice, chicken and stock,' said Mummy.

'It all takes so long!' I complained. Usually I'd have lost patience by now, but watching the stock come alive with such flavour was fascinating; it was as if the aroma of the stock was a magic potion with the ability to distract me from my woes.

'So, tell me what's bothering you, Somi. Is it about a boy?' my mother asked.

I was taken aback, because she'd never usually ask me something like this so directly. I sensed that she had noticed my moods lately and had been looking for the right opportunity to talk to me. It was as if the act of cooking with her had softened me, and the words just slipped out effortlessly.

'Mummy, Danesh is leaving for America. I don't know how it's going to work with him gone,' I blurted out.

Mummy smiled, put her hand on my shoulder and squeezed it.

'If he really loves you, he will work it out and keep in touch,' she said. 'But you're both so young. Just get on with your life, Somi. You have a future ahead of you. Don't waste it over a boy.'

'But he's the one for me, Mummy.'

'There will be many boys, Somi. Like I said, if it's meant to be, nothing will stop it from happening. You should concentrate on what makes you happy: find your passion, make your future.'

'I don't know what I'm passionate about yet.'

'Well, don't think about it, it'll come to you. Let's cook the pullao now. Watch each step and breathe in each moment; when you cook it on your own, you'll remember the smells and replicate the recipe in your own way.'

'What does that mean?' I asked.

'You'll see.'

Next, she strained the cooked *yakhni* stock into a bowl, placing the chicken on a plate and discarding the onion, garlic, ginger and spices. In the same pan, she heated a mix of ghee and oil, and when it was hot, added some more coriander and cumin seeds and green and black cardamom, letting them splutter before adding thinly sliced red onions. Black cardamom, the dark and smouldering cousin of green cardamom, lends a campfire smokiness to anything it is cooked with, and Mummy loved it with chicken.

'Watch as I take my time to brown the onions – I'll move them around in the pan so they brown evenly,' she said. 'This is really important, because the darker the onions are, the more of a brown tinge you get in the pullao rice. This acts like a natural dye for the rice, and the spiced stock flavours it.'

My mother used to keep browned onions in the fridge, ready to be added to the base of a korma, used as a garnish, or ground into a paste for marinades; they were one of her secret ingredients. I watched as she patiently cooked the onions. Initially it looked like a lot, but slowly they cooked down, turning soft with brown-tinged edges. The air filled with the sweetness of browned onions – one of my favourite smells in the kitchen, reminding me of everything from festivities to a casual weekend at Nani Mummy's. It took me back to my childhood on the ships, when Mummy would cook biryani in her electric frying pan in her makeshift galley in our cabin. These memories made me feel safe and happy.

As soon as the onions were dark brown, Mummy added the chicken, stirring it through, then adding the drained rice.

'Be careful not to over-stir the rice at this point, because the soaked rice breaks easily,' she said, 'and if you break the rice, it won't turn into fluffy, long grains.'

Carefully, she added enough of the stock to cover the rice, brought it to the boil and then returned it to a simmer, covering it and leaving it to cook.

'Mummy, how much stock is enough?'

'Cover the rice so that every grain is under the surface, with about half an inch of stock above it. That should be enough if you've soaked the rice for an hour, but check it after about seven or eight minutes to make sure you don't need to add more stock. Usually I get it spot on, but that comes with practice and trusting your eye.'

As we waited for the rice to cook with the stock and chicken, I walked around the house and noticed that the aroma of the pullao had permeated my hair and every room in the house. It was a heady smell but with a touch of buttered popcorn and candyfloss, which came from the rice. I'd discovered that I had a really strong sense of taste and smell; my nose was so sensitive that smells others found faint seemed to linger for hours, annoying me to the point where I'd end up with a migraine. With smells like body odour being so prevalent in Karachi because of the heat, not to mention the strong, cheap perfumes some people doused themselves with, my heightened senses could be more of a curse than a blessing; but the mouth-watering smells of roasting spices, browning onions and fresh herbs brought me to life. It was as if I could smell the very soul of each ingredient and marry them together in my mind, knowing how they'd taste with each other.

Sometimes I'd smell the flavours of our meal cooking in the kitchen as I sipped my chai – the smells around me would be contained in the teacup. I didn't pay much attention to it then, but I would later learn that this gift I possessed would help me to become an instinctive cook, enabling me to recreate flavours or a recipe from my sensory memories. With time, I came to trust my senses more than any written recipe.

When the pullao was ready, Mummy lifted the lid and steam rose from the pan. It smelt like home, like love and the comforting taste that only my mother could bring to food – buttery, earthy and grounding. It was that chicken pullao that lifted me from feeling down about Danesh to feeling hopeful that if we were meant to be, it would work out.

I discovered that there was something deeply therapeutic about cooking with my mother, or even just being in the kitchen with her. That day, when I first shared my innermost feelings with her, and it came so effortlessly, I realised that this represented a time of connection, of sharing and togetherness. I felt most comfortable in her company in the kitchen, which was this moveable home she'd created in my childhood; it didn't matter whether it was in our house in Karachi or on-board a ship when I was young, she could create a home with just her presence and her flavours.

My parents often went out to parties on weekends and, as I grew older, they'd sometimes let me stay home alone. One evening, as they were going out, Mummy took out a bowl of chicken from the fridge and placed it on the kitchen counter.

'While we're out, why don't you have a play with this and try making a chicken pullao on your own, then we can have it for lunch tomorrow?' she said.

'But I don't remember everything you showed me!'

'You remember the flavour, right?' she said. 'Well, let that memory guide you.'

I stood staring at the chicken, rice and spices. I didn't know if I could do this.

Earlier that day, Danesh had called to say goodbye. I could hear the excitement in his voice as he began a new chapter in his life, whereas I was left here, waiting for him, and the tears rolled down my cheeks as he told me he'd write and call. I was overwhelmed by a cocktail of bitter emotions – and now my mother wanted me to cook. I just didn't know if I had the emotional energy; it was cooking with Mummy that I knew would make me feel better, and I wasn't sure if I could do it by myself.

... in our house in Karachi or on-board a ship when I was young, my mother could create a home with just her presence and her flavours.

All dressed up on my first Eid

I took a deep breath; I knew the rice needed time to soak, so I rinsed it gently, but then I got distracted while I was picking the spices, chopping the onions and peeling the garlic. I didn't even think of how much I was adding – my heart just wasn't in it. When I cooked the rice, I lost track of time. The rice was stodgy, sticky and over-cooked; it was the kind of rice my mother wouldn't serve her worst enemy, the sort of rice she'd ask me to bin and cook again.

I sat down in the middle of the kitchen floor and sobbed. I think what upset me most was that Danesh had essentially told me not to live my life, but simply to wait for his return. Though I would've done anything for him, in my heart I knew that his demands were unfair. *To hell with him!* I told myself. I felt better after that cry, and so I popped the Bee Gees cassette into my dad's hifi system and danced to 'Stayin' Alive'. I went to soak some more rice; I had some *yakhni* stock left too, and I made the pullao again. This time I mindfully recreated each step and, as I did so, I slowly began to forget the immediacy of my heartache.

As soon as I took off the lid, I knew it was perfect. Each grain of rice stood proud, and the air was filled with that familiar comforting aroma of Sunday mornings.

I discovered that cooking with my whole heart not only made me feel good, it also made my food taste better; and that this curse of a sensitive nose could become my 'superpower', one I could harness to give me hope and happiness when I needed it the most.

EID AND ETIQUETTE

We always had Eid dinner with Mummy's side of the family, and that meant going to Uncle Iqbal's house for a big family gathering. Uncle Iqbal was Nani Mummy's elder brother and he lived a few streets away from us. He was a larger-than-life character, in terms of both size and his jovial demeanour; he was well-read and always had a cigarette in his hands. Uncle Iqbal had that kind of belly laugh that filled a room with positive energy.

In the late 1950s he had been posted to Washington as a commercial attaché, and as a result he had a real penchant for all things American. When he returned to Pakistan, he'd built a massive grey lime-washed house, modelled on mid-century American homes and it was quite a novelty; it was as if you'd walked into a 1960s film set. He'd imported everything from America, right down to the dustbins and the boxes of Kleenex tissues in every room. In the garden was a large magnolia tree, and Nani Mummy told me that even that had come from Washington as a seedling. He'd had fake fireplaces made, with mantelpieces bearing candle stands, family photos displayed in intricate photo frames and a brass carriage clock. At the back of his house, he had a tiled swimming pool that I don't think was ever used and cages housing birds, rabbits and a peacock. We all called it Uncle Iqbal's Zoo, and as a child I loved hanging out with the animals.

His Eid dinners were lavish feasts, and members of the extended family would emerge from the woodwork for them. We'd all congregate in his drawing room, which had an upright piano on one side with a black-and-white picture of his late wife Aunty Sakina in a gold-ridged frame on top of it. Years later, he'd married Aunty Sadaqat, a softly spoken lady who was a good wife to him. The piano itself belonged to Uncle Iqbal's daughter's (Mummy's cousin, Chand), who used to play it.

I enjoyed going to these dinners because there'd be other distant cousins to hang out with, but mostly I wanted to chat to Uncle Iqbal's granddaughter, Aliya, who visited from Saudi Arabia a couple of times a year. Aliya was my second cousin, but we were close as she was like me: a little rebellious and a little quirky. Aliya lived in Saudi because her father worked in a bank there, and she attended the American school in an expat compound. She talked about high-school proms and corsages, just like I'd seen in the movies. I was in awe of her accent, her very un-Pakistani ways and her American accessories, like Goody barrettes and Lady Speed Stick deodorant. She was sporty, with smooth tanned skin, auburn ringlets and an almond-shaped face. She always wore cool Ked sneakers and shorts, and I was full of envy that she was allowed to wear whatever she wanted.

Eid meant I had to wear something flashy and festive – usually, a *shalwar kameez* or *tung pajama*, long slim-legged trousers with fabric that bunched up just above the feet. I quite liked those, but I hated the *kameez* tops embellished with itchy gold *gota* ribbon. The timing of Eid was determined by the lunar calendar, and when it fell in the summer, this was an excruciating experience. The gold thread would bite into your underarms, making them hot and scratchy and the sweat would drip down your back, causing the *kameez* to stick uncomfortably to your skin.

Everyone sat in Uncle Iqbal's drawing room like they were in a doctor's waiting room. The rust-coloured velvet sofas were lined up against the wallpapered walls, each one sporting an abundance of cushions embroidered with flowers like those you saw in paintings by the Dutch Masters. All shapes and sizes of family members would be squashed side by side, waiting for dinner to be served. Most of the extended family who attended these dinners we'd only see at Eid or weddings, and we had little in common, so we'd make small talk, feigning interest in each other's health and wellbeing.

Then, as soon as dinner was served, they all rushed to the drawing room like a bunch of cats let out of a cage. There, the chairs were pushed up against the walls and the oval, vintage mahogany dining table was laid with a delicate lace tablecloth and an expansive buffet. Everyone hovered over the usual Eid suspects: a roast leg of lamb, *roghni* naan, chicken korma and pullao, all cooked by their family cook and presented on silver serving platters set over tealight food warmers. The scent of gladioli and tuberoses in vases mingled deliciously with the aromatic spices from the food. The children held out for dessert: strawberry ice cream, with mangoes in summer and pomegranates in winter, and of course there'd always be *seviyan* vermicelli dessert and lots of colourful *mithai* sweetmeats.

After dinner, most of the more distant family members slipped away, leaving Nani Mummy's siblings and their families to chew paan and talk family politics. I'd sit on the Persian rug in the middle of the drawing room playing board games with my cousins, but I'd also eavesdrop on the adults' conversations about who was having an affair or who owed money. Every now and then Nani Mummy would glare at me with a raised eyebrow, signalling with her hands that I should sit in a more ladylike fashion on the floor, or that I should fix my *dupatta* scarf so it didn't trail behind me when I walked. She'd call me over sometimes to advise me that my tomboyish ways weren't making a good impression: 'Somi, please sit properly. What are people going to say? You're a young lady now, behave like one.'

I hated being told to act like 'a young lady'. I had always been a little blasé about how I sat, walked or talked. I disliked conforming, and the more someone nagged me the less likely I was to obey. One time, as I sat there playing Monopoly with my cousins, I heard Aunty Tanveer, a short, dark-skinned woman who loved to wear bright-orange lipstick and strong perfume, calling Nani Mummy 'Aunty Pindi' (Pindi is short for Rawalpindi). A few of Nani Mummy's relatives called her this and it always annoyed me. *Who calls someone by the name of a city?* I thought. And on this occasion, I just couldn't bear it. I got up off the floor and walked over to her: 'Her name is Iqbal Sultana Ghani, not Aunty Pindi!' I said.

As soon as I had said it, my heart nearly jumped out of my mouth; all eyes in the room were on me. I trembled at the thought of the consequences but at the same time, I felt a sense of relief as the idea of other people having their own pet names for my Nani Mummy made me envious and angry.

'Somi, apologise to Aunty Tanveer. That's not a very nice way to speak to an elder,' said Mummy, who had heard my outburst and walked over. Soon afterwards, she made her excuses and we left.

I felt embarrassed, and I didn't see Nani Mummy for a couple of days. I knew she wouldn't tell me off, but in a way that was worse, because I knew she was disappointed in me. I finally mustered up the courage to go over. Nani Mummy was sitting on her bed, reading an Urdu digest. She smiled and told me to make a cup of tea and sit with her.

'Popplu, do you even know why they all call me Aunty Pindi?' she asked.

I was too ashamed to say anything.

'It's because, out of all the siblings, I spent the most time living in Rawalpindi, so Aunty Pindi became my nickname. You shouldn't feel bad about it. After all, no one else calls me Nani Mummy,' she said. 'You're a big girl now, and you should be polite to others. You know how to behave well, so why not be who you are? Besides, Popplu, soon you'll be of a marriageable age.'

I nodded sheepishly. When Nani Mummy pulled me up for my occasional impoliteness she made me realise that my obstinate behaviour was sometimes uncalled for. While I hated hearing that I'd soon be of a marriageable age, I knew it wasn't my place to be snappy with elders.

It was in moments like these that I felt the constraints of social expectation: in Pakistan, young people weren't supposed to express their opinions candidly, and it certainly wasn't the behaviour expected of young women. But standing up to make my voice heard was a part of my nature – one I found hard to give up even years later, for it was a way of exerting my independence and dislike for conformity.

Yakhni chicken pullao

Weekend comfort in a bowl, this is my mother's signature chicken pullao recipe (pictured overleaf). 'Yakhni' *refers to the stock used in the dish, which is infused with nourishment from the chicken on the bone and the spices.*

Prep time: 20 minutes + 1 hour soaking
Cooking time: 1 hour and 20 minutes
Serves 4–6

- 250 g (1¼ cups) basmati rice
- 100 ml (3½ fl oz) sunflower oil
- 1 teaspoon black peppercorns
- 1 cinnamon stick
- 2 star anise
- 1 teaspoon cloves
- 1 black cardamom pod
- 3–4 green cardamom pods, bruised
- 4–6 skinless chicken legs (thighs and/or drumsticks), on the bone
- 2 teaspoons cumin seeds
- 1 teaspoon coriander seeds
- 2 bay leaves
- 1 large red onion, thinly sliced
- 1 teaspoon finely grated ginger
- 1 teaspoon crushed garlic
- salt, to taste
- 1 green chilli, deseeded and chopped

For the raita

- ½ long (telegraph) cucumber
- 260 g (1 cup) Greek-style yoghurt
- 1 teaspoon cumin seeds, roasted in a dry frying pan and ground
- ½ tablespoon salt – ideally black salt (*kala namak*)
- ¼ teaspoon sugar
- 1 tablespoon chopped coriander (cilantro)

When the pullao was ready, Mummy lifted the lid and steam rose from the pan. It smelt like home, like love and the comforting taste that only my mother could bring to food – buttery, earthy and grounding.

- Rinse the rice, then leave to soak in a bowl of water for 1 hour.
- Meanwhile, heat half of the oil in a large saucepan with a lid over medium heat. When it is hot, add the peppercorns, cinnamon, star anise, cloves and black and green cardamom pods, then fry for 30 seconds, or until fragrant. Add the chicken and seal for 1–2 minutes, then add 400 ml (14 fl oz) water. Bring to the boil, then lower the heat to a simmer, cover the pan and cook until the chicken is tender, around 30 minutes. Keep the water in the saucepan topped up, as you'll need this liquid later to use as a stock.
- For the raita, grate the cucumber, then use your hands to squeeze out the excess liquid. Put the cucumber into a small bowl with all the remaining ingredients and mix well. Set aside.
- When the chicken is done, lift it out of the pan, then fish out and discard the whole spices but reserve the stock. You will need roughly 250–300 ml (1–1¼ cups) stock. Set both chicken and stock aside.
- Heat the remaining oil in the same saucepan. When it is hot, add the cumin and coriander seeds and the bay leaves and fry for 30 seconds, then add the onion, ginger and garlic. Fry, stirring, over medium-low heat for 5–6 minutes or until the onions are caramelised and brown.
- Drain the rice and add it to the pan, along with the cooked chicken and the salt. Stir gently for 1 minute, then pour in enough stock to cover the chicken and rice (you can freeze any remaining stock for use in other dishes).
- Stir well, then reduce the heat to low and cover the pan with a tight-fitting lid. Leave the pullao to cook for 10–12 minutes, or until the stock has been completely absorbed and the rice is cooked. If the rice isn't cooked, add a tablespoon of water, cover the pan and cook for a further 1–2 minutes until the rice is done.
- Fluff up the pullao with a fork, then stir gently and garnish with the green chilli. Serve hot, with the raita on the side.

Pea and browned onion pullao

An equally satisfying meat-free version of my mother's pullao.

Prep time: 15 minutes + 1 hour soaking
Cooking time: 45 minutes
Serves 4–6

250 g (1¼ cups) brown basmati rice
2 tablespoons ghee
2 teaspoons cumin seeds
1 star anise
1 teaspoon coriander seeds
1 black cardamom pod
1 teaspoon black peppercorns
1 large red onion, cut into half moons
1 teaspoon crushed garlic
1 teaspoon finely grated ginger
150 g (1 cup) fresh or frozen peas
salt, to taste
2 green chillies, deseeded and finely chopped
Greek-style yoghurt, to serve

- Rinse the rice, then leave it to soak in a bowl of water for 1 hour.
- Melt the ghee in a heavy-based saucepan (one that has a tight-fitting lid) over medium heat. Add the cumin seeds, star anise, coriander seeds, black cardamom pod and peppercorns and fry for about 30 seconds until fragrant, or until the cumin seeds begins to pop.
- Add the onion, garlic and ginger and fry, stirring, over medium heat for 3–4 minutes, or until the onion is soft and light brown. Add the peas, salt and chilli and fry for a further 30 seconds.
- Add the drained rice and stir to mix well, then pour in enough water to just cover the rice. Reduce the heat to low, cover the saucepan with the lid and cook for about 4–5 minutes until the rice is par-cooked and the water is almost absorbed. If the water has been totally absorbed, gently stir in another couple of tablespoons. Cover the pan with foil, securing it firmly around the edges, then replace the lid. Turn the heat down as low as it will go, then let the pullao cook in its own steam for about 10 minutes, or until the rice is cooked through and all the water has been absorbed.
- Serve hot, with yoghurt on the side.

A CELEBRATION MEAL
inspired by Nani Mummy's Eid spread

CHAPTER 11

Dadi's free spirit

My Dadi's health is fading,
and to escape the pain I revisit
memories of the way she used
to blend her spices and herbs,
realising that in her stories there
are lessons about how process
and patience lead to true flavour.
When Dadi passes away, I cope
with the loss by carrying on the
legacy of her recipes.

Karachi, 1989–1992

SHIFTING SCHOOLS, CHANGING FUTURES

It was my first year of A-levels and I'd moved to The Lyceum, a recently established A-level school in Clifton. I didn't want to stay on at St Michael's as many of the good teachers were leaving; besides, I'd had enough of Mrs Smith's passive aggressive behaviour. For the first time in years, I was excited about school and the prospect of choosing my own subjects. I knew I'd have to keep my promise to Daddy of taking law as one of my subjects, but it was made up for by the fact that I could study history and literature too. I had a chance to make new friends, and students in my class were planning their future, picking colleges and universities abroad. I felt a little out of place in those conversations as I had decided to stay and wait for Danesh, much to my parents' disapproval. Daddy wanted me to do A-levels and then go to London to sit my bar exams, but I was adamant about staying in Karachi.

Every month, Danesh would call me and a handwritten letter would arrive a few weeks later. My heart would leap when I saw that familiar writing on an envelope bearing an American stamp franked with the words 'Stamford, Connecticut'. I'd hold it up to my nose and take a deep breath; sometimes Danesh would spray the letters with his aftershave and a faint whiff of Calvin Klein would remain on the paper. Initially his letters took up six pages of a legal yellow notepad, filled with stories about university life and how much he missed me. But as the months passed by, the six pages became three and then dwindled to two. Over time, the letters and calls became more infrequent.

When he did call, it always seemed to be at the worst times. Daddy would be sitting by the phone, or Mummy would be speaking to one of her cousins for hours, and he'd not be able to get through. The ideal time was during the nine o'clock news, when both my parents would be glued to the television. I'd jump when I heard the phone ring, and if I could speak to him for a full ten minutes, everything felt perfect for the time being. At seventeen I was living a life of sparse phone calls and occasional letters, and the hope that my twenty-year-old boyfriend was being faithful to me in America.

His promises kept me going – but he wasn't happy that I was now at The Lyceum. He thought it might be better for me to go to an all-girls school instead: 'Why don't you transfer to St Joseph's College?' he asked. 'Both my sisters are there and it's great. You don't have to do A-levels if you're not going abroad, just stay there for four years and get your B.A. degree instead – I'll be back before you know it.'

'But I won't get in now, it's already mid-term,' I replied. 'I really love the subjects I'm taking and I have friends here.'

'Well, if you want to make me happy you should consider it. My sisters will help you adjust and you can study similar subjects there – imagine how much fun it would be!'

So, I began to push my parents to take me out of The Lyceum and get me into St Joseph's.

'I bet that boy is making you do this,' said Mummy.

'No Mummy, I'm doing it because so many of my friends are there, and besides I don't like The Lyceum,' I lied.

'You're throwing away your future for him. He's not worth it.'

The first women's college in the city, St Joseph's College was set up post-partition by the Catholic Church. It stood proudly amid the crumbling edifices of the Saddar area of Old Karachi, almost unscathed since 1948. Outside there was the constant drone of chaotic traffic; the carts of street-food vendors blocked pathways, the sound of their shouted slogans competing with the racket from rickshaws with broken silencers.

I found out in my first week that St Joseph's was all about the tuck shop. Here were delicacies I'd never come across before, like a starchy chicken and corn soup thickened with cornflour and scattered with shavings of chicken and tinned corn kernels: it was gloopy and tasteless, and it was only ever eaten with a whole packet of chilli chips dumped into it. Party Slims chilli chips were every teenage girl's must-have snack, fiery hot, thin-sliced matchstick crisps that contained unidentifiable spices, as well as lots of MSG and chilli powder. These would soak in the soup and become soft, adding a degree of texture and heat. I never much cared for it, but I'd eat it to fit in. Another such noxious snack was the *guttar ki chaat* (literally, 'chaat snack made with gutter water'). Behind the tuck shop, a man dished out watery tamarind sauce with a few chickpeas floating on top, and once again chilli chips came to the rescue to heighten the experience.

We'd grab plates of all that was on offer and sit on the bleachers, gossiping freely. I'd always been opposed to the idea of a single-sex institution, but it was hard to deny that it was rather liberating in reality. The lack of awkwardness and self-consciousness I felt without boys around quickly helped me to gain confidence.

In my first year I became the history society president and allowed myself to explore my creative streak; it all began with redecorating our common room.

Apart from the bleachers, this was the only other place we could hang out between classes. Housed in a concrete block, it was like a large, soulless church hall, with tattered sofas lined up against the wall, pale yellow paint peeling off the walls and a strong smell of sweat and cheap talcum powder. This was the place where we were meant to get respite from the heat outside and sit between classes. After enduring this space for a few weeks, I had an idea.

'What if we redid the common room?' I asked my friend Sahr.

'What do you mean, redo it?'

'I mean let's do some interior design, try and find out if we can raise some funds and make it into a cool place to hang out,' I said.

I became consumed with the idea. I got permission to set up a common room society and began thinking of ways to raise the money we needed. At the school's annual *mela* (fair) my friends and I had a stall with our home-made glass-bottle gardens, friendship bracelets, tie-dye *dupatta* scarfs, chaat and samosas for sale. In one day, we raised enough to do up the common room. I drew up plans. I had the sofas upholstered in red, black and white fabric; I sourced jute rugs and coffee tables; I sketched out a mural to be spray-painted.

I'd never done anything like this before and it opened up a whole new side of me that I didn't know existed. I approached my father with the idea of studying interior design and even took a course over the following summer, but he was still hoping law would be my career path: 'All this arty stuff is a lovely hobby. I'm so glad you've found one, but you need to focus on your exams. It's all very well that you're pursuing your artistic side, but it won't pay the bills.' I felt deflated by the lack of support and I never revisited my interest in interior design again.

It was only with hindsight that I realised how many of my life-changing decisions were made by men – firstly through Danesh's expectations of me as his girlfriend, and then by my father and his hopes for my future career.

'Mummy, Danesh is coming to Karachi,' I said, excitedly, knowing that he would be there for the whole summer. 'Can I please see him? He could come over and we could just chat. I won't go out with him.'

It was July, and the sun had been beating down all day. The verandah felt like the surface of a hotplate as I nervously paced the granite in my bare feet. Danesh was on his way to see me; Daddy was away in India, and Mummy had said Danesh could come over for an hour. I wore my light pink three-quarter-length knickerbocker trousers with a white shadow-work cotton top. As I stood by the door watching his green Charade pull up, a man stepped out of the car that I didn't recognise. His hair was shorter, he'd shaved his moustache and his eyes had a faraway look, as if he was trying not to meet my gaze for too long.

It was obvious that things had changed. Danesh greeted me with a formal hug and then spent the next hour asking me questions about mutual friends from school and what my plans were after college. When I asked about his life in America and our future together, he just dodged the questions.

In my heart I knew that things were ending, and not because I wanted them to. Danesh went back to America at the end of that summer and months passed by before he called.

One weekend morning, the phone rang. It was Danesh.

'Hi Usmani, how are you doing?'

'I'm ok. What's going on? I've been waiting to hear from you for months now,' I said, my voice shaking in anticipation of the inevitable.

'Well, I didn't know how to tell you this, and I've been trying to find the words. Look, I think it's best we break up. The distance isn't working. I have a life here and you have a life there. We are young – if we are meant to be, it'll work out later.'

I wanted to say: *What about the promises and the sacrifices I've made? After four years, are you just going to dump me on the phone?* But the words wouldn't come out. I just kept silent, listening to excuse after excuse. I felt as if I'd been kicked in the stomach, and tears stung my eyes.

'Ok, so you understand, yeah?' He was still talking.

'Yeah, ok. Bye, Danesh. Please don't call again.'

'Oh, don't be like that, please,' he said.

I felt like my heart had been cut out with a carving knife and thrown to the dogs. I hung up on him, sat down and cried like my life depended on it.

The next day, I returned to college and didn't say a word to my friends; the shame of being dumped, and the reality of what it meant, was too raw.

In history class, I stared idly out of the window. It was a wet day, and I watched as the rain drops streamed down the arched windows that overlooked the back gate of the school. Outside, a man pushing a wooden cart was selling *bhutta* (corn on the cob), with an umbrella tied to his cart to shelter his makeshift stove from the rain.

He was standing beneath an old block of flats, with peeling lime green paint and rusted iron grilles on the windows. People used to say that Freddie Mercury and his family had lived there when he was a child, but now it was unceremoniously decaying in the Karachi sun and rain, surrounded by a crumbling neighbourhood. The *bhutta* man was diligently preparing freshly peeled corn, popping it onto a grill over the coal fire that burnt in a cast-iron pot on his rickety wooden cart; his resilience in a torrential monsoon shower was fascinating. He seemed undaunted by his soaking Peshawari slippers and the drenched hem of his *shalwar*. Watching him char the corn and then rub it with a lemon half dipped in a mix of salt, chilli powder and pepper made my mouth water. The urge to walk out of the class and into the rain to get a *bhutta* was just too tempting, so I grabbed my bag and did just that.

I could barely hear the teacher's voice in the background demanding to know where I was going without permission. I was so focused on my need to taste the corn, to get away from what was expected of me – constantly. I just wanted to taste the corn's sweetness mixed with the heat from the tangy masala and then try to pull out the inevitable fibres stuck in my teeth. In that moment, escaping it all felt like the right thing to do. I was sick of doing what everyone told me to do.

THE SENSORY SIL BATTA

That same year, Dadi's cancer returned aggressively, and she was in and out of the hospital. She was so delicate and frail; the chemotherapy was making her disappear. For someone who loved cooking and food, it was a painful irony that she was unable to eat solid food. Tins of 'The Original Nurishment' liquid food were piled high on the shelves where she used to keep her *paandan*. She was tube-fed these meal replacements for weeks, and the choice of strawberry, chocolate and vanilla was wearing her patience thin, but at least they gave her some energy and she was able to talk for short periods of time.

One day I went to visit her and watched as she tried to sit up, smiling weakly, wanting to chat. I sat on a chair near her bed, scared I might crush her feeble body if I sat on her bed like I usually did.

'Somi, why don't you go to the market with Guddo and buy all the usual things?' she said.

'No, Dadi, I don't want to go without you,' I replied.

'Go, it'll give you some practice, and besides you are a better bargainer than Guddo,' she smiled, weakly.

'I'll go if you really want me to.'

Guddo Phuppo and I walked the familiar path to Hadi Market. Nothing changed in Nazimabad, except that each time there seemed to be more people on the streets. At the market, familiar vendors were shouting out their prices, and the dusty desert air was heavy with smoke from the street-food stalls and the aromas of raw rice and pulses from the wholesale shops. Usually I'd have chatted to my aunt, but I kept quiet. I wanted to tell her about Danesh, but still couldn't find the energy to talk about it. We walked into the shop where Dadi always bought her dry goods, and Guddo Phuppo ordered the usual weekly amounts. The shop carried everything from store-cupboard ingredients to videos and books. While I waited, I eyed pirated videos of *Back to the Future* and *Desperately Seeking Susan*, piles of *Archie* comics and Hardy Boys novels.

But to me, nothing felt the same in the market. Dadi's usual confident ways with the vendors and her quick-witted bargaining powers were legendary; I thought back to her tricks and smiled.

'I'll give you five rupees for this, not a penny more,' she'd say.

'No, Aunty, I can't give you such a big discount,' the shopkeeper would say.

'Ok then, I won't be giving you my business. Besides, the guy opposite you was giving it to me at four rupees per kilo. Right, I'm off,' she'd say, and pretend to walk away.

The shopkeeper would chase after her and accept the lower price. Dadi would wink at me, and whisper to me about how I must take notes.

And now I could see that my aunt had no bargaining power at all.

'Right, Guddo Phuppo,' I said, 'let me help.'

I turned to the shopkeeper: 'You know my Dadi, and you'd not be fleecing her this way. I'm giving you the usual price, otherwise we're going elsewhere. My Dadi knows the whole neighbourhood, and no one will buy daal from you again at that price.'

My aunt stood by, watching in amazement. In that moment, I realised how much I enjoyed bargaining. I was also good at it – a skill I'd picked up from both my grandmothers, and one you just had to have when shopping in bazaars. Best of all, it made me feel powerful.

In those final months, Dadi had some bad days and some good days. The doctor said that she couldn't have any more chemo, so she just had to take each day as it came.

On the weekends when she felt well enough, I'd go and visit, buying fresh herbs to take with me so I could practise making her chutney. I'd wash them in the large white porcelain sink outside and she'd tell me to grind them on the flat *sil batta* mortar, doing it slowly and with patience: 'If you rush any stage of cooking anything, your food will never have the real flavour of your hands.'

'What does that even mean, Dadi?' I asked.

'It means that you can only really flavour your food with the magic in your hands if you give each step of making a meal your full attention. Every time you prepare ingredients and cook them, you must look at the ingredients and thank them for being there, and then show them respect by cooking them well.' It was one of the last cooking tips she offered me.

Some years later, when I made her chutney in a blender and then did it again using a pestle and mortar, there really was a difference in flavour. As I imagined Dadi's frail body, her fine salt-and-pepper hair tied in a knot at her neck, grinding herbs and spices on the stone in her garden kitchen, I realised that making a chutney or spice paste by hand added a silent ingredient – a flavour that no machine could replicate, no matter how efficient it was.

THE GREATEST LESSON OF LOSS

It was a cold January for Karachi. The crisp winter breeze off the Arabian Sea carried the smokiness of the neighbourhood rubbish being burnt in the morning. Daddy was back in India for work, and the morning felt melancholic in the humidity, the skies heavy with rain that would probably never come. The telephone rang, and it was my Dada saying that we'd need to come over as Dadi had taken a turn for the worse. My mother told me to get ready to go to my grandparents' house.

'But Daddy isn't here, Mummy. What if something happens to Dadi?'

'We have to go, Somi, there's no time,' she said.

By the time we arrived, it was too late. Dadi's face was mere bones and thin skin, exposed from the neck up, the rest of her body wrapped in a white sheet, laid out on a mat on the floor. I wanted to run to her and shake her, but my body froze. The air was heavy with camphor and incense, smells associated with funerals in Pakistan. I held my breath as the aroma pierced my lungs. My throat was raw and my legs were shaking.

'Is she gone?' I asked, hoping that someone might just miraculously tell me otherwise. Everyone was weeping. I looked at her bed; there was still a hollow in the mattress from the gentle weight of her body.

Dadi taught me to cook with patience: 'If you rush any stage of cooking anything, your food will never have the real flavour of your hands.'

'Yes, Somi, she's in heaven now, she's at peace,' said my mother.

I felt my legs give way and I collapsed on the mosaic floor, sobbing.

We stayed there the whole day; her burial was to be before *mughrib* (sunset) prayers. Muslim burials need to be carried out before nightfall.

My father had taken a flight from Bombay back to Karachi before she passed away, and we were waiting for him to arrive. When I heard his car pull up outside, we were still in the bedroom, transfixed by Dadi's body, which was now lying on a stretcher-like cane carrier, wrapped in muslin with just her face exposed; a length of muslin lay unravelled to one side, ready to cover her head later. The colour had drained from her face, leaving it sallow and her cheeks even more sunken.

As Daddy walked into the room, he threw down his bag, ran over to the cane carrier on the floor and let out a terrible scream, like something out of a horror film. My heart ached with the pain I saw in him.

'*Amma! Amma!*' he cried, tears rolling down his distraught face. His expression was one of utter helplessness and despair – one I've never been able to erase from my mind. I'd never seen my father cry before. He was a man who kept it together through wars, torrential storms at sea and those few disagreements he had with Mummy. His was always the voice of reason and calm. I couldn't quite comprehend the sight of him on his knees, crying out to his dead mother. I saw a side to my father I had never seen before, and I realised that he was also a son.

I didn't ever see that side of him again, not even when his father passed away.

For the next few months everything felt flat. Sunday visits to my grandparents' home were never the same again. My aunts cooked all the same dishes that Dadi did, but something always seemed to be missing; the vigour of the women in the kitchen had disappeared and the food didn't taste right.

A year later, Dada fell ill with pneumonia, and he didn't recover. It was as if he had given up on life without the woman he'd spent nearly sixty years with. I was never that close to my Dada, but I could see that after Dadi died, he barely smiled, and his health began to deteriorate rapidly.

After Dadi passed away, I thought of her many roles. As well as being my grandmother, she was a wife, a sister and my father's mother.

One teatime, Daddy told me a story about his childhood in India, when the family had lived in a beautiful courtyard-style house in Jaunpur, in Uttar Pradesh.

Each afternoon his mother would sit him next to her and make banana *gulgulay* doughnuts. She'd mix flour with bicarbonate of soda and crushed banana pulp, adding a pinch of floral fennel and a little sugar. Then she'd heat up a wok-like *karahi* and fry small balls of fluffy *gulgulay* in hot oil. My father and his siblings would be given three or four each, and they'd sit and eat them under the large neem tree in the courtyard.

My father was never much of a cook, and no one in the family seemed to have Dadi's recipe. Many years later I decided to recreate the recipe from my father's memory of *gulgulay*, letting his description of their texture and flavour be my guide. After much trial and error, I finally pieced together a recipe that worked. I dropped spoonfuls of the batter in hot oil and they danced up to the surface, bobbing in and out of the oil, like irregular fluffy clouds. I imagined my father as a child relishing this treat made with his mother's love. I wondered why in all those years of visiting Dadi she'd never made me *gulgulay*, and now I couldn't even ask her for her recipe.

As I perfected my recipe, I realised that Dadi's lessons of patience and process in cooking had seeped into my style of cooking, effortlessly. I wished so much that I'd spent more time with her. We were never as close as Nani Mummy and I were, and it wasn't until I lost Dadi that I wished I'd learnt more about her – but in many ways cooking her food after she died helped me to feel closer to her. I knew I'd inherited her ability to take time over each step of cooking, and this was my way of keeping alive this part of my family's flavour legacy.

Dadi's coriander chutney

A staple in my kitchen – I eat this with everything! I love it with my lentil dumplings (recipe on page 84), for dipping chapattis into, or on the side with rice and daal; sometimes I even use it as a marinade.

Prep time: 5–7 minutes
Makes about 185 ml (¾ cup)

1 large bunch of coriander (cilantro), leaves and stems – about 200 g (7 oz) in total
20–25 mint leaves
1 green finger chilli, deseeded if desired
1 tablespoon brown sugar or jaggery
¼ teaspoon turmeric powder
1 teaspoon cumin seeds, roasted in a dry frying pan and ground
1 teaspoon salt
2 tablespoons unsweetened desiccated coconut
1 tablespoon ground dried pomegranate seeds (*anardana*) or 2 tablespoons fresh pomegranate seeds
juice of 1 lime
1–2 tablespoons full-fat Greek-style yoghurt

- Blitz all the ingredients in a blender or small food processor (or pound with a pestle and mortar) until smooth.
- This chutney is best used immediately, but can be stored in an airtight container in the fridge for up to 5 days.

As I imagined Dadi grinding herbs and spices on the stone in her garden kitchen, I realised that making a chutney or spice paste by hand added a silent ingredient – a flavour no machine could replicate, no matter how efficient it was.

Dadi's banana and fennel seed gulgulay doughnuts

This recipe is based on my father's recollection of his mother's doughnuts – I think I must have got it right, as he seems to think they taste just like my Dadi's!

Prep time: 20 minutes
Cooking time: 10–15 minutes
Makes about a dozen small doughnuts

50 g (⅓ cup) plain (all-purpose) flour
3–4 green cardamom pods, cracked open, seeds extracted and ground – you need ½ teaspoon ground cardamom
¼ teaspoon fennel seeds, ground
1 teaspoon bicarbonate of soda (baking soda)
2 tablespoons icing (confectioners') sugar, plus 2 tablespoons extra for decoration
1½ overripe bananas, mashed
2 tablespoons whole (full-cream) milk or non-dairy alternative
500 ml (2 cups) sunflower oil

- Begin by sifting the flour, cardamom, fennel, bicarbonate of soda and icing sugar into a bowl. Stir gently with a fork to combine.
- Add the mashed banana and, while mixing with the fork, slowly add just enough milk to make a very stiff and thick batter (you may not need it all). Leave the batter to rest for 10 minutes. Give it that time to get fluffy – I know my Dadi would have.
- Heat the oil in a wok or heavy-based saucepan over medium heat. When it is hot, add teaspoonfuls of the batter and cook, keeping them moving so they don't stick together, until they rise to the top, about 5–7 minutes.
- Drain on paper towels, then dust with the extra icing sugar and serve hot – with a cup of chai, just like my Dadi did.

Dadi would heat up her karahi and fry small balls of fluffy gulgulay in hot oil. My father and his siblings would be given three or four each, and they'd sit and eat them under the large neem tree in the courtyard.

CHAPTER 12

The secret to layering spices is serenity

I learn that patience is vital when cooking Pakistani food – being mindful with every step and every ingredient. The distinct flavour of my own food is distinguishable from that of others by the way spices are layered, and there are no shortcuts to achieving this depth of flavour.

Karachi, 1992–1995

THE KOEL BIRD IN THE TAMARIND TREE

The summer of 1992 was a hot one, the sort that made your neck itch. We'd stay in most days with the air-conditioning on at full blast. When the power failed, we'd sit in silence, letting the beads of sweat run down our faces and backs, finding little respite in the humid breeze from the open windows. Unrest had gripped Karachi once again, and although our home was far removed from the areas where violence was rampant, curfews were in place and fear stalked the streets.

The trouble was mainly confined to the localities of Nazimabad and Liaquatabad, where there was a concentration of MQM supporters. The movement was campaigning for Karachi to become an independent state, something neither the army nor the prime minister, Nawaz Sharif, wanted. 'Operation Clean-up' aimed to curb MQM strongholds, and the armed forces were given their orders: Muhajirs did not belong here, they were to be contained and not allowed to gain control. The city was effectively under siege. Newspaper headlines were of tear gas and gunfire, and the news on television was nothing but depressing: we'd watch as protestors engaged in running battles with the army and tanks rolled into Nazimabad, where my Dada and Dadi's house was.

My college was closed for months on end, and I could feel freedom slipping away. Curfews sometimes lasted all day, with two- or three-hour breaks in-between so we could rush to get supplies. The shopping centres lay empty, as eerie as haunted alleys. The markets where I used to go with Nani Mummy were mostly closed, with only small grocery shops open during the hours of curfew relaxation. Even then, it was safer to stay indoors, and the risk of getting caught up in a skirmish meant I wasn't allowed to meet friends or go out in the evening for shopping with Mummy like I used to.

All of this left me stuck at home, an only child, with no college, no friends and very little entertainment. For a restless nineteen-year-old, life in an already constrained society had become oppressive. I'd spend long days reading, daydreaming and hanging out with my mother or Nani Mummy. It was also around then that I began spending a lot more time in the kitchen, and what really caught my interest was watching Nani Mummy make *achar* (pickles) – her way of capturing the seasons.

Sometimes Karachi seemed to have only two main seasons: summer and monsoon season; winter was just like a cooler version of summer. The change of seasons itself wasn't as obvious as the seasonal produce: summer brought melons, lychees and mangoes; the monsoons filled the garden with herbs and gourds; and winter saw the markets piled high with Kino oranges, pomegranates and cherries. I didn't really appreciate the subtleties of the shifting seasons until much later, but I was connected to the seasons by the bounty each offered.

Spring in Karachi was very short, and if you didn't pay attention you'd miss it, but just before the cool, wintertime sea breeze gave way to the encroaching summer heat there'd be a few days when the air was filled with the song of the koel bird. Its melancholic mating call would float through the open window of my room, and the breeze that wafted in with it felt like silk on my skin and was the first sign of the changing season.

In Nani Mummy's garden, the early mango blossoms and the leaves of the tamarind tree would rustle in the wind, and I'd know it was time for the tamarind fruit pods to be plucked. The tamarind tree grew behind the garage, in nothing but rubble and raw earth. A sturdy, thick-trunked tree, in spring its branches hung lower than usual, heavy with ripened pods; its delicate tiny pale green leaves were just as tasty and tart as the fleshy pods, but fresher and more herb-like.

I was never allowed to go near the tree alone. Nani Mummy told me that the *choral* (witches) lived under it, but I knew she was just trying to deter me from going there because the tree was right by the quarters of her *chaukidar* (watchman), who looked after the outdoor areas of my grandmother's house and opened the gate for her. He lived there with his family, and Nani Mummy never liked me snooping around and invading their privacy.

I was also warned not to eat too much of the fruit: there were stories of how tamarind made young girl's breasts grow prematurely (something I really didn't want when I was younger but didn't mind when I was older); and there was the more prosaic risk of the sour fruit 'catching' your throat and making it sore.

Everything associated with that tree was forbidden – which was exactly why I was attracted to it.

The midday sunlight shone through its branches and the dappled light it cast was beautiful and inviting. I'd reach over and pull off a tamarind pod. Long and knobbly, its crusty brown casing broke easily to reveal a sticky muddy-brown pulp that followed the contours of the pod and hid a hard dark brown seed. I'd hesitate to take a bite of the pulp – the anticipation of its extreme tartness was both exciting and jaw-ache-inducing. As I sprawled out in the mottled shade beneath the tree with a book and carefully sucked the tamarind pulp from the seeds, its piercing sharpness would make my lips pucker.

Sometimes, despite all her warnings, Nani Mummy would bring the cane furniture from the verandah and come to sit under the tree with me. It was usually when she'd made a jug of *nimbu pani* lemonade, using the small *desi* lemons we'd picked, and sometimes we'd top it up with soda water or 7 Up.

'How come it's ok to sit under the tamarind tree with you, Nani Mummy?' I'd ask.

'Because the *choral* fear Nanis, and they won't get you if I'm here!' she'd say, laughing.

The truth was that she didn't want me picking the tamarind pods because she collected them each spring to make enough jars of chutney to last for several months. Nani Mummy told me that the trick to making the perfect tamarind chutney lay in balancing the taste sensations, and this came down to trusting your senses. She would heat the tamarind pulp with water and *gur* (sugarcane molasses) until it was soft, then sieve out the seeds. To the warm tamarind, she'd add roasted cumin, black salt, pepper, chilli and a little turmeric, tasting as she went along to make sure the sweet, sour, hot and salty flavours danced equally on the palate. This chutney brought life to anything it was eaten with.

Sitting in the shade together, sipping *nimbu pani* and sharing a plate of pakoras with tamarind chutney, we'd giggle about witches and gossip about cousins. My fascination with tamarind, and the tree it came from, has never left me; something about its tartness always feels slightly forbidden, the memory of those days with my Nani still fresh in my mind.

MAKING SUN PICKLES

In the middle of my Nani's kitchen stood a mid-century-style display cabinet, its glass sliding doors indented with frosted grooves as handles. Most of her cabinets housed her Wedgwood figurines and hand-cut crystal glassware, but this one was stuffed with jars of *achar* (pickles) and ferments. My mother never much cared for pickles, finding them bothersome and pointless, so I hadn't really tried them until we moved to Karachi, where Nani Mummy ate them with every meal. Mummy disliked the acidity and sharpness of the mustard oil used to preserve most of them, and she hated oily food, so unnecessary pickles laden with oil that seeped onto the plate was not her idea of embellishing a meal.

Nani Mummy, on the other hand, loved their little explosions of flavour. The food she cooked was filled with freshness, but never hot, as her pickles and ferments meant you could add a controllable degree of heat at the table. Each season, she made an array of them from her abundant harvest; there didn't seem to be a separate word for those pickles that were fermented in brine as opposed to those preserved in oil – she'd just call them all *achar*.

The corner of the kitchen where this cabinet stood had a sharp vinegary odour accentuated by the floral, curry-like aroma of fenugreek seeds; when she made *achar*, this smell lingered in the house, living in the upholstery, embalming the walls and permeating every pore of your body. A display of glass jars and bottles in muted hues of amber, dark brown and misty pale blue graced the cabinet's shelves. They contained a bounty of red carrot *achar*, its vertical slices of carrot stacked in a large pickling jar with a paste of mustard seeds, onion seeds, curry leaves and fenugreek; preserved lemons, green chillies and raw green mango; and round green *amla* (Indian gooseberries) bobbing in their brine, as they fermented with cloves, cardamom and black peppercorns.

I found the mindfulness of preservation comforting. Compared to when Nani Mummy was cooking daily meals for the family, there was less of a sense of urgency in the kitchen, and this gave me the opportunity to spend quality time with her.

In early summer we'd pick small mangoes from her tree, and if I didn't eat them all dipped into black salt, chilli and pepper, we'd use the rest to make *achar*. Nani Mummy would cut the *kayri* (raw mango) into bite-sized chunks and toss it with turmeric, salt and chilli powder. Next she'd bash brown mustard seeds with her pestle and mortar, revealing their yellow insides. Heating mustard oil in a pan, she'd add the mustard seeds, along with nigella, cumin and fenugreek seeds. Once the oil was fragranced with the spices, she'd pour it over the raw mango, mixing everything well, then it would be down to me to fill sterilised jam jars three-quarters-full with the mango.

'Don't fill it right to the top,' Nani Mummy would say. 'The *achar* needs to breathe, and the oil and salt will extract more moisture and fill up the jar to the top with time.'

'We're going to leave them on the windowsill now, before we put them away in the cupboard,' she'd say.

'Why? I thought you needed to keep them in a dark place?' I asked.

'They are sun-drenched pickles,' she'd say. 'The heat from the rays slowly preserves them, fending off bad bacteria. I like to call them sun pickles for that reason.'

These became the memories I tapped into many years later to remember Nani Mummy: her standing in the kitchen, peeling mangoes or washing lemons, getting ready to make *achar*. The bounty and sun of summer or spring, all bottled up to revisit later – a sort of time machine in a jar.

RISHTAS

At college I was surrounded by girls who constantly talked about their perfect wedding and all that marriage would bring them: the outfits and the jewellery, the freedom from their father's rules. As soon as they got a *rishta* (proposal), marriage mania took over; it was as if education was merely a stop-gap and all their aspirations of studying disappeared overnight.

For most girls in Pakistan, marriage was arranged, which meant their parents sought out good matches, often intent on bringing together two well-to-do families or forging business relationships; sometimes it was just about making sure the couple were well-suited for a marriage that might last. If they were lucky, the girl would get to meet the boy they were to marry beforehand; otherwise, the first time the bride and groom saw each other would be on their wedding day.

Since my break-up with Danesh, the very idea of marriage infuriated me; the thought of marrying *anyone*, let alone someone my parents picked, seemed ridiculous. *Why should someone else choose my husband? Why should my education benefit another? Shouldn't it be about what I wanted to do?*

Luckily I was able to avoid an arranged marriage. I knew my parents would let me choose a boy myself and get to know him, but they had started dropping hints about my 'marriageable' age. I'd overhear them discussing with my Nani how good it would be to get a *rishta* – ideally from an educated boy from a 'good' family – and I hated it.

'What am I going to do with her?' said Mummy. 'She never listens, she doesn't even want to learn to cook *desi* food. Besides, she's so anti-marriage. I've told her about a few good boys but she won't stand for it.'

'Let her be, Kausar,' said Nani Mummy. 'She will learn when she has to. You didn't learn until you got married, did you? And, if I remember correctly, you picked your own husband!'

Nani Mummy let out a laugh; Mummy smiled shyly.

'But you're right, it's important she learns now for her husband. What will people say if she can't?' Nani Mummy said. 'Anyway, have there been any new proposals for her lately? I hope she gets married while I am alive.'

Listening from behind the kitchen door, I was filled with rage. I stormed into the room.

'Please stop talking about me getting married and cooking for a husband,' I said. 'I'm never going to do either! Whatever I learn to cook, it will be for myself!'

I resisted doing anything that would qualify me as 'wife material'. I didn't want to be polished up to become some perfect bride who'd end up cooking for her husband and in-laws.

'Learn to make *saalan* – it's the least a girl should know how to cook when she gets married, and you're that age now,' Mummy would say as she stood by the stove, chopping red onions for the Pakistani thin stew that was a daily staple.

But I wasn't interested in cooking everyday Pakistani food; 'exotic' dishes like Thai green curry were more my forte. Mummy grew makrut lime leaves and lemongrass, and we could find coconut milk at Agha's Supermarket or Paradise, the two main shops in Karachi that sold imported ingredients. If there was a lull in supplies, we'd buy fresh coconuts, chop, blend and squeeze our own thick milk.

I did enjoy eating Pakistani food, though: everything from spiced mutton stews, masala vegetables and headily marinated barbecued meats – but nothing came close to the *aloo ki tehri* (turmeric potato rice) Mummy made on weekends. The original unwritten recipe had travelled with Dadi from her home in Uttar Pradesh. A classic Awadhi dish, it was quicker to make than biryani, and not as rich as a meat-based pullao. In the summer, peas would replace the potatoes, but each of my aunts brought their own style and spicing to the recipe too. True to her usual way of cooking, whenever Mummy cooked any of Dadi's recipes, *aloo ki tehri* among them, she made it entirely her own – and I'd wake up to the earthy aroma of turmeric and the freshness of dill, which she always finished her version of the dish with.

Food was my mother's first love; she would beg me to be a good girl and join her in the kitchen to learn to cook. I would wander in to taste the food that was on the stove or grab a snack, and sometimes Mummy and Nani Mummy would be dissecting the ingredients in a recipe, often squabbling about whether or not Mummy's version was better and more refined because of my Dadi's influence on her cooking.

What no one realised was that I was learning from these discussions about spices and the techniques used to infuse them into ingredients, the art of layering them and waiting for their true flavour to emerge. I may not have picked up on the way specific dishes were made from beginning to end, but somewhere in my subconscious a foundation was being laid for understanding flavour.

Since I made it very clear that marriage wasn't my goal, Daddy wanted me to focus on my career choices; he wanted me to be able to support myself and be independent. I knew that becoming a lawyer wasn't my dream. The thought of learning to bake French pastries sounded more exciting; even cutting hair seemed better than law. I begged to be allowed to go to Le Cordon Bleu in London – but, just like interior design, cooking wasn't a 'proper' career in Daddy's eyes, and he was dismissive: 'No daughter of mine will be a cook. I am not spending money for you to go to London and become a *khansama* (domestic servant). Law, medicine or engineering are real professions. As an only child you need to be able to stand on your own two feet. Creative stuff is frivolous; keep cooking as a hobby.'

'You need to make decisions about your future, Somi,' he would say. 'It would be wonderful to have you in the office. Why don't you come and work with me during the holidays? That way you can get a feel for law.' It was clear that my father wanted me to be a lawyer, and though he didn't force it on me, I always felt like I had to back down – not because Daddy was overbearing, but because he paid the bills and would be the one who'd fund my education. This was a battle I couldn't win, so any thoughts of a creative career were replaced with practicality as I concentrated on finishing my B.A. degree at St Joseph's.

I couldn't understand why my parents simultaneously wanted me to go abroad to study and to think about settling down. I thought only about escape. I didn't really know what it was that I wanted to do, but studying law would at least give me some freedom from the obligations, duties and family protocols that made it so hard for me to simply be myself.

Marriage would be an expectation that could wait, and that suited me fine.

GOLA GANDA AND DISCO DANCING

Guddo Phuppo was a fine balance of free-spiritedness and practicality. She was always clear that she didn't want to pursue a 'respectable' career of doctor or engineer, as my other aunts did, and she'd worked hard to become a schoolteacher, completing college and going on to do teacher training. I admired the way her passion for teaching fuelled her – and even though her marriage was arranged, she made sure she got to know her husband-to-be. She married on her own terms and she did what she loved; I wanted to be like her.

I remembered how we'd sneak out after Sunday lunches at my grandparents while the 'grown-ups' were busy talking. We'd go to roadside carts for those forbidden street foods my mother never let me eat: chaat or *gola ganda*, sweet rose-flavoured syrup poured over crushed ice, condensed milk and gelatinous basil seeds. There was something special about those moments with Guddo Phuppo. She was family but she didn't act like family; she never expected me to be a certain way, and she understood my yearning for freedom.

'*Chalo* (come on), Somi, let's slip away before anyone notices,' she'd say. 'We can go to Hadi Market to get some samosas, ice-cream soda and *gola ganda*. No one need ever find out!'

Always on street corners, *gola ganda* carts had a zinc bucket of ice in the middle, surrounded by psychedelic-coloured syrups in tall glass bottles: toxic-looking green for ice cream soda, a dark violet Vimto flavour, and the fluorescent red, rose-flavoured Rooh Afza. The vendor would fill a tall glass with crushed ice that he'd chipped off a block of ice with a small ice pick and then crushed in a dirty rag. He'd pour over your choice of the syrups, then add condensed milk and basil seeds that had been soaked overnight to plump them up. The slimy seeds made a squishing sound as they slid around in your mouth and down your throat, some sticking to your teeth to be found later.

Mummy never let me have *gola ganda* because of the unfiltered water used to make the ice and the dirty rag it was crushed in and the synthetic-coloured syrups – everything screamed a stomach flu or, worse, typhoid. But Guddo didn't care; in fact, she knew the risks and still did it.

'Don't worry, you won't get sick,' she'd say. 'We're Pakistani, our stomachs are iron clad!'

She wasn't wrong. For all the times I sneaked out and ate *gola ganda*, Hanifia burgers made from Hunter shredded beef with special spicy mustard chilli sauce, roadside and 'gutter water' chaat, I never fell ill – which also meant that I never got caught for breaking Mummy's rules of street-food eating.

Music played a big part in my life then. I'd ask family and friends to send me the latest *Rolling Stone* or *Billboard* magazines from America and mark up my calendar with the release dates of albums by Fleetwood Mac, Duran Duran or Madonna. With the lack of any official record shops in Pakistan, all we got were dodgy pirated cassettes, with the song titles printed on a dot matrix printer in a typewriter font. Later in the 1990s we'd get pirated CDs slipped inside colour-printed jackets, with the title scrawled on them in permanent marker; some had no titles on them, and you'd be left with an array of gold and silver discs slotted into incorrect sleeves.

I'd begun to love the latest pop music, but because Guddo loved disco I grew to enjoy that too. Sometimes on weekends I'd spend the night at Dadi's house and Guddo Phuppo would come back after a night out and pop a cassette on. We'd dance with abandon, singing at the top of our lungs to her favourite Tina Charles's song, 'I Love to Love', or listen to Pakistani pop sensations Nazia and Zohaib Hassan.

Then came the time for Guddo to get married. I was filled with envy. Not because she was getting married, but because I didn't want to lose the moments we shared together. I was uptight all through the wedding festivities: at the henna party, I went off in a huff because I wasn't allowed to be first in line to take the platters of gifts to the groom's family as that role is reserved for the bride's sisters. I was told to go to the back of the line and carry the *diya* ceremonial terracotta oil lamps instead.

After Guddo Phuppo was married, we lost touch and I hardly saw her. We spoke on the phone occasionally, but she had a new life – and a few years later, she moved to Sri Lanka with her husband and their two sons, Danish (she'd kept her promise to name him after 'my' Danesh) and Haris. I knew she was still fond of me, but once again I felt like I had no one who really listened to me.

It was a cool November afternoon. Sometimes the sea breeze would bring with it the threat of cyclone, and we had just heard on the news that Karachi's coast was at risk. As Karachi wasn't built for rain, cyclones always brought the city to a grinding halt. Because of bad drainage, the roads would quickly flood, turning into free-flowing rivers with wooden boats replacing cars.

We were fortunate to live in a hillier part of the city, away from areas of reclaimed land, but as soon as the first lightning struck, the electricity went. The distant moaning of the generators began in quick succession and the smell of petrol came in through the open windows. We didn't have a generator at the time and instead we sometimes used a battery-powered fan to help us sleep. I was fanning myself with a Japanese paper fan when I heard the phone ring in my parents' room.

I thought it was probably Nani Mummy calling to see if we were ok, but a few minutes later my father knocked briskly on my door: 'Somi, get up, I have some terrible news. Guddo died an hour ago.'

I couldn't manage any words because his hadn't sunk in yet.

'She was my baby sister,' he said. 'I've lost my baby sister.' My father's voice trembled.

I sat up in bed and turned to switch on my red and black lamp, forgetting that the electricity had gone. I finally managed some words: 'What's going to happen, Daddy? What's going to happen to Danish and Haris?'

'They have a father,' he replied.

The distance made the loss feel surreal. Once the truth started to sink in, I felt a sharp twinge of regret. I should've done more to keep in touch; I shouldn't have been resentful about losing our past relationship. I should've cherished the time we had more: I smiled thinking about our silly dancing, eating street-food snacks and laughing together. In the same study where my other aunts pulled all-nighters for their medical or engineering exams, we'd make scrap books or she would read my slam books from school, helping me to work out which boy had a crush on me from the cryptic messages written under 'who you'd kiss first'.

Years later, I wondered if she would have been friends with me when I was older. I thought of the things I could have done with her but never did. She was one of the best cooks in the family after Dadi, but she was too modest to talk about it. I tried hard to remember the way she used to cook okra with lots of onions, and I tried to cook it from my flavour memory of it. I knew she added tamarind, which was an odd thing to add to okra, but she loved tamarind as much as I did. We often used to buy Rita's tamarind sweets from the shops in Hadi Market, eating them with sugar and chaat masala. I heated oil and added black cumin to it, then curry leaves; slowly I recreated the recipe to find connection and my way back to my memories of her.

I remembered seeing photos of her when she was ill with cancer, boldly wearing a *hijab* head scarf during the last year of her life. I could see through her elegance to the sadness in her eyes, and I'd realised that I didn't know this woman anymore; I hadn't for years. My Guddo was the carefree one, when life's realities were still far away, but this woman had a life. Had she been happy? What had she enjoyed in her last months? Was there worry about the illness behind those sad eyes, or just disappointment that she'd never see her sons grow up?

As I cooked, I flashed back to trips to the markets with her, trying hard to remember the times we'd spent in the kitchen, and all I could remember was her laughter, cheekier and louder than anyone else's, and the way she scrunched up her nose when she tasted raw tamarind.

CRABBING ON THE ARABIAN SEA

'You've got mail from the London School of Economics (LSE) lying on the doorstep. Get Mummy, let's open it!' Daddy was alone in his excitement. The British stamp stared up at me. I picked up the envelope with apprehension and took a deep breath: 'I got a conditional offer to read Law.' My heart filled with resignation.

It was a pleasant winter's evening: a moist sea breeze caressed skin, easing the day's heat. Winter was always welcomed in Karachi – a time for parties, outdoor meals and trips to the beach. I wanted to get away from the house to escape chats about London and law, but it wasn't like I could go out with friends, or for a walk on my own, even though the streets were much calmer and safer since Benazir Bhutto had been elected prime minister in 1993.

The phone rang and I picked it up.

It was Asma: 'Do you think you'll be allowed out tonight?'

'I doubt it, you know my dad. But he's in a good mood about me getting an offer to go to uni, so I'll ask,' I said.

'Come on, give it a try – the weather is just amazing!' urged Asma.

I hung up, took a deep breath and bit my lower lip: 'Daddy, can I go crabbing, please?' I asked.

To my surprise, he nodded his head. 'Check with Mummy, though.'

I knew that Mummy would have something to say, even if she let me go. She thought Asma was a bad influence because she had boyfriends, went out to parties and wore revealing clothes: 'She has that fast look, always getting into trouble. I don't trust girls like her.' Reluctantly, though, she agreed that I could go with Asma and her friends, as long as we didn't go anywhere else afterwards and I was back by 10.30 p.m.

Getting to the harbour at Keamari was always an adventure. Driving through some of the oldest and poorest parts of Karachi on the way, we were welcomed by the rotten fishy smell of trucks carrying Bombay duck from the port. We ignored the usual mob of fishermen knocking on the car window and offering us their best rate for a crabbing dinner cruise. We left the bargaining to the boys and waded through the crowds to the harbour front with its crumbling clocktower.

'Who else is coming tonight?' I asked Asma, aware that the cruises needed a minimum of ten to depart and there were only five of us.

'Some of my brother's really cute friends,' she smiled cheekily.

'Last toilet trips before we board!' shouted the fisherman.

Wooden fishing boats lined the harbour and the fumes from the diesel were making me dizzy. I wrapped my pashmina tightly around my shoulders as the cold breeze came off the sea and stepped onto the plank leading to the boat. In the soft light of the boat's oil lanterns, I clocked a few unfamiliar faces on board as we settled down on semi-circular benches around a central makeshift 'dining table' – a plank atop the boat's engine.

The engine roared as we travelled away from the dock. I glanced back past the moon-glistening sea to the clocktower and the rows of fishing boats still in the harbour. In the dim light, I could barely make out the words on the menu card on my lap:

TODAY'S SPECIAL CRABBING MENU
Crab karahi * *Crab lollipop* * *Crab cutlets* * *Prawn masala* * *Potato bhujia*
Tomato chutney * *Naan* * *Paratha*

I felt a grumble in my tummy as a hand gently tapped my shoulder.

'The crab lollipops are the best,' I heard an unfamiliar voice say. I turned, and my gaze was met by a pair of hazel eyes set in a tanned, beaming face.

'I know, they're my favourite too,' I agreed.

How had I not noticed the boy sitting next to me? I recognised him as Juni, a popular radio DJ who had been dubbed 'a flirtatious party animal with a heart of gold' in a recent magazine article.

We talked about my conditional offer to read Law at LSE, and how I felt obliged to make my father proud by taking over his law firm one day: 'I'm going to London in August next year, and my dad can't wait for me to help him at work.'

'But is it your dream?' asked Juni. 'My parents just support me as long as I am happy. That's why I do the DJ stuff and work in the hotel – best of both passions!'

'I don't really know what I want to do,' I said. 'If I am honest, Law just seems like the best option.'

Juni's lack of a 'proper' career, and his love for R&B and reckless water sports, clearly set him apart from all the 'daddy's boys' I knew, who were intent on taking over the family business at the age of twenty-two. Then he told me about losing his brother Sunny in an accident, and his big hazel eyes filled with sadness; he told me how his mother had never recovered.

We'd dropped anchor a few miles away from the coast and the 'city of lights' looked particularly beautiful that night. There was a turmeric glow in the sky, stars twinkled. We fished for crab, but to no avail. Overfishing and pollution were pushing the crabs much further out to sea, so the fishermen were always prepared for this eventuality and they had a stash of freshly caught crabs on hand.

Dinner was prepared by the fisherman-chef in his crude kitchen in the bow of the boat, where a large stainless-steel *degchi* (cooking pot) and a wok-shaped *karahi* sat over a tiny coal fire. He was getting ready to make crab karahi, the recipe for which was the fishermen's closely guarded secret. I knew from previous crabbing trips that it was the most magnificent dish: lightly coal-smoky, lemony and intensely fiery, without losing the saline aroma of the crabmeat. It was one of the few Pakistani recipes I actually wanted to learn to cook, and I was determined to see how it was made – but I hadn't expected to be distracted by a boy.

'Juni, would you mind if I went to watch the fishermen cook their crab?' I asked.

'Oh, I do love a girl who likes to cook! Go ahead, I'll be here waiting for you.'

My heart skipped a little on hearing Juni's words. I casually walked over to the bow of the boat, trying not to look too conspicuous, determined to pick up small details and hoping to piece together the complete recipe. From the corner of my eye, I surreptitiously counted the number of lemon peels and pinches of spices. I peered into the *karahi* and saw tomatoes being added to ghee, along with liberal amounts of turmeric, cumin, chilli powder, fresh coriander, green chillies and lemon juice. In the *degchi*, a steamer was created with a handful of wood chips sprinkled with sea water and topped with a hand-cut paper doily. The fisherman-chef then placed the crab on top of the paper and covered the pan so that the crab cooked slowly, absorbing the smokiness of the coals beneath. The crab was then tossed into the *karahi* and the dish was finished off with finely chopped ginger. The fresh crabmeat smelt like the ocean and, as it soaked up the piquant sauce, it gradually turned almost sweet against the heat of the chillies and turmeric. I'd wanted to pick up this recipe for years and tonight I had finally learnt it, and much more besides.

I couldn't wait to join Juni for the meal. I had been worried that I might have lost my spot next to him, that some other girl would have taken my place. The food arrived on large stainless-steel sharing platters – the crab-claw lollipops were piled high, half of their juicy flesh exposed, the rest still in its orange shells. This was followed by spicy potatoes and the centrepiece of crab karahi, all heavily garnished with green chillies and coriander leaves. A large basket of naan and roti was placed alongside. Although the feast made my mouth water, my hunger had disappeared. It was supplanted by the awkward nerves of a first date – painfully conscious of how messy cracking open crab shells was going to be, I merely nibbled at the spicy potatoes and the naan.

We returned to shore soon afterwards; hours had rolled into what felt like only moments. Juni held my hand as I got off the boat, brushed my windswept hair from my face and my heart melted.

'Will you call me?' I asked.

'You bet,' said Juni. 'I'll be thinking about you until I do.'

The rest of the night was a haze of excitement and anxiety, and suddenly LSE felt like it was getting in the way of something. Was it crazy to think about leaving Karachi when I'd met a guy who might just be *the one*?

LAW OR LOVE

I was twenty-one and head-over-heels in love, and the world seemed exciting and new. Our whirlwind romance was stifled by the limitations of Pakistani society, but I had become adept at sneaking out of wherever I was meant to be. Juni would pick me up from friends' houses or from work in his navy Toyota saloon, his Wayfarers reflecting the sun, his white t-shirt making his skin glow.

The only dates possible in Karachi involved eating out – the most innocent thing you could do as an unmarried couple – and even then we'd get questioning looks. Food featured heavily on our dates for more than just the convenience of it. Whether it was a kebab roll by Boat Basin, an indulgent buffet lunch at Al-Bustan in the Sheraton or pistachio kulfi at Spinzer's, Juni loved eating, and he was on first-name terms with street-food stall owners and was fussed over by staff at hotel restaurants. I gained a stone within weeks of meeting him; I was ravenous with love.

It wasn't long before we came to a crossroads in our relationship, though. When Juni and I had been dating for three months, I could no longer ignore the fact that I was the one who needed to make decisions about our future. As I filled out forms for Butler's Wharf halls of residence at LSE, my plans felt like a burden, rather than the freedom they had represented just a few months ago. When Mummy and Daddy talked excitedly about London, I'd stay silent. They thought my relationship with Juni was a little crush that meant nothing.

Daddy made it clear that no man should stand in the way of my education: 'He works as a sales and marketing assistant in a hotel. Do you think any daughter of mine is going to end up with a guy like him?' Daddy was firm in his disapproval even before he met Juni – but it was much worse once he did. That fateful day was the first time I had ever seen my mother being rude to a guest.

My parents had a way of making the simplest encounter a formal event. Mummy set out Nimco snacks in a cut-glass bowl, chutney sandwiches, cumin biscuits and pineapple cake. Coke bottles sat next to the fancy crystal tumblers and a stack of Royal Albert porcelain side plates with starched napkins. It felt like a teatime interview at the White House.

As the clock struck 12.30 p.m., Juni, wearing a suit, walked up the stairs to my father's study. There to meet him were my father, stiff and upright, and my mother with her half-shy fixed smile.

'So, Juni, what degree did you study for?' asked Daddy.

'I have a diploma in hotel management, sir,' replied Juni.

'Somi tells me you work at the Pearl Continental; I know the CEO well.'

'Yes, I joined as an intern,' said Juni, 'but then I was offered a permanent position.'

'I know your grandfather from my navy days,' said Daddy. 'He is a good man.'

Daddy went on cross-examining Juni. I watched as my mother's expression went from a smile to a frown. Without explanation, she stood up and walked out of the study, closing the door with a thud. An already tense chat turned sour; my father fumbled his excuses and tried to make light of the situation. Juni's face was a picture of fear and embarrassment.

I followed Mummy to find out what had happened. She was standing in the kitchen, arms folded across her chest, her face as red as the chilli powder that covered the *dahi baras* (lentil dumplings) left on the counter, yet to be served. Making these was a labour of love, and I could sense her regret that she had bothered to spend time making them for Juni.

'You will have nothing to do with this boy once he leaves,' she said, her eyes bloodshot. 'What the hell do you see in him?' Her voice was shaking with anger.

'But Mummy, you haven't even given him a chance.'

'He's not right for you,' she said. 'He looks like a *lafanga* (rogue); Daddy will never agree to this match. Boys like him have no future. You're not going around with a boy like that.'

'He has a good future ahead,' I said. 'At least get to know him.'

I returned to the study to rescue Juni, who was still being quizzed by Daddy.

Hoping to reassure him, as he was leaving, I lied that he had impressed my parents. I had never felt more adamant about being with him.

I knew my parents' disapproval hurt him, but he never admitted it.

'Don't worry,' he said. 'My parents will love you.'

LEGENDARY ACHARI GOSHT

As I walked into Juni's family's apartment, which looked out over the Arabian Sea, I was met with a strong aroma of *achar* pickling spices. The small kitchen was right by the door, and straight away I could see the back of a short woman, hunched over a gas hob. Her hair was wavy, and she wore a starched white *kurta* shirt and *shalwar*.

When she turned around, I could see that heartbreak was deeply etched into Naseem Aunty's smile. (In Pakistan, 'Aunty' is the polite form of address for any woman much older than yourself.) The death of her middle son at eighteen had made her fiercely protective of her remaining children; Juni's mum was a woman who lived and breathed motherhood.

'Do you like to cook?' was the first thing she asked me.

'Not a lot, but I want to learn more,' I replied. 'I love the smell of spices in your kitchen. What are you cooking?'

Her disapproving silence made me nervous. I rested my back against a cupboard to support my trembling legs.

'My Juni loves food,' she replied, ignoring my question about the spices.

Juni replied for her: 'She's cooking her *achari gosht* – it's legendary.'

His mother playfully slapped his hand as he dipped a piece of naan in the pot to taste it.

'It was Sunny's favourite,' she said, her voice shaking ever so slightly.

Smoke billowed through the kitchen as she added fresh fenugreek leaves to a bubbling red sauce. I caught sight of a small bottle of whole spices, with a faint handwritten label that read '*achari* masala'. On the pretext of picking up some dishes, I walked over and peered closely at the contents. There seemed to be a mix of mustard, fenugreek, nigella and cumin seeds. She dumped them all into the pan at once, together with ginger and garlic, without waiting for each spice to impart their flavour first. My mother or my Dadi would never cook like this. I didn't like the way she treated the spices, but I was fascinated.

'What are the proportions of the spice seeds in your *achari* masala, Aunty?' I asked.

'Oh, I can't remember,' she said, brushing off my request.

She continued to stir the sauce vigorously, scraping a metal spoon against the pan.

'I'd love to know your recipe, Aunty, please!' I tried again, hoping she might feel compelled to tell me just to shut me up.

'A little bit of this and that. You'll have to watch me next time,' she said impatiently, stirring that spoon in the pan a little more loudly. Next she threw handfuls of chopped coriander and slivers of ginger into the sauce.

I gave up on asking her again. Instead, I kept one eye on the pan in case she added anything else to it, and I made myself useful in the kitchen, tidying dishes and cleaning counters, trying to impress her by being her son's dutiful girlfriend.

Dinner was served in a large room with a lounge suite on one side and Juni's parents' double bed on another. Food was brought in on one of the shiny hostess trolleys that all Pakistani brides seemed to have in their trousseau. It was golden, with two brown-glass shelves, and its wheels were squeaky from daily use. Under crocheted mats on the top layer were Pyrex bowls with basmati rice, potato *bhujia* and the *achari gosht*. The bottom tray had a watery-looking cucumber raita in a blue-and-white hand-painted Hala pottery bowl. Next to it was dessert, a glass bowl of jewel-like bright-red pomegranate seeds, with a tiny bowl of chilli powder and black salt to sprinkle on top.

'Ami, your food is the best. No one can cook like you!' said Juni, his hazel eyes twinkling with admiration.

But I felt that the *achari gosht* lacked the depth and balance of flavour I was used to, it seemed almost one dimensional in comparison. I wondered why Juni was so enthusiastic about it. *Wait until he tastes our food!* I thought, wondering if Mummy would ever cook for him again. I tried to find any fault I could in Naseem Aunty's food, partly because I felt rather envious of Juni's admiration for it.

We ate quietly and made small talk. Juni's father was funny and warm, and his younger brother and I took an instant liking to each other, but his mother continued to view me with suspicion. Despite her smiles and typically pushy Pakistani hospitality – insisting I have seconds, and then thirds – clearly she had begun to realise that she was no longer the only woman in her son's life. It was evident that there was already a silent competition between Juni's mother and me. I also felt stuck in the middle – between, on the one hand, a woman whose food the man I loved would always consider to be better than mine, and, on the other, my own parents, whose disapproval of him seemed unshakable.

Naseem Aunty never did give me the recipe for her *achari gosht*. I never really cared for it myself, but I wanted to learn how to make it, as I knew how much Juni loved it. When I was visiting Juni, I'd find reasons to go into the kitchen, hoping to pick up her techniques as I walked past. I would breathe in aromas, trying to figure out how deeply she browned her onions and when she fried the meat, and noting how much of the elusive *achari* masala she added. I'd go home and try out each step I had learnt. It took time until I mastered the entire recipe, but the day came when it tasted better than Naseem Aunty's – and there I was, cooking Pakistani food, and to please a man. That is to say, I was doing exactly what I'd sworn never to do just a few months earlier.

As I grew more focused on Juni and less focused on going to LSE, my parents became dead-set against this match. Despite my parents' apprehensions, I was sure we could make it work – we would be happy, and that would prove how wrong they were. By now Juni and I had discussed marriage, and he had made it clear that his parents would expect us to live with them; I felt anxious about the prospect. But it wasn't just the thought of sharing a house with in-laws that worried me; it was the thought of living with a woman who seemed to know little about the art of layering spices, and who didn't share recipes.

Achar with carrot and green chilli

This pickle (pictured overleaf) is based on my Nani's basic quick achar *recipe – use it to create your own pickles by changing the vegetables and flavourings. Split mustard seeds can be bought in Asian shops, but you can make your own by grinding brown mustard seeds with a pestle and mortar. For the tamarind, it's best to use a dried block, rehydrating it and then sieving the pulp as described on page 147, but you could use ready-made tamarind concentrate if you're short of time.*

Prep time: 30 minutes + several hours drying/ marinating time
Makes 1 x 1 litre (4 cup) jar, or 2 x 500 ml (2 cup) jars

450 g (1 lb) carrots (not baby carrots), peeled and cut into strips about 3 mm (⅛ inch) thick
3 tablespoons split mustard seeds
½ teaspoon chilli powder
2 tablespoons Himalayan pink salt
¼ teaspoon turmeric powder
4 tablespoons light brown sugar
2 tablespoons tamarind pulp or concentrate
8 green finger chillies, split and cut into 2.5 cm (1 inch) pieces
5 cm (2 inch) ginger, cut into fine strips
6 tablespoons sunflower oil

- Half-fill a medium-sized saucepan with water and bring to the boil. Pop in the carrots and cook for no longer than 2 minutes, then take them out and drain on paper towels. Let them dry for a few hours at room temperature – in the sun would be preferable – until they are totally dry.
- Put the mustard seeds, chilli powder, salt, turmeric and sugar into a non-reactive bowl, then give them a good mix with a wooden spoon. Add the tamarind and the oil and mix well.
- Now add the carrots, green chillies and ginger and mix well. Cover the bowl with a plate and leave in the fridge for at least 24 hours, stirring it a couple of times during this time. This allows the flavours to develop and soak into the vegetables and mature slightly – the colour of the vegetables will darken, which is fine.
- When ready to bottle up, sterilise your jar or jars by rinsing out with boiling water and drying thoroughly. Using a wooden spoon, carefully spoon in the pickle, but don't fill the jar right up to the top – you need to leave about 3–4 cm (1¼–1½ inches) of breathing space above the pickles.
- Seal and store in the fridge. If you always use a clean non-metallic spoon to take out the pickle and ensure the sides of the jar are kept clean, the *achar* should last for at least 6 months.

Achari gosht

A recipe I learnt by watching Naseem Aunty cook her legendary achari gosht. *The name of this intensely flavoured dish (pictured on previous page) comes from* achar *(pickle), as the spices used are generally associated with pickling. Eat with naan or basmati rice.*

Prep time: 20 minutes
Cooking time: 30 minutes
Serves 4–6

2 tablespoons ghee or sunflower oil
3 red onions, thinly sliced
1 tablespoon finely grated ginger
1 tablespoon crushed garlic
4 tomatoes, roughly chopped
300 g (10½ oz) full-fat Greek-style yoghurt
500 g (1 lb 2 oz) chicken on the bone, such as thighs, cut into 12 pieces
salt, to taste
½ teaspoon Kashmiri chilli powder – or more, if you prefer it hot
1 teaspoon turmeric powder
juice of 1 lemon
4–6 green finger chillies

For the pickling spices

1½ teaspoons fennel seeds
1½ teaspoons brown mustard seeds
1½ teaspoons cumin seeds
1½ teaspoons nigella seeds (*kalonji*)
½ teaspoon fenugreek seeds

To garnish

handful of chopped coriander (cilantro) leaves
1 tablespoon finely shredded ginger

I would breathe in the aromas, trying to figure out how deeply Naseem Aunty browned her onions and when she fried the meat, noting how much of the elusive 'achari masala' pickling spices she added.

- In a dry, heavy-based frying pan, roast all the pickling spices until they begin to pop and become fragrant, which takes about 30 seconds or so. Keep aside about 2 teaspoons of the roasted seeds and leave them whole, then grind the rest to a powder using a pestle and mortar or electric grinder.
- Heat the ghee or oil in a heavy-based saucepan over medium heat. Once it is hot, add the reserved whole seeds and the onions and fry, stirring, until the onions are light golden. Add the ginger and garlic and cook, stirring constantly, until their raw smell drifts away, about 2 minutes.
- Now add the tomatoes and cook until they become soft and the juice oozes out of them, about 7–8 minutes.
- Add the yoghurt and stir until it splits and then comes back together – about 5 minutes of rigorous stirring is involved.
- Add the chicken, salt, chilli powder and half of the turmeric. Stir well, then cover and simmer for about 20 minutes.
- Meanwhile, in a small bowl, mix the ground pickling spices with the remaining turmeric and the lemon juice to make a paste.
- Carefully make a lengthways slit in each of the chillies, keeping the ends intact, then fill the slits with the spice paste. Add any leftover spice paste to the chicken and stir well.
- Now add the stuffed chillies to the pan, stir gently and turn the heat down to low. Keep cooking for another 5–10 minutes, or until the chicken is cooked through.
- Serve hot, garnished with chopped coriander and shredded ginger.

CHAPTER 13

Wedding korma is never made with cream

I choose the menu for my
own wedding, and I learn
that wedding kormas are
rich with aromatic spices and
saffron. I soon realise that
the festivities are to appease
others, and that I might just
be signing up for a controlling
mother-in-law.

Karachi, 1996

THE ENGAGEMENT

My idealistic vision of a marriage proposal was to be alone with Juni, for it to be about us and no one else. I dreamt of him proposing to me at the beach or maybe even on a crabbing trip to recreate the night we met, but I knew that would never happen. Marriages in Pakistan were always about tradition, beginning with the proposal. Our engagement would have to begin in the culturally accepted way, which meant that his parents and mine would first have to meet over chai and make small talk without any mention of our 'proposal'. Then, after a couple of meals back and forth, Juni's parents would need to formally ask for my hand in marriage.

On the day of the proposal I found Mummy in the kitchen. Having spent a week shopping and cooking, she was intent on serving a huge spread for the special dinner. Mummy still had her doubts about Juni, but nothing would deter her from creating a feast for my prospective in-laws. When we first went to Juni's together, Naseem Aunty had made her famous *achari gosht* and biryani, and I could already sense a gentle cooking rivalry in the conversations between her and my mother.

Out to impress, Mummy was making *koftay*, intricate, richly spiced meatballs that took time and skill: 'Help me make them,' she said. 'This is my recipe, and you should learn it so you can show off to your in-laws once you live there.' Just a few months earlier, I would have ignored such demands, but now I saw food as a way to keep Juni on my side, and I wanted to learn as much as I could from her before I got married.

'You know we still aren't happy about you wanting to marry this boy?' said Mummy. 'We still think you're wasting your life. You'll regret it.'

'No, I won't,' I replied. 'You just don't think anyone is good enough for me. No one is going to live up to your expectations.'

'Somi, it's not that. The fact is you're still young. Besides, you're giving up LSE for this boy.'

I wanted to say that law wasn't my passion, and that in this culture there was no other way to be with someone you loved. I couldn't just live with Juni, which meant that marriage was the only way to get to know him. For me, marriage felt like freedom; like agreeing to study law in London had felt before. But the words never came out. Not because I was scared, but because I felt it was useless to say them. *What choice do I have?*

Mummy passed me the spice jars and told me to take out as much of them as I felt the recipe might need.

'How will I know how much? I asked.

'Trust yourself. You've eaten these so many times, you know what they are meant to taste like.'

I looked at the minced beef in the large stainless-steel bowl. Gauging by eye what felt like enough, I used my fingers to pinch up spices: I took a couple of pinches each of cumin, white poppy seeds and coriander seeds and started to heat them in a dry frying pan.

'How long do I roast them?'

'Until they smell *done*,' said Mummy, vaguely.

'What on earth is *done*?' I asked.

Mummy laughed. 'Done is when they smell like my *koftay*!'

The kitchen was filled with the warm aroma of festivity and celebration, of the dinner parties Mummy loved to host. I began to understand what she meant by 'done': it meant that they smelt like they were supposed to – of the flavour in her hands.

She inspected the seeds and smiled, then used her pestle and mortar to grind them to a powder, adding splashes of water as she went: 'Poppy seeds are really tough to grind, so you'll have to add a little water to make a paste. Even then, they are stubborn, but they add a unique, unidentifiable flavour and that's the secret to my *koftay*.'

We mixed this paste with the meat. Mummy added finely chopped mint, then told me to add some ginger and garlic paste, garam masala and salt and knead it together until the mixture felt like a dough. As we both took tablespoons of the mixture and rolled them into balls, she showed me how to make sure their surface was smooth without any cracks. Using the fingertips of one hand on the palm of the other, she rolled them expertly, bashing them against the flat of her palm every now and then to get rid of any creases. Soon a platter filled with beautifully uniform meatballs: they smelt earthy and fragrant; the freshness of mint came through, mingling with the earthiness of warm spices.

'We'll make the *saalan* next – the *koftay* will slowly cook in it,' Mummy said. 'The liquid will infuse them with flavour and cook them gently.'

She sizzled whole spices in hot oil, then added a paste of browned onions, ginger and garlic, stirring and adding splashes of water to avoid it burning: 'You must always cook the ginger and garlic until the raw smell disappears. If you don't, you'll get that awful taste of uncooked garlic in your mouth.' Those extra few minutes Mummy took with her cooking made all the difference to the intensity of flavour in her food.

I'd always wondered why my mother's *saalan* was so red, and she showed me how deeply vibrant the colour became when she added her brick-red chilli paste. Made from rehydrated dried Kashmiri chillies, this would give the *saalan* the sharp fruitiness of chilli, but very little heat. Next, I mixed in a little room-temperature yogurt – but then watched in horror as it began to split: 'But that looks terrible! How come it hasn't all been incorporated into the *salaan* like yours usually does?'

'You need to be patient. It's a stage it needs to go through,' Mummy explained. 'It takes time for the water to evaporate from the yoghurt. Once that happens, the oil rises to the top and it no longer looks split.'

And she was right. As I stirred the *saalan*, the heady spices and the yoghurt came together to form the perfect stew.

Mummy was on the other side of the kitchen, looking after the shami kebabs, mutton biryani, mixed *sabzi* (vegetables) and daal that she was also making for the dinner. She always threw herself headlong into creating any meal, and I was glad she was doing it for Juni and his parents because, more than anything, I wanted them to know that I came from a home where food was just as important as it was to them.

My new-found determination to cook well made me like a sponge for recipes and cooking tips. I wanted to write them all down so that I'd have them when I moved in with my in-laws, but this was proving to be less than easy. No one in my family could ever just recite a recipe. Neither my mother nor my grandmother would remember what they added to a dish if they weren't right there cooking it, so the only way I could learn a recipe was to be in the kitchen with them.

When I asked Nani Mummy how she made her biryani so fluffy, she saw through me right away: 'You were never interested in cooking it before, what's all this about?'

Everyone in my family knew about the proposal, but Nani Mummy was the only one who was supportive of it. 'I know you like him and you want to impress him – it's good you're marrying someone you like. And don't worry, I'm certain your parents will come around to liking him eventually,' she said.

'But I want them to be happy for me. Daddy is annoyed I'm giving up on going to London to study, and Mummy just thinks Juni is useless.'

'Your Nana never thought anyone was good enough for your mother, either, but you have it tougher. Remember you're an only child; it's a hard decision for them – you're their *ladli* (precious one).'

The curse of being an only child haunted me: the overprotectiveness, the expectations, and the burden of fulfilling their dreams for me. For once, I just wanted to have freedom from it all, and I thought that marriage might offer that.

From the moment Juni and his parents arrived at our house, Juni and I couldn't stop smiling. We sat in our formal drawing room, where Mummy had laid out open cucumber sandwiches and mini lemon tarts. After about half an hour of small talk, Juni's father took the opportunity to raise the subject of marriage. Juni and I smiled at each other, exchanging excited glances, while the parents talked about how wonderful it would be for the families to come together.

I wasn't sure if any of them were genuinely pleased, or if they were putting on a brave face, but at this point, I didn't care. It was happening. I'd finally be engaged to Juni.

The dinner table was laid with starched, neatly folded, lace-trimmed Irish linen napkins on bone-china plates, with cut-glass tumblers and silver cutlery on the side. In the centre of the table were candles and an ikebana floral arrangement of tuberoses and gladioli. In the array of serving dishes, bright-red *koftay* glistened in the candlelight, saffron-flecked biryani clung to uniformly cut pieces of spiced mutton and neat shami kebab patties were laid out on a silver-handled platter. I looked at the *koftay* with pride, waiting for someone to comment on how perfect they were.

Naseem Aunty was eyeing the food with one eyebrow raised, and I could tell she was judging its presentation.

'Kausar, you really didn't have to go to so much trouble!'

'Oh no, it's not a problem. It's a happy occasion, so I wanted to create a festive meal,' my mother replied.

'You made this all yourself?' asked Naseem Aunty.

'Yes, I don't have any servants and I don't like people cooking for me, so I do all the cooking,' said Mummy.

'And I made the *koftay*!' I interrupted.

'Wow, I couldn't do without a servant. My boy does all the cleaning and chopping for me,' Naseem Aunty said, pointedly ignoring my interruption.

After the meal was finished, Juni signalled with his eyes that I should follow him into the kitchen. We collected the empty plates from the table, but what we really wanted to do was go into the kitchen to kiss, something we couldn't do in front of our parents.

'I can't believe it, Juni – we're getting married!' I said.

Juni did a happy dance, with his signature R&B-style moves: 'I know! Everything is going to be perfect. I love you.'

Over the following weeks and months, there was a lot of planning to be done. The wedding was to take place in December – peak marriage season in Karachi and only eleven months away – which left us with barely enough time to organise a Pakistani wedding.

Although my mother and Naseem Aunty's relationship seemed polite enough, I could sense a slight competitiveness just below the surface, and even the preparations for our formal engagement party exposed the underlying tensions. They had quite different ideas of how the celebrations should unfold. Naseem Aunty made it clear that she wanted to invite everyone in her extended family, whereas Mummy wanted a classy, smaller affair with just close family and friends.

The party was to be in our living room and there was only space for about thirty people, so Mummy was annoyed at the idea of such a disproportionate number of Juni's family attending: 'I don't see why they need to all be here. After all, this is the bride's event and it's a small engagement party. I don't know why your future mother-in-law needs to invite her whole family over.'

Every other day I'd be whisked away by Naseem Aunty or Mummy to choose outfits, interview florists and look at venues for the wedding. I was living pre-wedding excitement, day and night, and I'd forgotten all about going to London. Since I hadn't gone to LSE, the compromise had been to finish my B.A. at St Joseph's and then study law in Karachi, so I was doing my law degree at S. M. (Sindh Muslim) Law College and had taken a break for my wedding.

In just a few months I had become the kind of girl I used to roll my eyes at: all I could do was talk about my wedding – but to my surprise, my college friends seemed more concerned with Juni's background than the fact that I was in love with him.

'So what is this Juni?' asked Aisha.

'What do you mean, what is he?' I replied.

'I mean is he Punjabi or Sindhi? And is he Shia or Sunni? What is he?' she went on.

'I don't know. He's just Pakistani.'

'*Uff*, you silly girl – no one is *just* Pakistani, you have to be from somewhere,' she said.

'Well, last time I checked, we were all Pakistanis!'

'No, that's wrong. I'm Sindhi because my parents grew up in a Sindhi village; and you're Punjabi and Muhajir, because your mother is Punjabi and your dad's family migrated from India.'

'I don't think that makes sense. I have never lived in Punjab and I didn't migrate. I'm Pakistani – that's it.'

I just couldn't understand this urge to put everybody into boxes, or the deeply rooted ethnic and religious segregation in Pakistan.

GOLD THREAD AND CRIMSON SILK

Most Pakistani weddings have at least three events: the *mehndi* (henna party), *shaadi* (the wedding day itself) – both of which are paid for, and organised by, the bride's family – and the *valima* (reception and banquet), paid for by the groom's family.

Naseem Aunty sprang into action, controlling every single aspect of the *valima* right from the beginning. I wanted to wear something contemporary and I made some suggestions about designers I liked, but she pushed me to agree to go to Mrs Kazmi, a traditional designer, justifying it by saying that a more conventional piece would mean I could wear it 'for ever'.

On the day of our appointment, it was clear that, although Naseem Aunty wanted me there to help her choose, ultimately it was going to be entirely her choice: '*Beta*, I'm hoping we can pick the fabrics for your *valima* outfit today – I was thinking we could go with a crimson theme.'

'I was hoping for a more pastel theme, actually,' I said.

'Oh, but you're wearing white on your wedding day, Somi, and that's so untraditional for a Pakistani bride anyway. Why don't you just choose something traditional for the *valima*?'

At the opulent Lahore-Fortress-style doorway that led to the designer's showroom, we were greeted by a tiny man in a *sherwani* (a knee-length formal tunic jacket). Inside, there were ornate carved-rosewood sofas and books on Mughal fabric art lay on a large glass-topped coffee table; the walls were adorned with framed samples of the intricate *dabka* gold-wire embroidery work this designer was known for.

'So, let me do the talking, you can go and get your measurements done, then I will help you pick out the fabrics,' she said.

We spent the rest of the hour going through stacks of colour-coordinated fabric and different finishes of silk – but ultimately, no matter what I suggested, we kept returning to shocking pink and purple options. Naseem Aunty liked bold colours with loud designs, whereas I liked classic neutrals and pale, pastel colours and miniature floral designs – there just didn't seem to be any common ground. I was desperate for her approval as I knew that it was key to Juni's happiness, so I settled for not looking like myself at the *valima* and surrendered to the crimson.

Juni and I were also starting to plan our honeymoon: 'It would be great to leave the day after the *valima*,' I said.

'I don't think Mama is going to like that,' said Juni.

'What? Why? Besides, what on earth has our honeymoon got to do with your mother?'

'Well, you know I'll have to ask her if it's ok. She has expectations that we'll meet the family straight afterwards,' said Juni. His gaze fell to the floor as he tried hard to ignore my anger.

The wedding was to take place in December – peak marriage season in Karachi and only a few months away.

On my wedding day

And, just like that, our honeymoon became her business too. I began to feel uneasy. It was becoming increasingly clear that my mother-in-law was going to be very involved in my marriage, but my desire to get married shrouded so many of those warning signs.

THE SHAADI MENU

I began to focus my attention on the things I could control, like what I would wear for my *shaadi* and, more importantly, what would be on the menu. Food was one of the main attractions at Pakistani weddings, and so I knew at least here I'd have some control over choices. Mummy and I had decided that the *mehndi* would take place in Nani Mummy's garden, and the wedding venue would be the ballroom at the Sheraton. I picked up the menu we had received from the caterers and began ticking off my choices:

MAIN DISHES

*Fish boti tikka * Haryali chicken * Mutton biryani * Beef boti * Beef shahi biryani*
*Shaadiwala chicken korma * Mutton pullao * Raita * Salad*
Naan / Sheermal (saffron flatbread) / Taaftan (butter flatbread)

DESSERTS

*Gulab jamun * Kulfi falooda * Gajar halva with rabri (carrot halva with clotted cream)*
Lab-e-shireen (custard dessert with jelly and fruit)
*Khubani ka meetha (Hunza apricot dessert) * Zarda (sweet rice)*

'Mummy, what on earth is *shaadiwala* korma?' I asked.

'Well, wedding korma is a little special,' she said. 'You know it's served at nearly every Pakistani wedding banquet?'

'Yeah, the typical korma; why does it always have to be there?' I asked.

'It's been on the menu at weddings since the time of the Mughals and in Persian courts. It's a traditional way of creating an extravagant, rich, slow-cooked dish, where the meat is braised with spices, so it becomes deeply infused with their flavours. When we lived in South Wonston, I couldn't believe that everyone thought all kormas included cream – but no Pakistani would ever put cream in their korma!' Mummy said.

My mother's wedding-style chicken korma was something she cooked for Eid dinners and lavish parties. A floral, heady dish, it was elegant and rich, finished with organic *kewra* (screwpine extract) and the best-quality saffron.

Wedding kormas rarely came close to home-cooked korma: they were usually hastily prepared, using inferior ingredients, and were almost always too spicy and oily.

I'd seen how differently people in my own family made their kormas, and I was worried that the caterers' version might not meet our expectations. My Dadi had made a korma that was rich and fragrant, steeped in Mughal tradition, with deeply browned onions and meat (usually mutton) cooked for hours, all bathed in a dark brownish-red sauce with oil floating on top. In contrast, Nani Mummy's korma was true to her Punjabi style of cooking – it was less heavily spiced, and so it tasted lighter and fruitier. My mother's was my favourite: the sauce was a deep auburn, with tender chicken and a glistening sheen on the surface, but it never tasted oily. The fragrance of her korma was unique too. It was floral from the cardamom and cloves, fruity and earthy in one bite, and because she added saffron towards the end of cooking, it lingered on the palate.

'I really want that on my menu,' I said, my mouth watering. 'I want the food to be just as lavish as the flowers or my outfit!' Mummy and I agreed that we would get the catering chefs to cook the chicken korma her way, and we also made some tweaks to the other dishes, settling on fish boti tikka, mutton biryani and *taaftan*, plus salad, raita and naan, followed by *zarda*.

As the months passed and the wedding day drew nearer, I began to wonder whether Naseem Aunty wasn't only intent on controlling the wedding preparations but that this might just be who she was. I was starting to sense that my life wasn't going to be easy when I was living with my in-laws. I felt conflicted about Naseem Aunty. There was a part of me that wanted her to think I was perfect for Juni, but on the other hand I felt as if she was always going to be a barrier between us, and I resented her interference. We never said anything directly to each other, but I could already sense a storm brewing.

Mummy's wedding-style chicken korma

Most wedding kormas are oily and one dimensional, but my mother's version (pictured on previous page) is aromatic and multi-layered; it is best served with basmati rice or naan, and a kachumber-style salad of chopped cucumber and tomato. If you can't find crispy fried onions in your local supermarket or Asian shop, make them yourself by frying three thinly sliced red onions in 100 ml (3½ fl oz) sunflower oil, in batches, then draining on paper towels.

Prep time: 15 minutes + marinating time, from 1 hour to overnight
Cooking time: 40–45 minutes
Serves 6–8

1 x 1 kg (2 lb 4 oz) chicken, skinned and cut into 8 pieces, or 8 skinless thighs, on the bone
400 g (1½ cups) full-fat Greek-style yoghurt, plus 2 tablespoons extra
1 tablespoon finely grated ginger
4 garlic cloves, crushed
1½ teaspoons Kashmiri chilli powder
1 teaspoon salt
4 tablespoons ready-made crispy fried onions
large pinch of saffron threads
1 ice cube
3 tablespoons ghee or sunflower oil
4–6 green cardamom pods, bruised
1 cinnamon stick
5 cloves
1 teaspoon black peppercorns
2 bay leaves
1 teaspoon cumin seeds, roasted in a dry frying pan and ground
1 teaspoon coriander seeds, roasted in a dry frying pan and ground
¼ teaspoon grated nutmeg
2–3 drops screwpine extract (*kewra*) – optional

To garnish

1 tablespoon chopped coriander (cilantro) leaves
1 green finger chilli, deseeded and finely chopped
2.5 cm (1 inch) ginger, cut into fine strips

- In a bowl, combine the chicken pieces with the yoghurt, ginger, garlic, chilli powder and salt. Leave to marinate in the fridge for at least 1 hour, or as long as overnight.
- When ready to cook, put the onions into a small blender or food processor with a couple of tablespoons of water and grind to a paste.
- Put the saffron into a small bowl (about the size of a pinch pot) with the ice cube and leave to melt and infuse while you cook – we'll be adding this saffron-infused water right at the end of the cooking.
- Heat the ghee or oil in a heavy-based saucepan over medium heat. When it is hot, add the cardamom pods, cinnamon, cloves, peppercorns and bay leaves and let them infuse the ghee. This will only take about 30–40 seconds – keep the spices moving to stop them burning.
- Quickly, so the spices don't catch, add the onion paste and 4 tablespoons of water. Cook until the water has evaporated and the paste is shiny and thick.
- Add the chicken with its marinade and stir well. Turn the heat up to high and cook, stirring, until the yoghurt thickens and dries up, then add some more water (about 5 tablespoons or so), cover and cook for about 20 minutes. Keep an eye on it: if it gets too dry, you might need to give it a stir and add a little more water.
- Next add the ground cumin and coriander, turn the heat up to high, and fry, stirring, until the oil rises to the surface. Stir in the saffron water, nutmeg and screwpine extract (if using), then cook over low heat, uncovered, for a minute or so.
- To finish, turn off the heat and immediately add the extra yoghurt, but don't stir it through. Garnish with the coriander, green chilli and ginger, then serve immediately.

CHAPTER 14

Mithai isn't dessert

In Pakistan, mithai (sweetmeats) are about sharing joyous times. I learn to cook Nani Mummy's sheer khurma and discover that it's an offering, not just a dessert or a drink.

Karachi, Winter 1996

WHITE FOR THE WEDDING

'Make sure you're rubbing the *ubtan* (skin scrub) on your face as well,' said Mummy.

'Argh, I hate the stuff on my face, it's so messy!' I said.

'Well, you need to have fair, clear skin for the wedding, so just keep doing it.'

In Pakistan, a fair complexion was considered the ultimate in beauty. Stemming from a colonial mindset, this fascination with fair skin was widespread in the media, and you were made to believe that you couldn't be happy or successful without the right skin colour.

A whole beauty industry had grown up to exploit this belief, with women who were *sanwli* (dusky-skinned) encouraged to torment themselves with skin-lightening products. Face creams branded 'Fair & Lovely' were bestsellers, street-side apothecaries sold every manner of face-bleaching treatments and mothers mixed up whitening concoctions for their daughters. Although my mother was never one to use anything unnatural like bleach, many of my friends would make a monthly trip to the beauty parlour for a 'skin polish': a horrifying mixture of Jolen creme bleach, body lotion and rose water that stung and itched would be applied to make the complexion a few shades lighter, with the bonus of blonde facial hair.

Mummy took appearances seriously, and she was constantly telling me to stay out of the sun. After each school sports day, I'd undergo a rigorous 'de-tanning' ritual. Kitchen beauty potions, such as fresh cream split with lemon juice, would help to exfoliate the tanned skin; oats ground and mixed with yoghurt and lime juice made a whitening mask. Amid this obsession with being *gora* (white), it was hard being the odd one out, so I succumbed to the pursuit of fair skin – and it seemed even more important now that I was getting married.

'You don't want to look dark on your wedding day, so please don't go out driving during the day,' said Mummy. 'If you need to go out, leave it until after sundown.'

'Yes, Mummy, and I'll make sure I use the *ubtan* too.'

But it wasn't all bad – the *ubtan* ritual wasn't just about making your skin fairer, it was also about softening your face and clearing away any blackheads and blemishes – like a daily facial for the four weeks leading up to the wedding. Made with red lentils, dried rose petals and orange peel, ground together and mixed with oat flour, herbs and roots, Mummy's usual *ubtan* smelt like an intoxicating floral masala, good enough to eat.

For my wedding *ubtan*, Mummy added potent rare herbs as well, following a recipe she got from a friend. She mixed the resulting powder with yoghurt and lemon juice and rubbed it all over my body as I wriggled with the coldness of it; the yoghurt was fresh from the fridge and the acidic lemon juice stung my skin. When it had dried, she scrubbed it off in circular motions until my face and body were red and glowing. A month of this was meant to make my skin look pale and luminescent on my wedding day. A white wedding meant something rather different in Pakistan: it was all about the skin, not the dress!

The time before the wedding was flying by. The days were filled with bazaar trips for last-minute shopping. In the evenings there were open-house *dholki* ('drum beating') events with food, music and dancing. Choreographed dance moves to Bollywood songs were all the rage, with a friendly rivalry developing between the groom's and bride's families on the night of the *mehndi*. My friends organised dance practice sessions, and though I was never a fan of Bollywood music, the earworm tunes began to stick in my head.

Dawn, my friend from South Wonston, had come to Karachi for the wedding and was staying with us. We caught up over henna-application evenings and choosing glass *choori* (bangles) to match her Pakistani outfits. She was intrigued by my decision: 'Are you happy about getting married so young?' asked Dawn. 'I mean I know you love this guy, but can't you just live with him or even just wait?'

'Well, this is the thing: in Pakistan, we can't live with anyone before marriage,' I said. 'And as for being too young, lots of girls get married younger than me. Anyway, it's too late to do anything else now. I can't call off a wedding a few weeks before. Marriage here isn't just about the couple, you see, it's a family thing. Besides, I do want to be with Juni.

Strangely, it was only her questions that made me stop for a moment and think about how dramatically I'd changed – from someone who wanted to be free to go and study in London, someone who'd never settle for the sake of settling, to a marriage-obsessed twenty-two-year-old who was about to become a bride. But, with everyone fussing over me, any doubts I might have had melted away easily in the enthusiasm and excitement of the build-up to the wedding.

SHARING SWEETNESS

While I began to wince at the sight of *ubtan* halfway through the month-long ritual, I was happy to eat as much *mithai* (sweetmeats) as our family received. In Pakistan, most happy occasions were celebrated with *mun meetha* ('sweetening the mouth'), but nothing compared to the amount of *mithai* exchanged and eaten in the days before and during a wedding. The *mehndi* was as much about rituals and receiving blessings as it was about the application of henna and the music. Traditionally, the bride and groom sat together on a carved daybed shaped like a wooden swing, piled high with cushions and garlanded with marigold and jasmine flowers. Family and friends would come to greet the couple and wish them well, feeding them *mithai* and offering them envelopes of present money called *salaami* – but not without ritually circling these gifts three times around the heads of the bride and groom to ward off the evil eye.

On the day of the *mehndi*, Mummy made up large platters of presents for Juni and his family to take home: four massive baskets full of colourful glass bangles, tie-dyed silk *dupatta* scarves and small packets of sugared almonds, dried dates and gold-coin chocolates. Yet more cellophane-wrapped baskets held silver boxes of her home-made *panjiri ladoos*.

Nani Mummy's side of the family were Punjabi, and whenever a woman got pregnant they gave her *panjiri*, a traditional granola-like sweet made with semolina and nuts (though whenever Nani Mummy or Mummy made it, we'd end up eating most of it before it got to the expectant mothers). For the *mehndi*, Mummy had decided that she'd make *panjiri* into *ladoo* sweets.

Heating up a large wok-style pan with a little ghee, she roasted coarse semolina with some ground cardamom until it turned pale brown and gave off a sweet, hazelnutty smell, then she roasted pistachio and almond slivers with dried fruit, tossing them until the nuts were lightly charred. In another pan she heated a little more ghee and fried *gond* (Arabic gum crystals) and *makhana* (lotus seeds) until puffy: the gum resembled tiny pieces of citrine, but when you bit into them they stuck to your teeth like toffee, and the fried lotus seeds looked like popcorn but quickly melted in your mouth. Usually I'd steal some of these to eat, but I was told to stay away this time!

With all the cooked ingredients now in the large pan, she kept adding ghee until the mixture became a mass. She took a couple of tablespoons of the warm mixture and rolled it into a neat, uniform ball about the size of a tennis ball, setting it on a large silver platter to cool and harden while she continued shaping the rest of the mixture. Once the *ladoos* were firm, she placed three in each silver cardboard *mithai* box, sealing it with an ivory ribbon. The whole house smelt floral and festive.

Desserts weren't generally a thing in our house, as my mother didn't have much of a sweet tooth, but Nani Mummy loved to indulge in a *ladoo* or *chum chum* sweetmeat. She would never make them, however. The base of nearly all Pakistani *mithai* was *khoya* – milk solids cooked until thick and creamy – and she maintained that this was something best left to the *halvai* (*mithai* chef): 'I really don't want to be slaving over milk for hours, stirring, simmering and making *khoya*.'

Besides, we'd have a steady supply of *mithai* boxes delivered to our homes every month. There was always a birth announcement, engagement, wedding or exam success that needed to be celebrated with the sharing of *mithai*. We both had our favourites. I loved *batisa*: made from chickpea flour flavoured with coconut and cardamom, it looked like slivers of ice compressed to give the texture of flaky pastry. Nani Mummy loved *petha*, boiled alum and sugar-preserved sweet pumpkin, and *chum chum*, a white sausage-shaped *khoya* sweet soaked in sugar syrup. Sometimes we'd have more *mithai* than we could eat, and tiny red ants would march in single file to the large boxes of sweetmeats left on the kitchen counter, infesting any that we didn't get to in time.

Though we never made *mithai* at home, we did make our own halva. Mummy would peel and grate blood-red Pakistani carrots, then boil them in cream and milk with cardamom pods and cloves, adding sugar to sweeten. As the halva cooked *bhuna* style in the oil that split from the cream, the fresh morning air would be filled with the fragrance of sweet, spiced carrots. I loved to eat hot carrot halva with cold *khoya* and a scattering of vivid-green pistachio shavings and thinly sliced blanched almonds.

And every Eid, Nani Mummy would make her special *sheer khurma* ('milk with dates and saffron'). A couple of days beforehand we'd go to the army reserve supermarket, which smelt of gritty lentils in jute bags and Castille soap, and pick out *choara* (dried dates), almonds, pistachios and packets of *seviyan* roasted vermicelli. Then, at Eid, I'd get up early in the morning, eager to have two mugs of it, still warm, for breakfast; she'd serve it in delicate Iranian tea glasses with gold-painted rims, but I never thought the dainty glasses held enough. She told me that *sheer khurma* wasn't a dessert or a drink – it was an offering of all the best you could afford, a gift of love and appreciation for your guests.

A week before the wedding, my excitement was tempered by a sinking feeling in my heart that I couldn't shift. Nani Mummy had been in and out of hospital, but she kept reassuring me that she was fine and she didn't want her illness to overshadow anything.

One afternoon, when I went to see Nani Mummy, I found her lying on the bed with her hand on her forehead, taking deep breaths.

'Are you ok, Nani Mummy?' I asked.

'Yes, Popplu. I'm just feeling a little dizzy – nothing to worry about.'

'Are you telling me it's back?'

'Somi, look, don't worry, really, I am fine,' she said, noticing how the colour had drained from my face. 'I will be there for your wedding no matter what,' she replied. 'I'm not going anywhere just yet.'

I didn't want to be worried, but I was. I didn't want her to be ill. Not now. Not ever again. She had been in remission for five years and she was coping so well, the doctor's reports had all been positive. She'd be fine, she always was.

With only a couple of days to go until the wedding, Mummy woke me up in the morning. I assumed we needed to head out somewhere for last-minute preparations, but instead she entered my room looking solemn.

'Somi, Nani Mummy isn't doing too well, just pray she can make it to the celebrations this week,' she said.

'I thought she was ok – what's suddenly happened?'

'Well, you know this disease, it returns so quietly and then takes over. Be kind to Nani Mummy and be patient if she isn't herself,' said Mummy. 'But smile, it'll be ok.'

I wanted to just push it all aside, the reality of her cancer returning, to believe that she'd be ok again, as she had been twice before.

All I could think was that I needed to go and see her. I went over to her kitchen, just like I always did, past the Sindhri mango tree in her garden; the leaves on the banana tree looked yellow and brown at this time of year, and the pomegranate blossoms had turned into fruit. I had always given her a hard time about keeping caged birds, but her yellow, green and blue parakeets were busy eating seeds in their chicken-wire cages.

I could see Nani Mummy through the kitchen window, and she was in her usual place at the white enamel stove, cooking something. As I walked in, the kitchen was warm from the glow of her stove and the midday winter sun.

'Nani Mummy, are you ok?'

'Of course, I'm just a little weak. Come, sit, let's have some chai,' she said.

I sat with her on the bed, where we always had our chai and rusks. As I dipped rusks in the tea, soggy crumbs filled the cup and I fished them out with a teaspoon. The smell of *Daily Jang* newspapers mingled with the earthy brew of Lipton tea and fresh bakery rusks.

'Nani Mummy, I want to know how you make your *sheer khurma*,' I said.

'*Beta*, why? It's not Eid yet,' she replied.

'Because I want to know how to make it, so I can make it for Juni and carry on the tradition in my new family.'

'That's a good enough reason! I'll teach you now. Finish your chai and we'll cook it even though it's not Eid,' she said.

'Are you feeling strong enough?' I asked.

'As long as you do all the hard work, I can instruct you and you can do it yourself,' said Nani Mummy.

In the kitchen she had a rosewood sofa with light-green handwoven cotton seats and large burgundy cushions. She kept it there so we could hang out together while she cooked and sometimes have a cup of tea. She put her feet up on the sofa and pointed to the top cupboard where she kept her dry ingredients.

'Take out the *seviyan* and crush them into tiny pieces, then chop the nuts. Remember it's a drink; you want to chew the bits a little, but not let them choke someone!' she said.

I did as she asked, and then she told me to take out her special Iranian saffron and pound it with her pestle and mortar just to break it up a little. I broke open green cardamom pods and chopped the nuts into dainty slivers. I opened tins of evaporated and condensed milk, which she said made the drink thick, sweet and creamy. I took the buffalo milk out of the fridge to bring it to the same temperature as the tinned milks so it wouldn't curdle when it was stirred into them. She told me to soak the *choara* (dried dates) before cutting them into quarters and taking out the pits.

'Heat the pan and remember we only use a very little crushed *seviyan*. It thickens up and becomes a pudding if you use too much. Now, we'll roast the nuts in a dry pan to add flavour to them.'

Nani Mummy watched me, and as I did each step, she smiled and nodded, saying *shahbash* (well done) each time. I wanted to keep looking back at her for approval, but more than that I kept looking back because I wanted to savour every second. I didn't know it then, but this was to be one of our last moments of pure togetherness in the kitchen; a bond only we shared, unalloyed by expectations or commitments. The kitchen was always the place I'd find Nani Mummy, and it was where she'd teach me so much more than just how to cook a recipe: she'd tell me stories about the dish, how she ate it when she was a child, and the ways in which food was more than mere sustenance. Years later, whenever I'd miss her, I'd conjure up memories of us being together in the warmth of her kitchen, with its omnipresence of spice in the air and the flavour of home that she created with her hands.

ALL THAT GLITTERS

It was December. Wisps of smoke from the charcoal barbecue set up for the wedding feast rose through the crisp, coastal air to the bridal suite, where I waited to be given away. My mother and a couple of girlfriends were there to keep me company.

Sparing my red lipstick, I bit into the gritty *panjiri* sweet I'd slipped into my bag, knowing it would calm my nerves before the big event. I could feel the weight of the silver-threaded and diamanté-encrusted *gharara* skirt as it pierced into my *ubtan*-softened skin. Behind me was an ornate bed, adorned with roses, marigold and jasmine, and I all I could think of was how suffocating it would be to sleep beneath a canopy of flowers. Trying not to trip in my bare feet and floor-length skirt, I went and tugged off the Bollywood-style flower garlands, throwing them over the side of the bed.

'Why are you doing that?' asked my friend Asma. 'Don't. It's meant to make your wedding-night bed smell gorgeous.'

'You really think a bed decorated with flowers is my kind of thing?'

'Well, Sumayya, marriage wasn't either!' she laughed. 'But finally it's happening, finally you'll be with the man you love forever – lucky you.' I noted the slight hint of envy in her voice.

As I sat back down, waiting to be called down once the *barat* (groom's side) had arrived, the reality and finality of marriage hit me: was this really the beginning of my new life, for the rest of my life? My heart began to beat faster, but I dismissed it as nerves. I had a lavish celebration ahead of me, with people to smile at, beautiful jewellery to wear and a dowry to match.

Stop being silly, Somi! I told myself. This was what I'd wanted; no one forced me here, and I'd planned each moment of the day, or at least the moments that were in my control. A knock on the door brought my mind back into the room. My cousin had come to tell me it was time. I took a sip of water, put on my ridiculous

Jimmy Choos with their four-inch heels, and was met at the door by my father. At the time, few brides in Pakistan had their father give them away in the Western tradition, but it felt natural to me.

'I'm proud of you,' said Daddy.

'Why, Daddy? I'm only getting married!'

I knew in my heart that his pride was laced with disappointment. He'd wanted me to go to London and become a barrister or do my master's degree in law, but instead I was marrying a man he didn't especially like. Yet he still took the time to reassure me that he'd have my back. A wave of sadness swept over me, and suddenly I was on the verge of tears. I remembered all the Urdu films I'd seen where a bride leaving her father's home on her wedding day starts crying dramatically. I'd always thought I wouldn't be like that, but here I was.

Arm-in-arm with Daddy, I walked precariously in my heels on the springy red carpet, as Pachelbel's Canon in D Major played softly. My heart was thumping and I was fighting back tears. I felt such mixed emotions: excitement, as I saw past the crowds to Juni, waiting for me; and sadness that I'd be leaving my parents' home. Keeping a smile plastered on my face, I brushed past Nani Mummy and she clasped my hand with her fragile fingers. Her gaze was full of tenderness and support, but I felt as if the other two hundred pairs of eyes in the ballroom were watching me with a mix of envy and wonder, whispering to each other and making judgements about me, my outfit and my decisions.

It all began to feel less scary as I got closer to Juni. As he rose from the regal red velvet sofa, surrounded by a halo of floral arrangements, he broke into a smile and I caught sight of his heart-melting dimples. On a stage covered with Persian carpets, Juni and I sat together on the large Victorian-style sofa, greeting family members, friends and people I'd never seen or heard of before. As hundreds of guests traipsed past, I felt like a showpiece. I was wearing a long skirt called a *langha*: made of ivory silk, it looked beautiful, but it was uncomfortable to sit in for hours, and my jaw hurt from the constant smiling.

With the *nikkah* (religious ceremony), the wedding was a long, drawn-out event, and the entire evening went by in a blur until *ruksati*, the moment a bride leaves her parents' home to embark on her new life. I'd seen so many brides weeping when the time came, and I didn't want to be one of them. I linked arms with Juni and we walked along the corridor and down the steps to the waiting car. My parents stood back as my new 'family' embraced me, welcoming me into the large Mercedes decorated with ribbons and flowers. We sat in the back while Naseem Aunty sat in front with the driver. Looking out of the window, I saw Nani Mummy as we drove away, with tears falling unapologetically down her face, and I cried. Standing next to her, my parents smiled and waved. It felt so strange. I was with the man I wanted to spend my life with, and I should have been happy to be a part of his family, yet I felt intense despair. All I wanted to do was jump out of the car and hug Nani Mummy and my mother and father.

We went to Juni's parents' house for ritual readings from the Quran and to drink milk that had been blessed, before we returned to the bridal suite, where we were staying for the next couple of nights. Finally, I could take off the heavy outfit, make-up and the thousand hairpins that had been holding up my hair. Exhausted, Juni and I collapsed onto the flower-adorned bed and fell asleep instantly.

And that was it, the beginning of my new life and the end of my old one. It was a life I had chosen, and I felt happy to be with the man I loved, but I also felt anxious that marriage might not lead to the freedom I craved. Looking back, I realise that my decision to marry so young was a direct contradiction of my deep desire for unconformity – but falling in love had changed everything. If I wanted to be with Juni, I had no choice but to marry him, so I had decided to conform just a little.

My family's wedding ubtan (face and body scrub)

A beauty preparation (pictured on previous page) that just had to be included, as my mother made it when I got married. Amba haldi, *also known as mango-ginger or wild turmeric, is closely related to regular turmeric and can be found in some Indian shops. It is used in skincare for its healing properties, but if you can't find it, just omit it – don't use regular turmeric as it will stain your skin. Look for sandalwood powder in Asian shops or online.*

Prep time: 2–3 days
Makes about 500 g (1 lb 2 oz)

- 450 g (2 cups) red split lentils (masoor daal)
- 250 ml (1 cup) whole (full-cream) milk
- zest from 2 oranges, peeled off in strips
- 2 egg whites
- juice of 2 lemons
- handful of edible dried organic rose petals
- 55 g (2 oz) rolled (porridge) oats
- 55 g (2 oz) sandalwood powder
- 1 tablespoon *amba haldi* powder – optional

Mummy originally found this ubtan recipe in some obscure women's magazine in 1969 – she still has the tattered cutting – but it has been in our family ever since, evolving as we added our own ingredients.

- On day one, soak the lentils in the milk overnight.
- The next day, drain the lentils, spread them out on paper towels and leave in a warm place – either near a fireplace, in a warm (switched off) oven or in the sun – to dry completely.
- Do the same with the orange peel. It should take between 12 and 24 hours for them both to dry, depending on the temperature and humidity.
- When the lentils and orange peel are dry, put the egg whites into a bowl and whisk lightly, just until frothy. Tip the daal into the bowl and stir to coat all over, then spread out on paper towels and leave in a warm place to dry again – this should take about half a day.
- Now soak the lentils in the lemon juice for about 1 hour, then drain and spread out on a baking tray lined with paper towels. Leave to dry in a warm place for a third and final time. You need to make sure the lentils are completely dry before grinding them, or the residual moisture will make the scrub go mouldy over time.
- Grind the dried orange peel and rose petals to a fine powder in an electric grinder and set aside.
- Using a food processor (or working in batches in an electric grinder), blitz the lentils and the rolled oats to a fine powder. Add the ground orange peel and rose petals, along with the sandalwood powder and *amba haldi* (if using). Either blend everything together in the food processor or mix thoroughly in a large bowl.
- Transfer to an airtight jar and keep in a cool, dry place for up to 10 days, or in the fridge for up to a month.
- To make into a scrub, mix with the following ingredients, depending on skin type. For one full face application, take 2 tablespoons of the scrub and, for dry skin, add enough fresh cream to make a thick paste, plus a few drops of almond oil. If skin is oily, add 1 tablespoon of rose water and ½ tablespoon each of lemon juice and yoghurt; for combination skin, use the same ingredients as for oily skin, plus a few drops of coconut oil.
- Leave the scrub on your face (or body) as a mask for 10–15 minutes, until it feels dry but not tight on the skin, then gently scrub off, working in the direction of the heart. Don't wash your face (or body) with soap, just rinse and pat dry – your skin should be smooth, glowing and soft.

A bride's panjiri (semolina granola)

Although this is based on the ladoo *(sweets) my mother made for my wedding, rather than using more ghee to make the nut and semolina mixture into sweets, I like to eat it as a granola, without milk. Lotus seeds and Arabic gum crystals can be found online and at some Asian or Middle Eastern supermarkets.*

Prep time: 15 minutes
Cooking time: 15 minutes
Makes 1 x 500 ml (2 cup) jar

- 2 tablespoons coconut flakes
- 2 tablespoons ghee
- 2 tablespoons unsalted pistachios, roughly chopped
- 2 tablespoons unsalted almonds, roughly chopped
- 2 teaspoons Arabic gum crystals
- 2 tablespoons lotus seeds (*makhana*)
- 6 green cardamom pods, cracked open, seeds extracted and ground
- 200 g (1 cup) coarse semolina
- 2 tablespoons dried apricots, roughly chopped
- 55 g (¼ cup) caster (superfine) sugar

- Roast the coconut flakes in a dry wok or frying pan over medium heat until light brown, then remove from the pan and set aside.
- In the same pan, heat 1 tablespoon of the ghee and fry the nuts, stirring frequently, until they are light brown, then set aside on paper towels.
- Next, fry the Arabic gum crystals until puffy, then set those aside on paper towels too. Do the same with the lotus seeds.
- Add the remaining ghee to the pan and reduce the heat to very low, then toss in the cardamom and semolina and fry for 5 minutes, stirring it constantly so it doesn't burn on the base of the pan.
- As soon as the semolina turns medium brown, stir in the reserved coconut, nuts, Arabic gum and lotus seeds, along with the apricots and sugar.
- Once everything is just warmed through – make sure the sugar doesn't melt – turn off the heat and allow the *panjiri* to cool before serving. It will keep in an airtight container for up to 3 days.

Traditionally, panjiri is given as a therapeutic offering or nutritious snack.

CHAPTER 15

Goodbye, Nani Mummy

I learn that home isn't always
a place for sharing happiness.
When I lose Nani Mummy,
I learn that food is a part of
my mourning and has a role to
play in solemn occasions too.

Karachi, December 1996–January 1997

THE HONEYMOON IS OVER

We spent our honeymoon in Sri Lanka, but the days after we returned were taken up with the seemingly endless events my mother-in-law had planned for me to meet her relatives. For these, I had to dress up in the glitzy outfits she'd bought me as part of my wedding *barri* – the presents given to the bride by the groom's family.

Before we left for our honeymoon, our friends and family had given us traditional gifts of *salaami* money at our *valima*, to help us build our new life together, and Naseem Aunty had held it for safekeeping. When we got back, we wanted to use the money to repay our credit cards after the honeymoon, and to put towards a deposit for a flat if we were to move out in the future. But when Juni reluctantly went to ask his mother for the money, he returned with the news that she wouldn't be giving it to us.

'What? Why on earth not? It's our wedding gift! Surely she can't just keep it?' I said.

'You can't talk to her about it because she's made up her mind,' Juni replied, looking down sheepishly.

'What's her reasoning for keeping the money, Juni?'

'Mama says that since they spent so much on the *valima*, they'll be keeping this money for themselves. What's wrong with that?'

'What's wrong with it is that it was our wedding gift from our families, to wish us well in our new life together.'

Because I didn't want a fight, we didn't talk about it again. But that was the beginning of the sour feelings between me and my mother-in-law. There was an air of discomfort that I couldn't shake – a tacit understanding that everything I brought into the home was somehow automatically hers.

The only sanctuary was Juni's room, which was now our bedroom; my parents had given us a new bed with a beautiful green wooden headboard, Liberty-print bed linen and a handwoven throw. The coastal breeze and the roar of the surf would seep through the cracks of our window at night.

The first few mornings I was excited by the prospect of waking up to a view of the Arabian Sea, and I'd get up earlier than Juni to watch the waves rolling in, caressing the silver sands of Seaview Beach, and the flocks of seagulls on the horizon. It reminded me of my childhood at sea, and the salty air would fill my senses with nostalgic comfort.

The winter had been colder than usual. It was the 31st of January, a Friday. At about 5.30 in the morning, I stirred in bed, my sleep interrupted by the faint ringing of the phone in my in-laws' bedroom. I wondered why anyone would call so early and my heart jumped. *What if it's bad news? What if…*

There was a knock on our bedroom door and I heard my mother-in-law's voice: 'Somi? Wake up, Somi.' As I opened the door, I rubbed my eyes and saw her solemn expression. She put her hand on my shoulder and squeezed it gently.

'Somi, your Nani's passed away.'

I heard the words but they didn't make sense. The world around me seemed to pause – I didn't notice Juni's consoling words or my in-laws' hugs. It had been a while since I last saw Nani Mummy but she had seemed so full of life that I never imagined she'd go downhill so fast. I racked my brain, trying to remember when I'd last spoken to Nani Mummy. Closing my eyes, I saw her face at the wedding and I felt the hot sting of tears. I thought back to that day, when Juni and I were seated on the stage, being presented to the guests at our *valima*. I was eating biryani from a white scalloped porcelain plate, nibbling at pieces of chicken and trying to avoid spoiling my lipstick. As Nani Mummy walked over, the folds of her grey satin sari glistened under the fairy lights. She sat down next to me and held my henna-covered hands.

'Popplu, so you're finally married. You happy now?' She held on a little tighter, and my rings pinched as she squeezed my hand.

'Yes, Nani Mummy, finally,' I said, 'I'm happy!'

'I'm glad. Now you can stop worrying – everything will be ok.'

She had a plate of biryani too, and as she stuck her fork into a piece of chicken, she said: 'Remember the time we went to that family wedding and I spotted a rather big black cardamom on a plate?'

'Ah yes – and it wasn't black cardamom at all…' I replied.

'…it was a dead cockroach!' we chorused, collapsing into laughter.

'Thank God we didn't eat it!' I said.

'Hmm, I wonder what a cooked cockroach tastes like?' she mused, throwing her head back and laughing.

Did I speak to her again after that? I couldn't remember. *Was that the last meal we shared?*

While I struggled to absorb the news, I knew we also had to deal with the practicalities of death, and I called my mother to find out about the arrangements for the burial. She was as stoic as ever, but her voice was shaky, and I knew she was only just holding it together as she tried to reassure me: 'We're of strong stock, Somi. Nani Mummy was the same. We will get through this, and you know she's in a better place.'

Juni and I drove to Nani Mummy's house and I joined the women of our family who had congregated in her bedroom. Mummy couldn't face seeing her mother's body, but I knew that Nani Mummy would want me to be there. She always said: 'Be present. Be strong.' It still hadn't sunk in that she was gone, and I also needed to see her body to accept the reality of her death.

Her body was on the bed, and she looked the same as she always did when I walked into her room, her heavily veined hands crossed over her round belly, her hair perfectly coiffed. It seemed as if she would open her eyes at any moment and smile at me. But instead she lay there, still and pale, and with no jewellery. She always wore jewellery: either pink pearl studs surrounded by tiny diamonds or half-carat solitaire diamonds in her ears; and on her hands a pearl ring and the quarter-carat diamond deeply set in a gold band that she never took off her finger, which meant that soap got stuck in it when she washed her hands. 'This is Nana's – your great-grandmother gave it to him when we got married,' she'd told me once. 'It'll be yours when I'm gone.'

From somewhere seemingly far away, I heard the voice of one of Nani Mummy's nieces: 'Somi, come and help with her bathing and the ablutions.'

'Ok, but I'm not sure what to do,' I said.

Her body had been moved to the corner of the bed, undressed now and covered with white muslin. The distinctive smell of a Pakistani funeral hung in the air – the floral, sour and strangely comforting scents of camphor and incense. This was the room where I'd always felt safe. When my parents told me off, Nani Mummy would be sitting here, smiling and welcoming me with open arms.

Outside I could hear the chanting of prayer. The women had gathered where we used to sit with our chai and pakoras on hot days, overlooking Nani Mummy's prized petunias in planters on the verandah. Now all the furniture was pushed up against the walls, and the floor was covered with white sheets. The women sat cross-legged on the sheets, surrounded by large sacks filled with exactly ten thousand shiny tamarind seeds, to be used as counters for the prayers. As the women quietly read *Surah Ikhlas* from the Quran, the room echoed with the sound of the seeds being dropped onto plates and the sighs and wails that marked the end of each prayer. The air was thick with sandalwood incense. The women asked me to join them, but it looked almost clinical with the sheets laid out, and I couldn't bear to stay there. It was calmer in her bedroom, and I wanted to be closer to her body.

Surah Ikhlas was one of the first prayers Nani Mummy had taught me, and I thought back to the way she used to read *Ayat-ul-kursi* three times every night to protect us from anything bad happening, blowing the prayer up onto her finger and then twirling her finger three times in the air. Little rituals like these were particular to her, and I found myself doing the same as her body was carried in for bathing, so that all would be well.

In Nani Mummy's bathroom, as my aunts prepared to wash her body, I remembered how I'd helped her to bathe when she was sick, her feeble body naked on a plastic stool as she steadied herself by placing her hands on the tiles. A faint scent of Yardley's English Lavender mingled with the overpowering smell of the camphor the women were using to clean the body. As I watched them place her body on the tiled floor, I noticed that her face had grown paler and a distinct round white mark was visible on her forehead.

'What's that on Nani Mummy's forehead?'

'Oh that's called *nur*,' said one of my aunts, 'it means she's going to heaven because she was such good person.'

I didn't know if my aunt was just trying to console me and give me something positive to hold on to, but I accepted her explanation. While they washed Nani Mummy's body, I looked in the cabinet where she kept her powder puff and Max Factor nude lipstick. Opening the lipstick, I saw that the tip was worn down and I remembered how I used to make fun of the way the top bit of her lipsticks became flatter with each application. I smiled at the memory and returned it to the cabinet; I didn't want to disturb the way she'd left things.

When she was bathed and embalmed in camphor, we took her body back to the bed and wrapped it in fresh muslin. When the time came to cover her face, I was asked to do it. Her body seemed smaller but it glowed, as if all the pain and disease had left her shell of a body and disappeared. It comforted me to think that she wasn't suffering anymore. I kissed her forehead and covered her face for the last time. I knew that I'd never see her kind, soft face again, and I held back tears.

Then I left and did what I knew Nani Mummy would want me to do. I went to the kitchen where we used to cook together to make sure that the food was ready.

Food was important at funerals: it was all about feeding the mourners properly, so they had energy for the rituals, and celebrating the person's life with a meal. In the white tents where the food was being served, the caterers were laying out platters of *taftaan* flatbread and *janaza* (funeral) biryani. At funerals, there always seemed to be overcooked chicken bobbing out of saffron-coloured rice – but the caterers usually cut corners by using orange food colouring and lots of *kewra* (screwpine extract) to add a floral note that mimicked the flavour of real saffron. Nani Mummy and I would always turn our nose up at it. Making a biryani without saffron felt like cheating, and I couldn't help wondering how Nani Mummy would feel about a saffron-less biryani at her own funeral.

As I looked at the biryani on its big stainless-steel platters, I remembered that the last time I cooked with Nani Mummy was to make *bakra* (goat) biryani for Eid ul Azha.

Held each year after the Hajj pilgrimage, this festival involved making a sacrifice to honour the Hazrat Ibrahim (PBUH). Nani Mummy would get a goat a few weeks beforehand and each morning I'd hear its bleat and see its sweet, trusting face beneath my window as she fed it greens.

'Why do we have to do *qurbani* (sacrifice)?' I'd ask Nani Mummy. 'I don't like that we keep an animal like a pet and then kill it.'

'It's part of our religion, Somi. The goat is not a pet – it's a sacrifice we do in memory of Hazrat Ibrahim (PBUH) and to honour the sacrifice he was prepared to make.'

Nani Mummy was religious and she always followed rituals devoutly, finding a way to gently explain such things to me if I didn't understand them.

'Well, I still think it's sad!' I said. 'I don't want an animal to die.'

On the morning of Eid, I'd hear the final bleat of the goat as he was given his last meal, and by mid-morning the slaughterman and butcher would have done the deed. Later that day, I'd go to Nani Mummy's house and she'd be cooking biryani with goat meat from the sacrifice.

'Come and help me, Somi,' she'd say.

'No, I refuse to have anything to do with that meat!'

'Don't be silly – just help me chop the vegetables and choose the spices,' she'd say. 'We have to eat, don't we?'

I'd begin by finely chopping red onions and peeling ginger and garlic. We picked the spices carefully, as the intensity of red meat needed to be balanced with dark spices: the woody notes of star anise and the floral sweetness of cinnamon sticks, rather than the lighter and woodier cassia bark. She'd make a marinade of yoghurt, chopped coriander and mint, green chillies, ginger and garlic to tenderise the goat; sometimes she'd add grated raw papaya to break down the meat further.

Once the base of spices and onions was made, the meat would go in with its marinade. I'd refuse to look at it at first, but as it cooked the sweetness of the spices and the mouth-watering aroma of browned onions would soon break down my stubbornness.

When it was half cooked, she spooned in par-boiled rice and then poured over saffron soaked in hot milk, followed by a little *kewra* (screwpine extract), lots of herbs, ghee and slices of lemon. We'd make a paste of atta flour and water and roll it into a sausage shape to seal the lid on the pan and trap the steam.

'That keeps the steam inside, because we have to cook the biryani under *dum*,' she'd say.

'What's *dum*?' I asked.

'It's when you cook everything in the steam generated by the base of the dish. This technique infuses the spices and the flavour of the meat into the rice and the saffron into the meat,' she explained. 'It's a magical process that's been done for centuries. Traditionally, the dish is put into a pit filled with hot coals to cook, but we're going to do it in the oven.'

As the biryani cooked in the oven, the kitchen came alive with the perfume of dark, deep spices, and the rich gaminess of goat meat mingled with the sweet hay-like scent of basmati rice. When it was ready, I used a knife to break the seal and carefully removed the lid. Steam surged into the air, its intoxicating aroma reminiscent of the cut-grass, jasmine, roses and mint in my Nani's garden, then cleared to reveal perfectly cooked grains of rice standing on end, brightened with blobs of saffron. She stirred the biryani gently, explaining that I mustn't move the rice too much or else the grains would break.

The biryani at my Nani's funeral was nothing like hers. I went to see my mother, who was talking to some of the women inside.

'Mummy, the biryani is horrible. Nani Mummy wouldn't have liked it,' I said.

'Somi, this isn't the time.'

'I don't really care – this is her funeral and she'd hate the food.'

'People aren't here for food, they are here for prayers,' said Mummy, now getting slightly annoyed at my interruption.

'Oh, trust me, they are here for the food,' I said, as I pointed to where some of the men had already started eating, their plates piled high with biryani and raita.

While I was preoccupied with the men eating biryani, the prayers grew louder and I heard women calling out my grandmother's name. It was time for the men to take the body for burial. I looked back and saw six men from the family, including my father and my uncle, with Nani Mummy's body on a cane carrier, taking it down the steps past her petunias and marigolds in their terracotta pots.

Someone nudged me to read *Surah Fatheha*, the prayer for when the body is taken to the burial ground – but I just stood there, unable to move or speak. This would be the last time she'd leave her home, never to return.

Looking up at the carrier, I suddenly felt ridiculous for being angry about the biryani. *Why hadn't I sat with her body in the room until it was time?* I began to run towards the carrier, past the *motia* jasmine she loved so much, past her light-blue Fiat, to the gate.

'Nani Mummy! Come back, please come back!' I shouted, as tears rolled down my face and my neck. My mother ran after me and pulled me to her, holding me tight.

'Why can't I go to the burial, I want to go,' I screamed.

'Somi, women can't go to the burial – you know that. It's not allowed,' said Mummy, 'You have to pray from home and bless her spirit.'

'Well that's totally unfair! Why is everything so unfair? I hate you all for not letting me go for the burial.'

As the gate closed, I held on to it and shook it. Sobbing unconsolably, my heart felt as if it had sunk deep underground.

Nani Mummy died a day before her seventy-second birthday, leaving a gaping hole in my life.

SUNSET WALKS AND FROZEN PARATHAS

After Nani Mummy died, I went nearly every day to see my mother, and one day she came over to me and put something in my hand.

'She wanted you to have this,' said Mummy, handing me Nana's diamond solitaire ring that Nani Mummy always wore.

'Oh,' I said, looking at its glittering surface.

I slipped the ring onto my right index finger. It was loose, but I put another ring over it to stop it from slipping off. When I looked at it closely, I could still see some soap lodged in the setting.

Over the next few months I tried to cope with Nani Mummy's loss in my own way. I'd ask Juni to take me down to the beach at sunset and I'd walk barefoot on the silver sand, gazing at the sky. As a ring of fire surrounded the huge tangerine sun and it slowly sank below the horizon, it reminded me of the Kino oranges Nani Mummy and I would eat together under the winter sun. I'd keep walking until the rays of light faded into the sepia shades of a star-studded night sky.

I tried to remember small details about Nani Mummy. I could almost feel the softness of the saris in her cupboard and their silkiness against my nose as I breathed in their scent. I could almost smell the faint powderiness of lavender and feel the caress of chiffon on my cheek, reminding me of her wrinkly, soft hands. Closing my eyes, I could see her Singer sewing machine with white thread through the needle, her make-up still standing on the windowsill next to her dressing table.

I could see her behind my closed eyes; she was there in the kitchen, cooking *firni*, her ground rice dessert that was like a balm to my soul. She was crouching over the white enamel stove, surrounded by wisps of cardamom-infused smoke. As she turned around, she opened her mouth to say something – I could barely hear her voice, and she was pointing to the freezer.

The next day I went to her house. There were sheets thrown over the sofas and the bed, and her belongings were in boxes. I went straight to the kitchen and opened the freezer. In the first section I saw a pile of parathas wrapped in plastic, with a label written in Urdu, in her handwriting: 'Aloo paratha, made 10.09.1996'. I took out a paratha, defrosted and reheated it. As I sat on the sofa by the window, dappled winter sun shone through her guava trees and her pet parakeets sang in the distance. I bit into one of the last things she'd cooked. It tasted of her love and my salty tears.

Goodbye biryani

It takes time to say goodbye. I cooked this biryani (pictured overleaf) soon after my Nani passed; the rose petals and jasmine are a homage to her, as she loved growing these flowers. I usually serve my biryani with some beetroot raita on the side: just stir grated beetroot, roasted cumin seeds and chopped coriander (cilantro) and mint through plain yoghurt.

Prep time: 45 minutes + 1 hour soaking + marinating time, from 1 hour to overnight
Cooking time: about 1 hour 15 minutes
Serves 6

- 260 g (1 cup) full-fat Greek-style yoghurt
- 1 tablespoon chopped coriander (cilantro)
- 1 tablespoon chopped mint
- 1 green chilli, deseeded and chopped
- 1 tablespoon finely grated ginger
- 1 tablespoon crushed garlic
- 1 teaspoon salt, plus extra to taste
- ½ teaspoon Kashmiri chilli powder
- ¼ teaspoon turmeric powder
- ¼ nutmeg, ground
- 1 piece mace, ground
- 400 g (14 oz) skinless chicken breast or thigh fillets, cut into chunks
- 300 g (1½ cups) basmati rice
- 3 tablespoons sunflower oil
- 1 tablespoon ghee
- 6 green cardamom pods, bruised
- 1 black cardamom pods, bruised
- 1 cinnamon stick
- 2 star anise
- 2 bay leaves
- 1 teaspoon coriander seeds
- 1 teaspoon cumin seeds
- ½ teaspoon fennel seeds
- 1 large red onion, finely chopped
- 3 large tomatoes, coarsely grated, skins discarded

For the steaming and finishing

- 2 large pinches of saffron threads
- 1 ice cube
- 1 tablespoon screwpine extract (*kewra*) or rose water
- 1 tablespoon melted ghee
- 1 lemon, cut into slices
- a few mint leaves
- 1 tablespoon edible dried or fresh organic rose petals or buds
- 1 tablespoon edible dried or fresh organic jasmine buds

- In a large bowl, mix the yoghurt with the coriander, mint, green chilli, ginger, garlic, salt, chilli powder, turmeric, nutmeg and mace. Add the chicken and stir to coat, then leave to marinate in the fridge for 1 hour or overnight.
- When you're ready to start cooking the biryani, rinse the rice, then leave it to soak in a bowl of water for at least 1 hour.
- Put the saffron into a small bowl with the ice cube and leave to melt and infuse while you cook the base of the biryani.
- Heat the oil and ghee in a large, heavy-based saucepan with a tight-fitting lid over medium heat. When it is hot, add the green and black cardamom pods, cinnamon stick, star anise and bay leaves, together with the coriander, cumin and fennel seeds. Let them splutter and fragrance the oil for a minute or so, then add the onion and cook, stirring often, for 8–10 minutes or until light brown.
- Now add the tomatoes, increase the heat to high, and stir until the oil rises to the surface, about 10–12 minutes. Add the chicken with its marinade and cook until dryish and the oil rises to the surface again, about 10 minutes.
- Meanwhile, in another saucepan, parboil the rice for 5 minutes, then drain.
- Cover the chicken with a lid and cook for a further 10 minutes. You should end up with a thick curry with a film of oil on the top. If it seems to be getting too thick at any stage, add a few splashes of water, reduce the heat to low and cook until the oil rises back to the surface again. Taste and adjust the seasoning if needed. When it's ready, turn the heat down to very low.
- For the steaming, spoon the par-boiled rice on top of the chicken curry, then sprinkle with the saffron water, screwpine extract or rose water and ghee. Top with the lemon slices and mint.
- Cover the pan with foil, sealing it firmly around the edges, then cover with the lid and let the biryani cook in its own steam over a very low heat for about 5–7 minutes – if you have a heat diffuser it will help the rice to cook evenly. The key thing to look for is that when you remove the foil, steam should rise from the pan and the rice grains should be standing on end. Anything further and the rice will be overcooked.
- When the biryani is ready, use a dessertspoon to stir the rice into the chicken curry carefully, so as not to break the rice. Sprinkle with the rose petals or buds and jasmine buds before serving.

CHAPTER 16

Bitter, dark lemons

I learn that the kitchen can be a place where two women exert their power and indulge in conflicts – but as I begin cooking in my new home, I find peace and comfort. Memories of enjoying food with loved ones help me through my grief.

Karachi, Spring/Summer 1997

THE KITCHEN IS A BATTLEGROUND

I've never been able to clearly recall the months after Nani Mummy passed away. I'd begun a new life with the man I loved, the man who was meant to be my soulmate, but I'd also lost the person who I felt could have guided me through this transition.

Food had been such an intrinsic part of the time I spent with Nani Mummy: the buying of it, the cooking of it and the eating of it. It had been such a huge part of my childhood and my family's travels as well, so when I moved in with my in-laws, it was natural for me to crave the same freedom in the kitchen that I'd grown up with. I'd felt free in my grandmother's and my mother's kitchens, but here I was looked on with suspicion. My mother-in-law was particular about the way she cooked and cleaned, and the sort of food she served her family; I couldn't just take over.

Whenever I went into the kitchen, Naseem Aunty was there, and I felt uncomfortable in her presence as she always told me how to do things. She used a lot of oil in her food and there'd often be an oily smell of fried eggs or parathas in the air, and dirty dishes in the sink. The smell would cling to my clothes and the oil would stick to my fingers if I tried to clean a surface to prepare my food.

'Oh, don't clean the counters, the girl will come tomorrow and do it,' she'd say, expecting me to cook in a messy kitchen because she was paying the cleaning girl and wanted to get her money's worth.

One evening, when I was cooking chicken karahi, one of Juni's favourite dishes, she came into the kitchen and walked over to the stove.

'I wouldn't add roasted cumin to my karahi,' she said, lifting her chin up and peering into my pan.

'Juni's had it before – he loves it.'

'Hmm, well I think it makes it taste bitter; I never add it.'

'I only add it at the end,' I said.

'Well, it looks a bit dark, doesn't it?' she observed.

'Mummy taught me to extract all the flavour out of it.'

Naseem Aunty just raised an eyebrow and went to make herself a cup of tea, lingering in the kitchen rather longer than she usually would.

Sometimes I'd see that my pans had been moved, and they'd end up dented or scratched. Naseem Aunty always insisted it wasn't her, but that maybe it was her cleaner and she'd have a word with them – but I don't think she ever did.

In the evenings, we'd have to eat with Juni's parents in their bedroom, which felt like a step too far. We'd sit down to dinner around the food trolley next to their bed and Juni would go on about how much his mother's food was the best, which only made me more determined to get Juni to notice that his wife was a better cook.

As I battled with the pain of loss, my in-laws left me to mourn in peace – with no more family parties to face, I lived each day as it came, and I began to find the courage to raise the subject of moving out. It was a small flat we were sharing with Juni's parents and his younger brother, and after the loss of my grandmother, it became evident that there wasn't really anywhere for me to be alone and grieve for her. And, as much as I wanted to make Juni happy, our lack of time together as a couple was pulling us apart.

My conviction grew stronger by the day: 'I think we do need our own place, Juni. I don't mind living near to your parents, but it would be good for us to have our own home.'

But he was adamant: 'No, absolutely not. My parents want us here. Mama wants to enjoy seeing me married and get to know you. I've told you before – we can maybe think about moving out in a couple of years.'

'Look, I understand your reasons, but I'd like you to think of us as a married couple now; we're too old to stay with parents.'

'Mama loves you – you know that. You don't even have to cook, and you know Mama is the best cook in the world. She can teach you a thing or two!' Juni replied.

'The thing is, Juni, I want to cook,' I said. 'And I know how to cook!' He was oblivious to the silent rivalry between his mother and me, and how easily we'd slipped into the habit of competing for his affection through food.

In my search for some sort of freedom from expectations, I'd only discovered more of them – I now faced the expectations of a mother-in-law and a husband. This new home wasn't my home, and I resented that.

LOSS AND THE KITCHEN

If there is one thing I do remember about the time after Nani Mummy died, it was the intense desire to recreate her recipes. On any evenings that my in-laws went out with friends, they would leave cooked food for us, but instead I'd take the opportunity to cook unhindered, with my own pans, spices and utensils, carving out a space on the kitchen counter.

I'd been searching for the recipes that Nani Mummy cooked, but no one knew how to cook them, so I began calling my mother every day – just as she had done with her own mother for many years when she first got married. Mummy dictated methods to me over the phone with her usual vague measurements – 'a pinch' of this, or 'a little' of that – but I pieced together the recipes by writing down the ingredients and trying to cook them with *andaza*, much like she did. Sometimes I spent days just jotting down flavours I remembered from the simple lunches she made. I tried to recall Nani Mummy's matter-of-fact way of cooking, talking to me as she pulled out ingredients from the fridge or store cupboard. I even found myself craving dishes I didn't like: chana daal with onions, or turnip and mutton.

By cooking some of Nani Mummy's food in my mother-in-law's kitchen, I created a small sacred space for myself. I was only twenty-three; this was the first time I'd lost someone I dearly loved, and I'd just left the security of my parents' home, but food helped me to find moments of connection and consolation – it was my link to home.

When I was in my teens, Nani Mummy and I would go on monthly food adventures and sometimes Mummy would join us too. Usually, we'd go to Hyderabadi Colony, a vibrant area of Karachi where Hyderabadi migrants settled after partition. Hyderabadi cuisine is almost an artform, originating from royal abundance under the Delhi Sultanate and later incorporating Mughal, Turkish and Arabic influences, and the migrants brought their food traditions with them. The first businesses that sprouted in the area sold pickles and dishes such as *mirchi ka saalan* (chilli curry), *bhagar-e-baingan* (stuffed aubergines, slow-cooked in a masala of poppy seeds, peanuts, tamarind and coconut), *khatti* (sweet-and-sour) daal, *double ka meetha* (bread pudding with saffron and pistachios baked in a creamy milky custard) and, my favourite, *khubani ka meetha* (Hunza apricot dessert). These regional dishes were nothing like the Punjabi food that Nani Mummy cooked or the Awadhi food that Dadi cooked – but they inspired us to create our own versions at home. Shops spilled out onto the streets, their glass cabinets topped with precarious stacks of plastic pickle jars with red and orange plastic lids, the sharp sting of vinegar in the air. From afar, we'd spot the samosa stall, where a large vat of oil was set over a fierce fire, and as we came closer, the smell of freshly fried samosas would make our mouths water. I'd have four of them, their crispy shells enclosing a tangle of red onions, herbs and *powa* (dried flattened rice) – this would soak up all the moisture from the onions, leaving the pastry crunchy.

My main motivation for going shopping here were the Hyderabadi bangles that Nani Mummy would buy me – they'd click together on my arms and make me feel like a princess. Covered with colourful lacquer, and embedded with mirror fragments and diamanté, they could be found in shades to match every outfit. I'd be mesmerised by the play of light from the display units on the tiny mirrors on the bangles, creating stars of light on the walls.

But it was the food stalls that left a lasting impression. I was intrigued by the large *degchi* cooking pots, each filled to the brim with Hyderabadi delicacies simmering over flickering gas flames. We'd never eat there; we'd just have plastic bags filled with the dishes to take home and freeze.

'Give me half a kilo of *bhagar-e-baingan* and one kilo of *mirchi ka saalan*, and divide them into two bags each,' Nani Mummy would say; the desserts would be packed up in Tupperware containers she'd brought from home.

I tried to recall Nani Mummy's matter-of-fact way of cooking, talking to me as she pulled out ingredients from the fridge or store cupboard.

People who did eat there perched on plastic chairs around large tables laden with ten or more different dishes in massive portions. I'd watch big groups laughing and eating as we waited for our order, wondering how they could eat so much. At home, as much as we were fond of our food, we never ate big portions, preferring to graze on small portions and lots of different flavours.

Nani Mummy and Mummy would bring home the food, but they wouldn't eat it until they'd spent some time deciphering the ingredients. It was difficult getting recipes from any of our Hyderabadi friends because no one ever shared them – it was as if there was some kind of pact never to give away Hyderabadi cooking secrets.

'Let's get the *mirchi ka saalan* out,' Mummy would say, 'I want to taste it and figure out how they make it.'

As Nani Mummy poured it into a bowl, the air would be flooded with the dish's complex spicing, and I couldn't imagine how anyone could identify such an array of ingredients, but Mummy always could.

'Ah, I can tell they use peanut oil to make this,' Mummy would say, as she took a bite and flicked her tongue over her palate to dissipate the flavours around her mouth, 'and they've used roasted cumin and coriander, plus roasted peanuts, but I can tell there is a hint of fenugreek too.'

As they scrutinised the dishes one by one, neither of them wrote anything down; both Nani Mummy and Mummy cooked from memory and felt no need to write down recipes, not even ones they'd assembled by taste.

I missed exploring flavours with them. Even though I didn't realise it then, I was building memories of the distinct divisions of flavour that made up the cuisine I knew as Pakistani. Karachi was a sub-continent within a city, a melting pot of the flavours of the Indian sub-continent created through migration, and I felt privileged to have grown up in a city that offered such a variety of food experiences.

RICE AND PICKLES

Months after Nani Mummy had passed away, neither my mother nor her brother (my maternal uncle, Khawar Mamo) could face packing up her belongings. And even though I didn't live with my parents anymore, I couldn't find it in my heart to visit, knowing that Nani Mummy wouldn't be there.

My parents had built their own house next door to Nani Mummy's, on the plot my mother had inherited from her father. Designed by Khawar Mamo, who was an architect, it was a beautiful house, with tall corner windows and dark rosewood floors; Khawar Mamo and his family lived in a separate part of Nani Mummy's house.

After she died, my father and uncle decided to sell both houses at the same time – partly because the neighbourhood was becoming more commercialised, and partly because the place was full of poignant memories.

Finally, my father, aunt and uncle made a start on packing up Nani Mummy's things, and when the time came to clear the house, I mustered the courage to go over. I wasn't looking forward to this, but it had to be done.

Everything looked the same as it always did. I knew the *mali* (gardener) had been tending to the grounds, but seeing the petunias and snapdragons thriving, and her beloved *motia* jasmine full of buds that would open in the evening, still took me aback. We used to go to the nursery together every season to pick up small seedlings and bedding plants and create rainbow arrangements in the planters. Seeing her light-blue Fiat parked in the driveway, I remembered all the times we'd driven to Abajaan's house or the markets.

I walked past the mango trees and the now-empty parakeet cage to the back door. As I opened it, I was met by a stale, musty smell – a mix of mothballs, neglect and something I couldn't quite place, something acidic and almost bitter, like old vinegar. There were cobwebs on the white enamel cooker and a startled house lizard stared down at me from one of the walls. I hated those lizards. Over the years, a few had fallen off the ceiling of the verandah and down my back, their tails separating from the shock and wiggling about as if they had a life of their own. I shuddered.

I wasn't sure what I was meant to be doing here; no one had given me instructions, and I felt a little useless. My mother had said vaguely that I was to sort out the cupboards in the kitchen. I decided to trust my judgement.

I put down my bag on the familiar green sofa, and dust rose from it. I began opening the kitchen cabinets. Most of the food has been cleared out, but a few plates and cups remained. I took them out and started to clean the shelves. One by one, I went through each cabinet, emptying the kitchen of memories and moments long gone: plates we'd eaten from, the Pyrex bowls that Nani Mummy used for serving her pullao.

In the store cupboard, I found a jar of rice infested with tiny insects. Each week, she refilled the jar with basmati from the large sack at the market, and I remembered how she always soaked and washed her rice assiduously.

'Why on earth do you wash the rice so much, Nani Mummy?' I'd ask.

'You've got to get rid of any debris from the sacks,' she'd say. 'Also, as the sack rubs on the rice, it breaks down the starch – and when you wash it, it rinses that away too.'

'And you soak it so that each grain absorbs water, making it long, fragrant and fluffy,' she'd say. 'We won't have stodgy rice in this house – that's why your mother cooks perfect rice. I taught her how!'

I saw the reflection of a faint smile on my face in the glass jar as I thought about my family and our obsession with perfect rice.

As I erased the history of this kitchen, my heart sank at the finality of it all. The reality of Nani Mummy's absence was intensified by this empty kitchen with its bare shelves. She really was gone, and her kitchen was clear of the things she lived for: spices, daal and rice – and the ability to make them into meals to feed the souls of those she loved.

When I got to the large rosewood pickle cabinet on the other side of the kitchen, I realised it still had something in it. I slid open the glass door and was hit by a waft of the same acidic smell that had struck me as I had walked in, but it was more intense – it seemed to be escaping from a glass jar, the only one left on the shelf, and there was something dark inside it. Wary of the cockroaches that lurk in such dark spaces, I reached cautiously into the cabinet and pulled out the jar. It was one of those Nani Mummy used to make her pickles in, and it contained preserved lemons that had turned brown and murky with age. A thick, hazy liquid embalmed the lemons, but there was no sign of any mould. As I turned it round in my hands, I saw a tiny piece of masking tape with her handwriting on it: 'For Somi'. My mind raced. *When had she made these? Was she planning to give the jar to me before she died or did she expect me to find it later?*

I sat there for what felt like hours just staring at the jar. I remembered all she'd taught me about preserving and pickling, and how much joy it had given me as a teenager. At the time I hadn't really appreciated the beauty and the magic of it all. Left to create their own ecosystem, these lemons hadn't decayed, but had come alive as the salt drew out their juices and the lactic acid in the brine preserved them.

Age had changed the colour of those tiny, bright *desi* lemons from Nani Mummy's tree into darker version of themselves – a repository of moments and memories. I longed to open the jar, but didn't want to disturb the story of these lemons, the last to be picked and preserved by my grandmother. I slipped the jar into my bag and left with tears in my eyes.

MOVING OUT

Back in the kitchen at my in-laws' flat, I couldn't find the space to cook, either emotionally or physically. I walked into the kitchen one morning and Naseem Aunty was there, making parathas.

'*Beta*, when do you think you and Juni will have children?' she asked.

'We haven't talked about it yet,' I replied, surprised she'd sprung this on me. 'Besides, Naseem Aunty, we're really quite young.'

'Twenty-three isn't that young; many girls are mothers at your age,' she replied, casually tossing a paratha onto the *tawa* griddle pan, 'I think it'll help you as a couple. Also, *beta*, you can call me Mama.'

I couldn't call anyone else mother – I knew that, but I kept quiet.

'We can't wait to have grandchildren,' she continued, 'And we don't mind, you can still work with your father once you finish college, and I'll bring up the children.'

We'd only been married for six months – and I had no desire to have children right away – but the very idea of her bringing up my children infuriated me.

That evening, I told Juni about our conversation: 'Juni, your mother wants us to have kids now.'

'Oh, don't worry, she's just wanting grandchildren. It's not that bad an idea, though. Maybe we should talk about it?'

'Juni, I'd like our own home first, please. We aren't even independent – you can't expect me to have a kid here. Please, I'm serious, let's start looking for a flat. I'm unhappy here. Your mother constantly wants to be involved in our lives. I understand that she loves you, Juni, but I need space to grow with you.'

I'll never know how or why he agreed, maybe it was the sheer desperation that was written all over my face.

'Ok, we'll look into it, but you'd better not say anything to Mama. I'm still not totally sure, but let's take it as it comes – you must promise me that we'll find a flat that's within walking distance.'

That was all the permission I needed, and I became obsessed with finding a flat. I spent the next few weeks chasing estate agents, talking to my parents about helping out with the initial deposit. I felt crippled by Juni's demand that we stay close to his parents, as there wasn't much choice in the area.

At first, every apartment I viewed was shabby and surrounded by rubbish heaps or unfinished roads, but finally I found the right place: it was in a brand new block of flats, only ten minutes' walk away.

'Leave it to me – don't tell Mama anything,' he made me promise.

And so I did.

Aunty Naseem continued to talk about her plans for us while we lived there, and it felt deceitful to say nothing, yet I slowly packed my bags on the sly and started shopping for curtains and sofas.

The day when we were due to leave drew closer, and I realised that Juni still hadn't told his mother we were moving out. As much as I hated living there, it didn't seem fair that my in-laws didn't know, and I confronted him about it.

'I can't tell her; she'd be crushed,' he said.

'I don't understand. We will only be ten minutes down the road,' I said. 'We can visit every day, if she likes – but who wouldn't want their newly married son and his wife to thrive on their own?'

The evening before we moved out, I returned from dinner at my parents to find that Juni wasn't in our room. I heard crying from my in-laws' room, so I knocked on the door and let myself in. Naseem Aunty was letting out small sobs, her face buried in her hands as she sat next to Juni, his arms around her.

'Somi, you'd better leave,' said a solemn-looking Juni.

'What's wrong?'

'I'm talking to Mama. Please leave. Now,' he said firmly.

I went to my room, closed the door and waited. *Would she let us go? Surely, she couldn't stop us?*

Around midnight, Juni returned to our room.

'We need to pack up and leave in the morning,' he said.

'What? Just like that?'

'She wants us gone, and please do not try talking to her. She wants nothing to do with you,' Juni said. His voice was broken and hoarse.

He got into bed, turned his back to me and went to asleep.

NEW HOME, OLD HABITS

Country Club Apartments was a high-rise development, a new style of apartments in the Sea View area of Clifton. We'd rented a small one-bedroom apartment, with terrazzo floors and a simple functional kitchen. From the eighth floor the view was spectacular, and both the lounge and our bedroom overlooked the sea. After just a week in our new home, I felt free to be myself.

Juni had started a new job with a local bank, and each morning I'd get up early and make him breakfast: pancakes and parathas, sometimes boiled eggs and spicy potatoes.

We didn't talk much about his mother. I knew he'd been going to see her, but he had told me to stay away for now. Every now and then, he'd return from an after-work visit, looking down and defeated. I let it go. I suppose I was happy to pretend that we now had a perfect married life.

One evening, after spending hours cooking the keema and daal Nani Mummy used to make, along with my mother's mixed *sabzi* (vegetables), I laid the table and waited for Juni to come home. But soon it was way past dinnertime and there was no sign of him. Annoyed that he hadn't even called to let me know he wasn't coming home to eat, I gave up and put the food away in the fridge.

As I glanced at the kitchen counter, I spotted the jar of preserved lemons from Nani Mummy's kitchen. I realised I'd forgotten to open them to see if they were even edible. I grabbed the jar and a spoon – and a pot of sugar in case they were too sour to eat as they were – and went out on to the balcony. Sitting cross-legged on the marble, I took a deep breath of the salty, humid air and thought of Nani Mummy's weak fingers closing this very jar. I opened it to the familiar hiss of 'friendly bacteria', as she used to call them. The dark lemons shone in the moonlight, their smell a mix of piquant and acrid. I dipped the spoon in my mouth and then into the sugar. With the sugar-coated spoon, I fished out one dark, squishy lemon and bit into it. Sharp, tart juices hit the sides of my jaw, and as I tried to swallow, my tears mingled with the sweet sourness of the lemon. I broke down, repeating Nani Mummy's name softly and gazing up at the clear starlit sky, wishing she could hear me.

What would she think of me now? Would she have wanted me to be patient with my in-laws and not allow my husband to feel torn between his mother and me? Was this the sort of marriage she would have wanted me to have? I felt frustrated that I couldn't have these questions answered by Nani Mummy. I knew my parents would always support me, but it was the special bond I had with my grandmother that I missed – one with no judgement, only kind words. I sat there with my memories of her and those bitter, dark lemons, hoping I hadn't let her down.

Bitter lemon, mustard seed and garlic pullao

A recipe inspired by my Nani's preserved lemons. The combination of preserved lemon and mustard seeds is reminiscent of my Nani's Karachi kitchen and the aroma of her garden-grown lemons, resulting in an unusual and unique dish that fuels my nostalgia.

Prep time: 15 minutes
Cooking time: 15–20 minutes + 30 minutes soaking
Serves 6–8

4 tablespoons sunflower oil
½ teaspoon black peppercorns
1 cinnamon stick
5–6 cloves
1 tablespoon brown mustard seeds
½ tablespoon coriander seeds
1 teaspoon cumin seeds
5–6 fresh curry leaves
2–3 dried red chillies
1 large red onion, thinly sliced
1 tablespoon finely grated ginger
5 garlic cloves, thinly sliced
2 tablespoons full-fat Greek-style yoghurt
salt, to taste
350 g (1¾ cups) basmati rice, rinsed, then soaked in water for at least 30 minutes
1 preserved lemon (see page 132, or use shop-bought), sliced into thin rounds

To garnish

10 mint leaves, thinly sliced
handful of unsalted cashew nuts, roasted in a dry frying pan

- Heat the oil in a heavy-based saucepan with a lid over medium heat. When it is hot, add the peppercorns, cinnamon and cloves, along with the mustard, coriander and cumin seeds. Fry until fragrant but not burnt, about 10–15 seconds.
- Add the curry leaves and chillies – stand back, as they will pop! Next add the onion and cook until medium brown, stirring often so it browns evenly.
- Next add the ginger and garlic and cook, stirring until the raw smell leaves the pan, then add the yoghurt and salt and cook until the yoghurt thickens, about 3–5 minutes.
- Add the rice to the pan and stir gently until combined. Top with the lemon slices and enough water to just cover the rice – about 150–200 ml (5–7 fl oz), depending on the size of your pan.
- Turn the heat down to low, cover and let the pullao cook for 7 minutes, then check to see if the rice has absorbed all the water and is cooked through, with its grains standing on end. If not, give it another few minutes, then check again.
- If the water runs dry before the rice is cooked, add a little more water, then cover and cook until rice is done.
- To serve, gently spoon the rice out onto a platter and top with the mint and cashews.

CHAPTER 17

Cooking for consolation

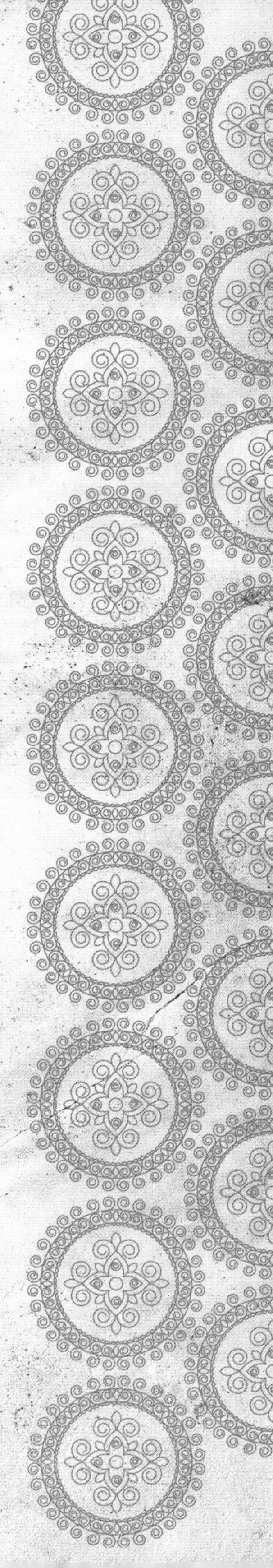

I finally find a way to assert myself through cooking; my confidence grows as I really begin to trust my senses with flavour. I make tough decisions by following my intuition.

Karachi, Autumn 1997

SEEKING SOLACE IN NEW PLACES

When I wasn't savouring time spent in the kitchen of our new home, I was finding distraction from the silent treatment I was receiving from my in-laws by going out to parties with Juni. Right up until I was married, my parents had insisted on a curfew of 10.30 p.m. – but no party in Karachi began before eleven.

While I relished the freedom of late nights, I didn't really enjoy the social scene. For the past few years, I'd been on the periphery of the 'party people' in Karachi. Seeking to be a part of this set was what most young people from my background craved. After all, there was little else to do in the city at that time: no nightclubs or bars open to the public, no cinemas nearby, no independent cafés where you could sit and have coffee with friends; meeting each other for meals and parties was our main source of entertainment.

For the most part, people in these 'cool' groups in Karachi defied cultural norms just enough to seem rebellious. Many of them lived dual lives: outwardly conforming by being courteous and religious in front of their families, and abstaining from drinking in public, while running wild and taking recreational drugs at parties. Girls would leave the house conservatively dressed, then change into a revealing outfit for a party; those who smoked would freshen their breath by chewing cardamom pods before they returned home. Only the so-called elite went to these sorts of gatherings, where alcohol flowed, girls wore backless dresses and the dance floors were packed; expensive chauffeur-driven cars would wait outside.

Of course, access to such circles was only possible if you came from a well-connected, relatively wealthy family, and then you had little choice but to try and fit in or be labelled a recluse. Even then, I always felt like an outsider; I wanted the choice to do something different, rather than merely acquiesce to this way of life.

Juni was a media sweetheart and his popularity was growing. Boosted to fame by independent radio station FM 100, he was the first DJ to play English and American music on the radio in Pakistan, introducing the masses to hip hop and pop-chart hits. Up until then, we'd only had Pakistani music and Urdu-language songs on the radio, so this was revolutionary. Juni also wanted to bring acid and house to Karachi.

His interest in DJ-ing at parties was growing too, and so was his legion of female fans. At one party, I was standing right next to him when two girls came over and pushed me aside so they could flirt with him – and he didn't stop them. I was beginning to feel slightly envious of the attention he was getting. Not only that, but he had already found his passion whereas I hadn't yet, and I felt threatened by his success.

I hadn't returned to college that semester, as I wanted to focus on my marriage. I had started working a few days a week in my father's law firm, and when I went to the High Court and watched him argue his cases before the judge, I'd contemplate life as a lawyer. Daddy encouraged me to keep an open mind, but I still felt confused. Although I wasn't sure this was ever going to be the sort of life I wanted for myself, I decided I had little choice but to continue, and I stayed enrolled at the law college.

My relationship with Juni had been shaky ever since we'd moved into our new place. Soon afterwards, Juni had been invited to go to Japan for three weeks as part of an exchange programme to represent Pakistan's media industry, and I'd thought that maybe this circuit-breaker might help us find our way back to each other.

I spent the weeks Juni was away trying to find refuge in my tiny kitchen – it began with small things beyond the usual cooking that I found pleasure in. I started going to the market to buy seasonal vegetables. Back in the kitchen, I'd open my spice cupboard and stare at the rows of tiny round stainless-steel tins for ages, thinking about flavour combinations in my head. Instead of calling my mother and asking her for recipes, I began trusting my ability to combine ingredients and create something of my own. I was finding confidence in my hands, and in my estimation of amounts. I began to trust my senses and my memory of methods.

I conjured up memories of mealtimes with my grandmothers and my parents, of festive lunches and family barbecues. As I stood in my kitchen and recalled the conversations between my aunts, mother and grandmothers about food – all that chatter and all the flavours – my self-confidence slowly grew, and I found contentment in the familiar sounds and smells of cooking. When spices hit hot oil or steam rose as I lifted the lid off a pot of pullao, I was taken to another time, another moment in one of their kitchens.

'Somi, come over and see us,' my mother said on the other end of the phone. 'You've been home alone for days now. What are you doing?'

'I'm cooking, Mummy,' I said. 'Just cooking.'

'Who for? Juni isn't even there.'

'For myself, Mummy,' I replied. 'I just want to connect with Nani Mummy in my own way, and I can think better when I cook – I really need to think about things.'

'I understand,' she said. 'Just call me if you need some help.'

And I just kept going. I made the pullao that Mummy always cooked on Sundays, the whole apartment echoing with the aroma of dark black cardamom and heady star anise. I painstakingly slow-cooked *haleem*, the meat and daal porridge my Nani used to make.

Our apartment wasn't far from the Sufi saint's shrine I used to go to with Nani Mummy. Devotees would come from far and wide to pay homage to the spirit of Abdullah Shah Ghazi, to pray for ailing family members or improved financial prospects, or just to soak up the positive energy. But the main thing I remember about my childhood visits to the shrine were the fortune tellers with their parrots. Each fortune teller sat on the pavement with an oil lantern they lit at sunset and their parrot on a perch next to a box of cards. Trained to pick out the Tarot-like cards for customers, Titu – the name given to all green talking parrots in Pakistan – would select two cards from the box, and I'd get Nani Mummy or Daddy to read out our fortunes from the indecipherable tiny Urdu script.

People visiting the shrine would give alms to the poor and homeless who gathered around the entrance, where makeshift shopfronts with aluminium shutters cooked up large vats of steaming *haleem* or chicken biryani. But instead of buying this ready-made food, we'd always take a huge pot of pullao or *haleem* to give to the needy at the gates of the shrine. While I was cooking my *haleem*, I remembered how we would share it out, in thick brown-paper bags with all the usual condiments: chaat masala, shredded ginger, lemon wedges, coriander, mint and crispy fried onions. I didn't know how to make a small pot of *haleem*, so I ended up making far more than I could eat alone.

I could have taken some to my mother-in-law, but I decided against it. We'd only seen each other once or twice since Juni and I had moved out, and always with Juni present. It hadn't gone well. Naseem Aunty was cold and formal, and we made stilted small talk over chai and cumin biscuits. I couldn't see how our relationship was ever going to be repaired, and it was obvious that I was the one getting in the way of the close bond between mother and son.

I couldn't be who they wanted me to be. I hadn't been brought up in an extended family household. Even though Nani Mummy had lived next door to us, it was more out of convenience than custom, and we didn't share each other's rooms, kitchens or homes. I hadn't appreciated how difficult this adjustment would be for me – living with another woman, sharing her home, her kitchen and her son. Although it was tempting for me to blame my mother-in-law, I think in many ways I was emotionally ill-equipped for becoming a Pakistani wife.

These are the thoughts that went through my head during those days and evenings when I recreated every single dish I'd watched being cooked in front of me: from the chicken Odesa that I first made as an impressionable child and the ribbon sandwiches Mummy made for my birthdays, to the hug of the *kheer* rice pudding Nani Mummy cooked with leftover basmati rice, buffalo milk and cardamom. Each scent, each flavour sent me to a space and time that I needed to relive to help me find answers. *Should I compromise and make concessions to try and find a way to be a better wife and daughter-in-law? Should I think about what I really wanted instead? Could I live with being divorced in Pakistan at twenty-three? Would there be a future for me?*

EVERYTHING CHANGES

Things weren't the same when Juni returned. I wasn't the same either. There was growing rift between us, and the intimacy had gone. To avoid confrontation, we didn't talk about it, and we tried to find reasons not to spend time with each other. I'd go to see my parents most nights when he was at work, returning to find the apartment empty.

Because I still loved Juni, I didn't want to give up just yet, though. And so I returned to the one way I knew how to express my love, hoping that my food might win back his affection. I began making all his favourite dishes: *nihari* (lamb shank stew), mutton biryani, *aloo gosht* and carrot halva. Our tiny kitchen was bursting at the seams with spices, extravagant Pakistani dishes and constant cooking.

As I cooked, I forgot about Juni's coldness and the grief I still felt for Nani Mummy. I thought back to when she'd taught me about 'the flavour in your hands': 'Some people just don't have *haath ka mazza* – it's not their fault really. Usually, it's when they are sad or broken-hearted, so they just can't connect to the food they are making. Cooking isn't just about putting ingredients together in a particular way, you know. It's about offering your soul in it too.'

'Do you think I have *haath ka mazza*, Nani Mummy?'

'Oh, most definitely you do. You'll see. As you grow up, you'll learn that the flavour you have is unique – it's created by heritage, the experiences you've lived and, most of all, the ability to trust your senses.'

At the time I didn't entirely understand what she meant, but now her words rang true. I made everything I knew Juni liked, in the hope that I could save us. One night I asked him to join me for dinner, begging him not to go to his mother's to eat. But as we sat around the small round table in our apartment, eating off Nani Mummy's bone-china dinner set, I knew there was no hope left.

September in Karachi marked the end of the monsoon season; the hot, dry wind called *loo* carried gusts of dusty air from the west. It was unbearable to go outside on such days, and the coast got the worst of it. As our apartment became oppressively hot and dusty, I felt less and less attached to it.

We'd been married about eight months. In that time, I'd lost Nani Mummy, paused my studies and lived with my in-laws, before moving out to try and create a home of my own. Instead of this being the most positive time in my life, it felt as if all the walls of safety I'd built had come crumbling down. I felt lost, insecure and scared.

But I had also grown up. I'd learnt to trust my intuition, and that I could control what my future looked like. I'd discovered so much about myself during those times I'd spent around the flavours I grew up with on the ship, during my travels, and in the kitchen with the women I loved; I'd taken my first steps to finding a true sense of belonging.

Cooking offered a way for me to find consolation, comfort and connection. Food made me feel safe, and it helped me to find the confidence in myself to make tough decisions.

It all happened so quickly. It was a Sunday in September, and Juni had gone to play football. When he came home that evening, my life took another path.

'I'm sorry, Juni – I want to go back to my parents,' I said.

'What? No, please no. We can work this out. Why so suddenly?'

'It's not sudden, Juni. You know this has been brewing, and I don't think we can make it work. It's not just about your mother, it's us – we don't have what it takes.'

'How can you decide this so quickly? We haven't even discussed it.'

'Are you going to deny it's not working?' I asked. 'I mean, are you happy?'

'No, but I'm sure we can work it out,' he said.

'There hasn't been any respect, Juni, from the beginning, and it can't be found later. I don't think I have it in me to try. Something about us just feels broken.'

I was adamant that I wanted to go home, at least for a while, to give us some time apart. But in my heart, I knew there was no chance of saving our relationship. In the eight months since the wedding, instead of growing closer we'd become strangers. We were so fundamentally different, and we hadn't been able to get to know each other well enough before we married.

Juni left for his mother's that night and I stayed in our apartment. My parents wanted to pick me up, but I insisted on spending one last night alone there. As I looked around at my simple kitchen, with its stainless-steel cooker, Formica counters and wooden cabinets, I smiled at the pans on the shelves and the Pyrex dishes I served my food in, just like Nani Mummy did.

I caught sight of a familiar utensil that Mummy had given me when we cleared out Nani Mummy's kitchen: it was the stovetop sandwich maker she had used to make keema 'flying saucers' for me when I came home from school. She'd use leftover spicy minced beef from the night before, as it tasted much better. She would butter the insides of the mould, then place a slice of white bread on one side. She'd fill it with keema before adding another slice of bread and closing the mould tightly, snapping the latch shut. Turning the gas ring up high, she'd hold it over the flame until you could hear the sizzling of butter against the steel of the mould, and the juices of the keema would begin to ooze out from the sides. When she opened it up, the bread would be a dark shade of caramel and indented with the triangle designs from the mould. Nani Mummy would cut it into two pieces, and we'd each have a half, dipped into chutney and eaten alongside a cup of chai. It was always meant to just be a snack, but it would fill us up and we'd chat for hours.

I couldn't remember the last time I'd eaten a keema 'flying saucer', and so I decided to make myself one as the last dinner in my apartment. I knew there was some keema in the fridge, there always was, and I followed in Nani Mummy's steps. As it cooked, I took in the familiar scent of buttery bread and spices. When I opened the mould and took out the sandwich, my heart sank fleetingly at the thought that Nani Mummy wouldn't be there to have the other half. I placed both halves on a plate and made myself some chai. I sat on the cane chair and looked out to sea as I ate.

I reflected on the power of my food memories and the solace I'd found in the kitchen with the women of my family. I thought of the way Mummy had cooked for me when Gogi had gone overboard, or the times Guddo Phuppo had taken me out for some chaat or *gola ganda* and always found the time to listen to me, and of Nani Mummy's open arms and all the treats, made with love, that had sustained me through my growing years.

As I packed my bags, I knew that these memories would heal me, filling the empty space in my heart, and offering comfort and direction at an uncertain time.

Beef haleem (beef and daal porridge)

Making this hearty Pakistani slow-cooked dish (pictured overleaf) always fills me with memories of serving haleem to worshippers at the Sufi saint's tomb in Karachi when I visited with my Nani. It is usually eaten with naan; any leftovers freeze well too.

Prep time: 30 minutes + overnight soaking
Cooking time: 3 hours
Serves 6–8

30 g (1 oz) each of moong daal, urid daal and chana daal
25 g (1 oz) pearl barley
500 g (1 lb 2 oz) braising steak, chuck, shank or sirloin, cut into chunks
2 star anise
2 black cardamom pods
1 cinnamon stick
1 teaspoon coriander seeds, roasted in a dry frying pan
1 teaspoon cumin seeds, roasted in a dry frying pan
2 bay leaves
2 teaspoons finely grated ginger
2 teaspoons crushed garlic
1 red onion, peeled and cut into quarters
1 teaspoon turmeric powder
1 teaspoon chilli flakes
salt, to taste
10 g (¼ oz) rolled (porridge) oats
2 lemons, cut into wedges, to serve

For the haleem masala

¼ teaspoon nigella seeds (*kalonji*)
½ teaspoon black peppercorns
1 star anise
1 small piece mace
1 small piece nutmeg

For the tempering

1 tablespoon ghee
1 red onion, thinly sliced
1 garlic clove, thinly sliced

To garnish

1 bunch of coriander (cilantro), leaves and stems, finely chopped
½ bunch of mint, leaves only, finely chopped
2.5 cm (1 inch) ginger, cut into fine strips
1 tablespoon chaat masala
3 green chillies, deseeded and finely chopped

- Soak all the daals and the barley together in a bowl of water overnight. The next day, drain and put into a heavy-based saucepan, along with the beef, star anise, cardamom, cinnamon, coriander, cumin, bay leaves, ginger, garlic and the quartered onion. Pour in enough water to cover everything, then bring to the boil, using a slotted spoon to remove any scum that forms on the surface.
- Reduce the heat, partially cover and cook until all the daals and the barley are soft and the meat can be mashed with the back of a spoon – this could take up to 2 hours. During this time, check the water level frequently and give it a good stir every so often to make sure nothing sticks to the base of the pan.
- Meanwhile, grind the spices for the haleem masala using an electric grinder or a pestle and mortar.
- When the haleem is ready, it should resemble a thick porridge with chunks of meat. Add the haleem masala, turmeric, chilli flakes, salt and oats and cook for another 10 minutes, then take the pan off the heat and cover.
- For the tempering, heat the ghee in a small frying pan over medium heat. When it is hot, add the sliced onion and garlic and cook, stirring often, for 8 minutes, or until brown. Pour this over the haleem, cover with the lid again and let it sit for a minute or so.
- To serve, spoon into a serving dish sprinkle some of the garnishes over the haleem, then place the rest in small bowls and serve alongside, for people to help themselves. Serve with lemon wedges for squeezing.

We'd always take a huge pot of pullao or haleem to the gates of the shrine. I remember how we would share it out in thick brown-paper bags.

Keema 'flying saucers'

The last thing I cooked before I went back to my parents, this is a snack (pictured on previous page) that Nani Mummy always comforted me with. If you have any leftover keema, or spicy minced beef, this makes good use of it. You should be able to find dried fenugreek leaves (methi) *at some Asian shops or online.*

Prep time: 15 minutes
Cooking time: 30–45 minutes
Serves 4–5

2 tablespoons sunflower oil
6 black peppercorns
6 cloves
1 cinnamon stick
1 black cardamom pod
1 bay leaf
1 teaspoon coriander seeds
½ teaspoon cumin seeds
1 red onion, very finely chopped
1 teaspoon finely grated ginger
1 teaspoon crushed garlic
2 tomatoes, very finely chopped
1 tablespoon concentrated tomato puree (tomato paste)
¼ teaspoon turmeric powder
½ teaspoon Kashmiri chilli powder
1 teaspoon salt
450 g (1 lb) minced (ground) beef
1 teaspoon dried fenugreek leaves *(methi)*
Dadi's coriander chutney (see page 187), to serve

To garnish

handful of chopped coriander (cilantro)
2 spring onions (scallions), finely chopped
juice of ½ lemon
1 cm (½ inch) ginger, finely chopped

For each 'flying saucer'

1 teaspoon salted butter
2 slices of bread, white or brown
tomato ketchup – optional

Nani Mummy would cut it into two pieces, and we'd each have a half, dipped into chutney and eaten alongside a cup of chai.

- Heat the oil in a deep saucepan over medium heat. When it is hot, add the peppercorns, cloves, cinnamon stick, cardamom pod, bay leaf, coriander and cumin seeds and let them splutter for 30 seconds until fragrant, then add the onion and fry, stirring, until light brown. Add the ginger and garlic and cook for 1–2 minutes, or until their raw smell disappears.
- Now add the tomatoes, tomato puree and a splash of water and cook for 7–8 minutes until the tomatoes are soft and the oil rises to the surface.
- Stir in the turmeric, chilli powder and salt and cook until the oil rises to the surface again, about 5 minutes. Add the beef and cook, stirring constantly, for 7–8 minutes, or until all the liquid has evaporated.
- Add the dried fenugreek leaves, then cover and cook over medium-low heat for 5–7 minutes, or until the meat is cooked through, dark brown and dry.
- Meanwhile, combine all the garnish ingredients in a small bowl.
- For each flying saucer, if you have an electric sandwich maker, butter both sides of the bread, then place 2–3 tablespoons of keema on one slice, plus some ketchup if you want, and close with the other slice. Press down gently to close and cook until golden brown. If you're cooking them on the stovetop, heat the butter in a frying pan over medium-low heat, pop in one slice of bread and brown on one side, spoon the keema into the middle and close with the other slice of bread, then turn over carefully with a spatula and fry on the other side.
- Eat immediately, scattered with some of the garnish and dipped in Dadi's coriander chutney.

DISHES THAT OFFER COMFORT AND CONSOLATION

CHAPTER 18

Andaza in my kitchen

I finally understand what
andaza means to me: the
art of sensory cooking
offers a way of finding
consolation, comfort
and connection in my life.

Karachi, December 1997

PINK SALT AND APRICOTS

Twelve months previously, I had been getting ready to be given away by my father. I could never have imagined that a year later I'd be back with my parents. I had been consumed with chasing a life I thought I'd wanted – the same life I'd previously spurned. Only after I began to live life as a married woman did I realise that I'd found myself somewhere I didn't belong. It's why I found strength in being at home. I sought comfort in the familiarity of the surroundings – but, most of all, returning to my mother's kitchen offered a sense of belonging. The kitchen welcomed me back with open arms, and my mother's food was my greatest consolation.

I felt embraced by the smallest details of my parents' place, the things that make a house into a home. I saw the keepsakes from our travels in a new light: the oil painting of a sombre Russian lady in an antique frame that Daddy had insisted on buying in Odesa; the wooden masks from the Ivory Coast that scared me when I was young. I noticed how inviting the open shelves in Mummy's kitchen were, with their rows of colourful spice bottles, and the herbs in pots just begging to be picked and savoured. On the dining table was a hand-painted Hala pottery bowl of fresh pomegranates and apricots, with *champa* (frangipani) leaves and flowers artistically arranged around it. In the past I'd mocked my mother's quaint touches, but now all I saw was a calming reflection of her grace.

I'd spent the past year living in places where everything felt different. My mother-in-law's kitchen had been so unfamiliar, from the peculiar aromas created there to my presence in it being unwelcome. And for the last few months I'd been scrambling to create a home in the soulless kitchen in our apartment – but it was there that I managed to unearth a source of healing through intuitive cooking. As I recalled the stories and unwritten recipes that had been passed on to me from both my grandmothers and my mother as a child, I realised that I'd also picked up unspoken guidance that I could call upon whenever I felt lost. As well as learning to cook from them, I had learnt that home is more than just a place – it's a feeling, an aroma, a taste. I'd learnt that I could trust my senses.

Returning home, I realised that my parents were my greatest refuge. From the day I'd asked them to come and pick me up, they hadn't once slipped in an *I told you so,*

as I'd feared they would. Instead, Daddy had reassured me: 'We're here for you. Don't worry about any of that. We only want to see you happy. We're coming to take you home.'

While Daddy had the benefit of being able to express himself with supportive words, Mummy offered comfort the way she knew best: through her cooking. As she stood at the cooker, browning onions for a pullao or korma, their sweetness and earthiness nursed me when I was at my lowest ebb. It wasn't easy being back, but her food was there to make me forget the pain. As she fried shami kebabs or cooked up a batch of Dadi's chana daal halva to eat with chai in the afternoon, my disappointment and heartbreak seemed to melt away.

'Sit at the table,' Mummy would say. 'Fill your belly and your heart. Everything will be better after you eat.'

'I'm going to be divorced. Food isn't going to fix that,' I'd say, aware that soon everyone would know that my marriage had fallen apart.

'Don't worry about what other people will say. What matters is that you're home with us and, *inshallah* (God willing), there will be good that will come from this,' she'd say, squeezing my shoulder. 'Come and have some fruit. I've deseeded *anar* (pomegranate) for you. We can have it with some chaat masala.'

There was always a big bowl of fruit on the table – her way of keeping me full in-between meals was by leading me towards the fruit bowl. We spent a lot of the time during those first weeks reminiscing about market trips with Nani Mummy. Fruit was our dessert of choice, and we'd always buy seasonal fruit to eat after dinner. Nani Mummy would deseed pomegranates so that each aril glistened – a deep shade of blood red, and without a trace of membrane around it. Sometimes in the winter we'd find pink guavas in among all the white ones, and I wished I'd spent more time savouring their floral sweetness and the way Nani Mummy cut them into perfectly uniform squares for me.

We'd come back with so much more than just fruit, though: everything from spices to vegetables and pink salt to apricots. At home we never had generic table salt – it was always the pink rock salt that we bought in raw crystal form in kilo bags from Empress Market. It came from the foothills of the Himalayas, in northern Pakistan, and the same stallholder sold Hunza apricots – usually bags of dried ones, but in August each year his wooden stall would be piled high with mounds of red-blushed fresh apricots. These were like no other apricots I'd ever eaten. When pressed, their soft, slightly furry skin would break apart, revealing orange flesh and a stone that encased the precious kernel from which much-sought-after apricot kernel oil was extracted.

'The oil is really good for your skin and hair,' Nani Mummy had told me once. 'And it's said that the kernels have anti-cancer properties.' We'd buy bottles of the oil and massage it into each other's hair to condition it; we'd also eat it with chapattis. When I first found out that she had cancer, I found myself wishing that she had eaten more apricot kernels and their oil, but it was too late for them to help her now.

The man who sold the pink salt and the apricots had weathered skin, and he smiled with his whole face. His green eyes danced with pride when he spoke of his village in Hunza. He'd describe how the hills would be ablaze with autumnal shades as the trees changed their colours with the turn of the season. He'd tell us about the apricot harvest, when the women would set out early with their empty baskets and by lunchtime they would return laden with the bounty. Later they'd de-stone the fruit and set the baskets with the apricots in the sun to dry.

'Grind some salt and dip the apricot in it,' the fruit seller would instruct us. 'It's a satisfying treat that gives you a balance of salt and sweet. Then add the salt to your chai – that's the flavour of my village. It always helps me find home when I'm far away; as soon as I take a bite and a sip, I can feel my children's hugs, see my wife's smile and smell the smoky air of the mountains. I can be at home, no matter where I am.'

His stories taught me that flavour and a sense of home are intrinsically intertwined.

The last summer that Nani Mummy and I spent together, we went to get those same apricots. I could never come to terms with adding salt to tea, so instead we just dipped the split apricots in the ground pink salt. The honeyed sweetness of the fruit contrasted sharply with the minerality of the salt: unexpected, yet beautifully balanced.

'You know, life is a bit like this,' said Nani Mummy. 'A little sweetness with hints of saltiness.'

'What do you mean?' I asked.

'What I mean is that life will bring you some sweet moments, but there are always unexpected twists and turns that will teach you a lesson – like the salt, these come out of nowhere, but they are there for a reason.'

I realised that this ability to trust my intuition ran deeper than my ability to create flavour.

NOSTALGIA AND NEW BEGINNINGS

A few months after I returned home, I decided to reapply to university in England. Since our separation, Juni had tried a few times to patch things up, but I'd been adamant about my decision. I wasn't bitter towards him; I just knew it would never work out between us. Looking back, I'm sometimes astonished at how mature my reasoning was, and I'm thankful to my younger self for sticking to my decision with such resolve.

I needed to get out of Pakistan. Going away also meant that I'd be forgotten for a while in Karachi. I could heal and return when I was ready. Studying law abroad didn't seem like such a bad idea anymore, either; maybe I'd find my way with it after all.

I had a lot of time to myself before I left for England, and I looked through Nani Mummy's belongings, if only to find nostalgic mementos that might help me hold on to her memory. I hadn't yet found my way back to the kitchen, not least because Mummy had been showering me with comfort food – and perhaps this was a time for me to be fed, to find nurturing in the food cooked by her hands.

During my search, I came across an old Fox's biscuit tin. Inside it was a box of recipes and snippets my mother and grandmother had collected over the years, cut out of women's magazines, newspapers and Nani Mummy's Urdu digest. There were cookies from *Woman's Own*, recipes for pineapple cakes, chutneys, pickles and peculiar rice dishes from different parts of the world. I looked at the cuttings with their weathered corners: stained with splashes of oil or cake batter, it was as if each one captured a moment in the kitchen, like a photograph. They were well-loved, well-used – and although I'd never seen either of them using the cuttings when they cooked, I realised that these must have been the inspiration for many of the dishes I'd grown up eating. They'd savoured the flavour of other family recipes from faraway lands, the stories of unfamiliar ingredients and the baking techniques they'd never have discovered anywhere else.

In the tin were pages torn out of a diary, with scribbles in Mummy's handwriting giving rough measurements or mere lists of ingredients, much like the way she cooked. These were recipes jotted down from the radio, and others she'd collected at markets and street stalls when we were sailing the world. This was a legacy of my mother's and grandmother's passion to keep learning about food, of their constant search for cooking inspiration.

One afternoon, when my mother and I were talking in her bedroom, I noticed a diary that I'd never seen before. It was dated 1979, and in its pages were hundreds of recipes, all written in different handwriting.

'What's that?' I asked.

'That's the *khalas*' cookbook,' she said, laughing. (Close female friends are affectionately called *khalas*, which means sisters.) 'It's a collection of recipes by the women from my home economics course,' she said.

'Well, it's quite a treasure – maybe one day I can make it into a cookbook. Though, as usual, there are no measurements.'

'Oh, you don't need measurements! You have *andaza* to guide you. And yes, maybe one day you can write a cookbook – but for now concentrate on law,' said my mother.

FREEDOM IN THE KITCHEN

That summer before I left for London to study, I returned to the kitchen. In the past, I'd turned to cooking for different reasons, whether it was to win a man's heart, to outdo my ex-mother-in-law, or simply to find solace as my marriage fell apart. But now I wasn't cooking for any other reason other than to prove to myself that I could cook, that I understood how to create comfort with my own hands. I realised that this ability to trust my intuition ran deeper than my ability to create flavour. As I began a new chapter of my life, I knew I could always rely on cooking to help me find a sense of home. Merely the remembered smell of a dish, or the way the spices looked together in a *sil batta* mortar, could take me back to another time and place.

The hope that lay ahead filled me with appreciation for the gifts I was given by the women in my family. I realised that I was a sum of all their parts, from my Dadi's free-spiritedness to Nani Mummy's nurturing, and my mother's ability to create a home anywhere.

Andaza had just been a word to me growing up. At the time it had felt like a lazy way of sharing recipes without methods and measurements, but now it meant so much more. The art of sensory cooking, the ability to create flavours intuitively, wasn't something I was taught, but something I picked up through my life in the kitchen. These became such an intrinsic part of me that cooking dishes I ate during my childhood came naturally, as if my heart and mind just knew how to create those flavours and recreate moments long-forgotten.

While heartache and loss had robbed me of my naivety, they had offered me something much more valuable: resilience, and an ability to create a taste of home no matter where I was.

Aubergine borani

This is one of the recipes I cooked when I returned to my mother's kitchen: inspired by the Afghani dish of borani, it makes a lovely side (pictured overleaf). As it is served at room temperature, it's perfect for relaxed meals.

Prep time: 15 minutes
Cooking time: 20 minutes
Serves 4–6

2 aubergines (eggplants), cut into rounds about 5 mm (¼ inch) thick
1 tablespoon Himalayan pink salt
2 tablespoons sunflower oil

For the tomato topping

2 tablespoons sunflower oil
1 small red onion, finely chopped
2 garlic cloves, thinly sliced
1 teaspoon finely grated ginger
4 tomatoes, finely chopped
salt, to taste

For the yoghurt and mint

260 g (1 cup) full-fat Greek-style yoghurt
½ teaspoon crushed garlic
1 teaspoon dried mint
salt, to taste

For the tempering

1 tablespoon sunflower oil
½ teaspoon cumin seeds
2 dried red chillies

To garnish

1 tablespoon chopped dill
1 tablespoon coriander (cilantro) leaves

- Sprinkle the aubergine slices with the salt and set aside for 5 minutes to draw out the moisture, then rinse and dry with paper towels.
- Heat an overhead grill (broiler) to high. Drizzle the aubergine slices with the oil, place on a baking tray and grill (broil) until brown on one side, then flip and brown on the other. Set aside.
- To make the tomato topping, heat the oil in a frying pan over medium heat. When it is hot, add the onion, garlic and ginger and cook, stirring, until light brown, then add the tomatoes and salt and cook until the tomatoes are soft and the oil rises to the surface. Set aside.
- For the yoghurt and mint, mix all the ingredients together.
- To assemble the dish, lay most of the aubergine slices on a serving plate and spoon over the tomato topping, then drizzle with the yoghurt and mint. Finish with the remaining aubergine slices.
- For the tempering, heat the oil in a small frying pan over medium heat. When it is hot, add the cumin seeds and chillies and fry for a few seconds, then pour over the dish.
- Serve at room temperature, garnished with dill and coriander.

The art of sensory cooking, the ability to create flavours intuitively, wasn't something I was taught, but something I picked up from my life in the kitchen.

Pink salt, saffron and Hunza apricot meetha

Based on the Hyderabadi dessert of khubani ka meetha, *this recipe (pictured on previous page) was inspired by the man who sold Hunza apricots at the markets, and my memories of the pink salt and apricots Nani Mummy would buy from him every season.*

Prep time: 30 minutes + overnight soaking
Cooking: 45 minutes
Serves 6–8

500 g (1 lb 2 oz) dried Hunza apricots
250 g (9 oz) caster (superfine) sugar
1 teaspoon Himalayan pink salt
pinch of saffron threads
1 ice cube
250 ml (1 cup) double (thick) cream
1 tablespoon icing (confectioners') sugar
1 teaspoon rose water
1 tablespoon blanched unsalted almonds, roasted in a dry frying pan, to decorate – optional

'You know, life is a bit like this,' said Nani Mummy. 'A little sweetness with hints of saltiness.'

- The day before, rinse the dried apricots, then put them in a bowl and pour in enough water to cover the apricots by 5 cm (2 inches). Soak them overnight, leaving the bowl uncovered.
- By the next day, they should have doubled in size and become plump. Drain the apricots, reserving their soaking water. Cut the apricots in half and carefully remove the stones, tearing the flesh as little as possible; keep the stones as well as the fruit.
- Put the apricots into a saucepan with their soaking water and bring to the boil, then cook over medium-low heat for about 30 minutes, or until all the water has evaporated. Give them a very gentle stir only if they start to stick – if you stir them too much, they will go mushy.
- Once all the water has evaporated, reduce the heat to low and add the caster sugar. Stir occasionally as the sugar melts, then cook for 5–10 minutes, stirring as little as possible. When the texture is thick, pulpy and sticky, turn off the heat and gently stir in the pink salt, then cover and leave to cool.
- As soon as the apricots are completely cold, place them in the fridge, where they will keep well for 3–4 days, or they can be frozen for up to a month and then thawed before serving.
- When you're almost ready to serve, put the saffron into a small bowl (about the size of a pinch pot) with the ice cube and leave to melt and infuse. Whip the cream with the icing sugar until it holds soft peaks, then stir in the saffron and rose water. Spoon the apricots into individual serving dishes, add a layer of the whipped rose cream and decorate with roasted almonds, if you like.

Acknowledgements

Writing this book has been a journey of self-discovery and evolution. It's a coming-of-age story close to my heart, and one I didn't realise was for the telling until I sat down to write it. Along the way I've been on a rollercoaster of emotions, but I've been cheered on by so many people – I feel humbled and blessed to have you all in my life.

I want to thank my mother and father for supporting my every crazy decision and for gifting me with a unique childhood. Daddy, for teaching me to never give up and to never let being a woman be anything but an advantage. Thank you, Mummy, for instilling in me such a beautiful connection to food and cooking, for bringing me up with such gratitude in life, and for teaching me the meaning of hospitality and hearth. Even though they are no longer with us, thank you to Nani Mummy, Dadi and Guddo Phuppo, for opening up a world of flavour, for giving me faith in myself, and for helping me gain confidence as a free-spirited adolescent in a conventional society.

I'd like to thank my incredibly astute child, Ayaana, who I hope carries these recipes and stories through life, and my very old companion and ever-loving cat, Chino, for sitting on my lap (and keyboard) while I wrote this book.

I feel blessed to have the support of my wonderful literary agent, Emily Sweet, whose belief in *Andaza* has helped make it a reality. Thank you so much.

My deep gratitude to my publishers at Murdoch Books, Corinne Roberts at the outset and later Céline Hughes, who have both championed *Andaza* and helped make the book a reality by taking a chance on a memoir such as this. To the wonderful team at Murdoch, including Kristy Allen and designer Sharon Misko, editorial manager Justin Wolfers, and my editor Alison Cowan, thank you. Thanks also to Sage Creative for food photography styling that complements the nostalgic theme of *Andaza*, and to photographer Alicia Taylor. Thanks to cover illustrator Kirstin Heldt for such an intriguingly beautiful cover. Each one of you has truly captured the essence of *Andaza* and created something unique.

To those who have supported the idea of *Andaza* from its inception: a massive thank you to Louise Haines, who helped shape much of the initial structure of *Andaza*. Thank you also to Jonathan Taylor, my initial mentor, who not only read through my first garbled chapters but also helped me become a better writer. A massive thank you to the Scottish Book Trust for awarding *Andaza* the Next Chapter Award 2021, and to the anonymous donor who supported the award. A big thank you to my mentor through this award, Malachy Tallack, who vigilantly edited each chapter to tight deadlines and supported me tirelessly, and thank you to Moniack Mhor writers' retreat, where many of these chapters were written, surrounded by the beautiful Scottish Highlands.

Finally I'd like to thank friends who have lent their support, either by letting me share their names within the book or testing the recipes (and who have been there for me when I cried and stumbled): thank you, Darren Rae, Moneeza Khan, Brian Mallaghan, Michaela Egger, Alison McKenzie and Sheena Langdon; and a huge thank you to Junaid Mumtaz and Danesh Raza, who, despite what life's thrown our way, have remained friends all these years. And to all those I haven't named, but who have supported my writing career to date, thank you from the bottom of my heart.

Finally, my deep gratitude and love to all the women in my family, who taught me to believe in the flavour in my hands and *andaza* in my soul.

List of recipes and menus

MENUS

Index

Published in 2023 by Murdoch Books,
an imprint of Allen & Unwin

Murdoch Books Australia
Cammeraygal Country
83 Alexander Street, Crows Nest NSW 2065
Phone: +61 (0)2 8425 0100
murdochbooks.com.au
info@murdochbooks.com.au

Murdoch Books UK
Ormond House, 26–27 Boswell Street
London WC1N 3JZ
Phone: +44 (0) 20 8785 5995
murdochbooks.co.uk
info@murdochbooks.co.uk

For corporate orders and custom publishing, contact our business development team at salesenquiries@murdochbooks.com.au

Publishers: Corinne Roberts and Céline Hughes
Editorial Manager: Justin Wolfers
Design Manager: Kristy Allen
Editor: Alison Cowan
Designer: Sharon Misko
Cover illustration: Kristin Heldt
Photographer: Alicia Taylor
Stylist: Steve Pearce, Sage Creative
Home Economist: Jessica Brook, Sage Creative
Production Director: Lou Playfair

Murdoch Books acknowledges the Traditional Owners of the Country on which we live and work. We pay our respects to all Aboriginal and Torres Strait Islander Elders, past and present.

ISBN 9 781 92261 619 7

A catalogue record for this book is available from the National Library of Australia

A catalogue record for this book is available from the British Library

OVEN GUIDE: you may find cooking times vary depending on the oven you are using. For fan-forced ovens, as a general rule, set the oven temperature to 20°C (35°F) lower than indicated in the recipe.

TABLESPOON MEASURES: We have used 15 ml (3 teaspoon) tablespoon measures.

Colour reproduction by Splitting Image Colour Studio Pty Ltd, Wantirna, Victoria
Printed by C&C Offset Printing Co. Ltd., China

10 9 8 7 6 5 4 3 2 1

MIX
Paper | Supporting responsible forestry
FSC www.fsc.org FSC® C008047